Christian Values in Communist China

This book argues that as new political and social values are formed in post-socialist China, Christian values are becoming increasingly embedded in the new post-socialist Chinese outlook. It shows how although Christianity is viewed in China as a foreign religion, promoted by Christian missionaries and as such at odds with the official position of the state, Christianity as a source of social and political values – rather than a faith requiring adherence to a church – is in fact having a huge impact. The book shows how these values inform both official and dissident ideology and provide a key underpinning of morality and ethics in the post-socialist moral landscape.

Adopting a variety of different angles, the book investigates the role Christian thought plays in the official discourse on morality and love and what contribution Chinese Christians make to charitable projects. It analyses key Christian publications and dedicates two chapters to Christian intellectuals and their impact on political liberal thinking in China. The concluding chapter highlights gender roles, the role of the Chinese diaspora, and the overlap of the government and Christian agenda in China today. The book challenges commonly held views on contemporary Chinese Christianity as a movement in opposition to the state by showing the diversity and complexity of Christian thinking and the many factors influencing it.

Gerda Wielander is a Principal Lecturer in Chinese Studies at the University of Westminster, UK.

Routledge Contemporary China Series

1 **Nationalism, Democracy and National Integration in China**
   Leong Liew and Wang Shaoguang

2 **Hong Kong's Tortuous Democratization**
   A comparative analysis
   Ming Sing

3 **China's Business Reforms**
   Institutional challenges in a globalised economy
   Edited by Russell Smyth, On Kit Tam, Malcolm Warner and Cherrie Zhu

4 **Challenges for China's Development**
   An enterprise perspective
   Edited by David H. Brown and Alasdair MacBean

5 **New Crime in China**
   Public order and human rights
   Ron Keith and Zhiqiu Lin

6 **Non-Governmental Organizations in Contemporary China**
   Paving the way to civil society?
   Qiusha Ma

7 **Globalization and the Chinese City**
   Fulong Wu

8 **The Politics of China's Accession to the World Trade Organization**
   The dragon goes global
   Hui Feng

9 **Narrating China**
   Jia Pingwa and his fictional world
   Yiyan Wang

10 **Sex, Science and Morality in China**
   Joanne McMillan

11 **Politics in China Since 1949**
   Legitimizing authoritarian rule
   Robert Weatherley

12 **International Human Resource Management in Chinese Multinationals**
   Jie Shen and Vincent Edwards

13 **Unemployment in China**
   Economy, human resources and labour markets
   Edited by Grace Lee and Malcolm Warner

14 **China and Africa**
   Engagement and compromise
   Ian Taylor

15 **Gender and Education in China**
   Gender discourses and women's schooling in the early twentieth century
   Paul J. Bailey

16 **SARS**
   Reception and interpretation in three Chinese cities
   Edited by Deborah Davis and Helen Siu

17 **Human Security and the Chinese State**
   Historical transformations and the modern quest for sovereignty
   Robert E. Bedeski

18 **Gender and Work in Urban China**
   Women workers of the unlucky generation
   Liu Jieyu

19 **China's State Enterprise Reform**
   From Marx to the market
   John Hassard, Jackie Sheehan, Meixiang Zhou, Jane Terpstra-Tong and Jonathan Morris

20 **Cultural Heritage Management in China**
   Preserving the cities of the Pearl River Delta
   Edited by Hilary du Cros and Yok-shiu F. Lee

21 **Paying for Progress**
   Public finance, human welfare and inequality in china
   Edited by Vivienne Shue and Christine Wong

22 **China's Foreign Trade Policy**
   The new constituencies
   Edited by Ka Zeng

23 **Hong Kong, China**
   Learning to belong to a nation
   Gordon Mathews, Tai-lok Lui, and Eric Kit-wai Ma

24 **China Turns to Multilateralism**
   Foreign policy and regional security
   Edited by Guoguang Wu and Helen Lansdowne

25 **Tourism and Tibetan Culture in Transition**
   A place called Shangrila
   Åshild Kolås

26 **China's Emerging Cities**
   The making of new urbanism
   Edited by Fulong Wu

27 **China-US Relations Transformed**
   Perceptions and strategic interactions
   Edited by Suisheng Zhao

28 **The Chinese Party-State in the 21st Century**
   Adaptation and the reinvention of legitimacy
   Edited by André Laliberté and Marc Lanteigne

29 **Political Change in Macao**
   Sonny Shiu-Hing Lo

30 **China's Energy Geopolitics**
   The Shanghai Cooperation Organization and Central Asia
   Thrassy N. Marketos

31 **Regime Legitimacy in Contemporary China**
   Institutional change and stability
   Edited by Thomas Heberer and Gunter Schubert

32 **U.S.-China Relations**
    China policy on Capitol Hill
    Tao Xie

33 **Chinese Kinship**
    Contemporary anthropological perspectives
    Edited by Susanne Brandtstädter and Gonçalo D. Santos

34 **Politics and Government in Hong Kong**
    Crisis under Chinese sovereignty
    Edited by Ming Sing

35 **Rethinking Chinese Popular Culture**
    Cannibalizations of the canon
    Edited by Carlos Rojas and Eileen Cheng-yin Chow

36 **Institutional Balancing in the Asia Pacific**
    Economic interdependence and China's rise
    Kai He

37 **Rent Seeking in China**
    Edited by Tak-Wing Ngo and Yongping Wu

38 **China, Xinjiang and Central Asia**
    History, transition and crossborder interaction into the 21st century
    Edited by Colin Mackerras and Michael Clarke

39 **Intellectual Property Rights in China**
    Politics of piracy, trade and protection
    Gordon Cheung

40 **Developing China**
    Land, politics and social conditions
    George C.S. Lin

41 **State and Society Responses to Social Welfare Needs in China**
    Serving the people
    Edited by Jonathan Schwartz and Shawn Shieh

42 **Gay and Lesbian Subculture in Urban China**
    Loretta Wing Wah Ho

43 **The Politics of Heritage Tourism in China**
    A view from lijiang
    Xiaobo Su and Peggy Teo

44 **Suicide and Justice**
   A Chinese perspective
   Wu Fei

45 **Management Training and Development in China**
   Educating managers in a globalized economy
   Edited by Malcolm Warner and Keith Goodall

46 **Patron-Client Politics and Elections in Hong Kong**
   Bruce Kam-kwan Kwong

47 **Chinese Family Business and the Equal Inheritance System**
   Unravelling the myth
   Victor Zheng

48 **Reconciling State, Market and Civil Society in China**
   The long march towards prosperity
   Paolo Urio

49 **Innovation in China**
   The Chinese software industry
   Shang-Ling Jui

50 **Mobility, Migration and the Chinese Scientific Research System**
   Koen Jonkers

51 **Chinese Film Stars**
   Edited by Mary Farquhar and Yingjin Zhang

52 **Chinese Male Homosexualities**
   Memba, Tongzhi and Golden Boy
   Travis S.K. Kong

53 **Industrialisation and Rural Livelihoods in China**
   Agricultural processing in Sichuan
   Susanne Lingohr-Wolf

54 **Law, Policy and Practice on China's Periphery**
   Selective adaptation and institutional capacity
   Pitman B. Potter

55 **China-Africa Development Relations**
   Edited by Christopher M. Dent

56 **Neoliberalism and Culture in China and Hong Kong**
   The countdown of time
   Hai Ren

57 **China's Higher Education Reform and Internationalisation**
   Edited by Janette Ryan

58 **Law, Wealth and Power in China**
   Commercial law reforms in context
   Edited by John Garrick

59 **Religion in Contemporary China**
   Revitalization and innovation
   Edited by Adam Yuet Chau

60 **Consumer-Citizens of China**
   The role of foreign brands in the imagined future china
   Kelly Tian and Lily Dong

61 **The Chinese Communist Party and China's Capitalist Revolution**
   The political impact of the market
   Lance L. P. Gore

62 **China's Homeless Generation**
   Voices from the veterans of the Chinese civil war, 1940s–1990s
   Joshua Fan

63 **In Search of China's Development Model**
   Beyond the Beijing consensus
   Edited by S. Philip Hsu, Suisheng Zhao and Yu-Shan Wu

64 **Xinjiang and China's Rise in Central Asia, 1949–2009**
   A history
   Michael E. Clarke

65 **Trade Unions in China**
   The challenge of labour unrest
   Tim Pringle

66 **China's Changing Workplace**
   Dynamism, diversity and disparity
   Edited by Peter Sheldon, Sunghoon Kim, Yiqiong Li and Malcolm Warner

67 **Leisure and Power in Urban China**
    Everyday life in a medium-sized Chinese city
    Unn Målfrid H. Rolandsen

68 **China, Oil and Global Politics**
    Philip Andrews-Speed and Roland Dannreuther

69 **Education Reform in China**
    Edited by Janette Ryan

70 **Social Policy and Migration in China**
    Lida Fan

71 **China's One Child Policy and Multiple Caregiving**
    Raising little Suns in Xiamen
    Esther C. L. Goh

72 **Politics and Markets in Rural China**
    Edited by Björn Alpermann

73 **China's New Underclass**
    Paid domestic labour
    Xinying Hu

74 **Poverty and Development in China**
    Alternative approaches to poverty assessment
    Lu Caizhen

75 **International Governance and Regimes**
    A Chinese perspective
    Peter Kien-Hong Yu

76 **HIV/AIDS in China – The Economic and Social Determinants**
    Dylan Sutherland and Jennifer Y. J. Hsu

77 **Looking for Work in Post-Socialist China**
    Governance, active job seekers and the new Chinese labor market
    Feng Xu

78 **Sino-Latin American Relations**
    Edited by K.C. Fung and Alicia Garcia-Herrero

79 **Mao's China and the Sino-Soviet Split**
    Ideological dilemma
    Mingjiang Li

80 **Law and Policy for China's Market Socialism**
   Edited by John Garrick

81 **China-Taiwan Relations in a Global Context**
   Taiwan's foreign policy and relations
   Edited by C. X. George Wei

82 **The Chinese Transformation of Corporate Culture**
   Colin S.C. Hawes

83 **Mapping Media in China**
   Region, province, locality
   Edited by Wanning Sun and Jenny Chio

84 **China, the West and the Myth of New Public Management**
   Neoliberalism and its discontents
   Paolo Urio

85 **The Lahu Minority in Southwest China**
   A response to ethnic marginalization on the frontier
   Jianxiong Ma

86 **Social Capital and Institutional Constraints**
   A comparative analysis of China, Taiwan and the US
   Joonmo Son

87 **Southern China**
   Industry, development and industrial policy
   Marco R. Di Tommaso, Lauretta Rubini and Elisa Barbieri

88 **State-Market Interactions in China's Reform Era**
   Local state competition and global market building in the tobacco industry
   Junmin Wang

89 **The Reception and Rendition of Freud in China**
   China's Freudian slip
   Edited by Tao Jiang and Philip J. Ivanhoe

90 **Sinologism**
   An alternative to Orientalism and Postcolonialism
   Ming Dong Gu

91 **The Middle Class in Neoliberal China**
   Governing risk, life-building, and themed spaces
   Hai Ren

92 **The Chinese Corporatist State**
Adaption, survival and resistance
Edited by Jennifer Y. J. Hsu and Reza Hasmath

93 **Law and Fair Work in China**
Sean Cooney, Sarah Biddulph and Ying Zhu

94 **Guangdong and Chinese Diaspora**
The changing landscape of qiaoxiang
Yow Cheun Hoe

95 **The Shanghai Alleyway House**
A vanishing urban vernacular
Gregory Bracken

96 **Chinese Globalization**
A profile of people-based global connections in China
Jiaming Sun and Scott Lancaster

97 **Disruptive Innovation in Chinese and Indian Businesses**
The strategic implications for local entrepreneurs and global incumbents
Peter Ping Li

98 **Corporate Governance and Banking in China**
Michael Tan

99 **Gender, Modernity and Male Migrant Workers in China**
Becoming a 'modern' man
Xiaodong Lin

100 **Emissions, Pollutants and Environmental Policy in China**
Designing a national emissions trading system
Bo Miao

101 **Sustainable Development in China**
Edited by Curtis Andressen, Mubarak A. R. and Xiaoyi Wang

102 **Islam and China's Hong Kong**
Ethnic identity, Muslim networks and the new Silk Road
Wai-Yip Ho

103 **International Regimes in China**
Domestic implementation of the international fisheries agreements
Gianluca Ferraro

104 **Rural Migrants in Urban China**
Enclaves and transient urbanism
Fulong Wu, Fangzhu Zhang and Chris Webster

105 **State-Led Privatization in China**
The politics of economic reform
Jin Zeng

106 **China's Supreme Court**
Ronald C. Keith, Zhiqiu Lin and Shumei Hou

107 **Queer Sinophone Cultures**
Howard Chiang and Ari Larissa Heinrich

108 **New Confucianism in Twenty-First Century China**
The construction of a discourse
Jesús Solé-Farràs

109 **Christian Values in Communist China**
Gerda Wielander

Christian Values in Communist China

Gerda Wielander

Taylor & Francis Group

LONDON AND NEW YORK

First published 2013
by Routledge
2 Park Square, Milton Park, Abingdon, Oxfordshire OX14 4RN

and by Routledge
711 Third Avenue, New York, NY 10017

First issued in paperback 2014

Routledge is an imprint of the Taylor and Francis Group, an informa business

© 2013 Gerda Wielander

The right of Gerda Wielander to be identified as author of this work has been asserted by her in accordance with the Copyright, Designs and Patent Act 1988.

All rights reserved. No part of this book may be reprinted or reproduced or utilised in any form or by any electronic, mechanical, or other means, now known or hereafter invented, including photocopying and recording, or in any information storage or retrieval system, without permission in writing from the publishers.

Trademark notice: Product or corporate names may be trademarks or registered trademarks, and are used only for identification and explanation without intent to infringe.

British Library Cataloguing in Publication Data
A catalogue record for this book is available from the British Library

Library of Congress Cataloging in Publication Data
A catalog record for this book has been requested

ISBN 978-0-415-52223-6 (hbk)
ISBN 978-1-138-91842-9 (pbk)
ISBN 978-1-315-87153-0 (ebk)

Typeset in Times New Roman
by Fish Books Ltd.

Contents

	Acknowledgments	xviii
1	An introduction to Chinese Christianity today: key questions and issues	1
2	Christianity and China's moral reconstruction	24
3	Christian love and China's 'harmonious society'	46
4	Charity: Christian love in action?	65
5	Protestant and online	85
6	Christian intellectuals: bridging the gap?	108
7	Politics and the transcendental	130
8	Christian values in Communist China: a conclusion	151
	Bibliography	168
	Glossary	184
	Index	189

In memory of Helmut and Josefa

Acknowledgments

In September 2005 I took myself from London to Nottingham for the annual conference of the British Association of Chinese Studies. At the time I had been an 'hourly paid' lecturer for a few years at a number of universities in southeast England. This together with my Austrian provenance, where I had undertaken both undergraduate and graduate studies of Sinology, meant that I felt very much at the margins and an outsider to British Chinese studies. But the conference in 2005 provided two essential catalysts of change. Sitting next to a colleague one morning waiting for the start of a presentation, she turned to me and asked why I wasn't presenting at the conference. I forget what I mumbled in response, but the question was well put. Why indeed? During the same conference I also met fellow University of Westminster lecturer Mark Harrison for the first time. (Surely there is a lesson in institutional culture in there somewhere?) Mark took great interest in what at the time were very preliminary musings about the role of Christian individuals in China's human rights activism. Once we actually knew of each other's existence, we met in London and Mark was instrumental in my putting together the first research grant application for the study presented in this book. I dare say that without his interest and support the whole thing may never have got off the ground and I am sincerely grateful for his input; as I am to Chloe Starr, who will long have forgotten our little exchange in Nottingham.

The first research grant application resulted in funds from the Taiwan Foundation for Democracy which financed the first major research trip to conduct interviews and collect sources in Hong Kong and China in September 2006. Subsequent trips to China were funded by the Universities' China Committee in London as well as internal staff travel funds from the Department of Modern and Applied Languages at the University of Westminster. In 2012 I was awarded a seven-month fellowship by the Arts and Humanities Research Council UK, which enabled me to concentrate fully on further research, including another visit to China to conduct interviews, and the completion of this manuscript.

My previous research resulted in the publication of three articles. 'Protestant and Online' was published in *The China Quarterly* in March 2009. Chapter 5 of this book is based on this article and carries the same title, but is otherwise a significantly updated and revised version of the original. My thanks go to *The China Quarterly* for permission to use the parts of the article which I have retained. In

November 2009 an article entitled 'Bridging the Gap: An Investigation of Beijing Intellectual House Church Activities and their Implications for China's Democratization' was published by the *Journal of Contemporary China*. Chapter 6 of this book is based on this article and retains the first three words of the title, but is otherwise completely revised, updated and complemented with significant new material. In January 2011 *The China Journal* published my article 'Beyond Repression and Resistance – Christian Love and China's Harmonious Society', parts of which have found their way into several chapters of this book. I thank the University of Chicago Press for granting permission to use all these parts.

In addition to detailed textual analysis, the research presented in this book is based on semi-structured interviews – I prefer to call them extended conversations – with about 70 individuals, the majority of them in mainland China, but including several in the UK and Hong Kong. Some of these conversations belong to the most personal and most memorable experiences of my life as a Chinese studies scholar. There is something special about the trust extended by people who share their thoughts and life experiences with a stranger they may never see again. The honesty and enthusiasm with which so many individuals engaged in these at times spontaneous conversations with me was encouraging and often moving. The majority of them are not mentioned by name in this book (where names are given, they are pseudonyms), but the truth is that without them this book would not exist and I am immensely grateful for these encounters.

My gratitude is extended to Qiu Zhonghui and She Hongyu at Nanjing's Amity Foundation and Tian Meimei and her colleagues at Amity's NGO Training Centre, who provided me with a warm welcome every time and generously shared their time and knowledge as well as introducing me to other people and institutions I would otherwise not have met. They include staff at Gospel Times in Nanjing and Beijing, for whose time and interest in my questions I am very grateful. Thanks go to Nicola Jordan, who made me aware of Beijing Huiling. Her hint resulted in several hours with its founder Meng Weina, who is one of the most impressive, outspoken and generous women I have met.

Many academics and colleagues have supported and inspired me during the course of this study. Special thanks go to Richard Madsen, Stephan Feuchtwang, Christopher Hancock, He Guanghu, Nanlai Cao, Lian Xi, Fredrik Fällman, Chloe Starr, Alex Chow, Cathy Zhang, Susan McCarthy, and Derek Hird. Several of them were kind enough to read earlier versions of the following chapters and provided invaluable feedback and corrections. Needless to say, that all remaining errors and shortcomings are entirely my own.

My sincere thanks go to Reverend Dr Kenneth Brownell and his wife as well as Dorothy Hannah of the East London Tabernacle Baptist Church for extending their hospitality to me. My gratitude is also due to Ken Ko of the Chinese Pastor Association in London and all his colleagues for inviting me to their quarterly meeting.

I originally proposed *Everything Depends on Love* as the title of this book, which was vetoed by Routledge's commissioning editor for not indicating clearly enough what this book is about – no doubt a wise decision. Still, much of this book talks about love: its importance in Chinese Christian theology, its significance as a source of moral behaviour, its value as motivation for charitable behaviour. But more importantly, much of this book also depended on friendship and love. Special thanks are due to two friends in Oxford, who do not wish to be named, who provided me with many contact details and introductions in China; without their generous help this study would have been so much the poorer. Very special thanks are also extended to my good friend Hong for her interest in my research, her proactive and practical help in London and China, and her honesty in our conversations. She helped me immensely with this study for which I am hugely grateful and which I hope to be able to reciprocate one day. Thanks are also due to my friend Michel Hockx for many years of intellectual and emotional support – and for introducing me to the secrets of zotero, which proved an invaluable tool in the preparation of this manuscript.

This could not be a book about love without mentioning the support of my family: my husband Konrad and my children Nora, Sara and Viktor for taking my repeated absences in their stride and for cheering me on, believing that something worthwhile would come out of it. My mother Maria and my father in law Gottfried are thanked for all the love and support they have provided, which among other ways expressed itself in the form of practical, hands-on help with the children over the many years of my studies of China. This book is dedicated to the memory of my father Helmut and my mother-in-law Josefa, who sadly did not live to share my sense of pride and joy in writing it.

1 An introduction to Chinese Christianity today

Key questions and issues

For a number of years in the early 2000s I taught a course called 'Democracy and Human Rights in Contemporary China'. Due to topicality of the subject matter, teaching preparation included the close monitoring of human rights publications and reports. In this context, one particular phenomenon started to catch my eye, namely that an increasing number of those involved in the struggles for human rights and democracy were lawyers (rather than writers or intellectuals, as characteristic of earlier chapters of China's democracy movement), and that among these lawyers, a fair few seemed to be Christians. This led me to wonder whether there was a correlation between political activism and Christian faith among this new generation of Chinese 'democracy activists'. As I was engaged in these preliminary musings, David Aikman's book *Jesus in Beijing* was published. Its impact on the study of Christianity as well as on Chinese Christians was substantial. The book, which was well researched, constituted the first non-academic and eminently readable account on the state of Christianity in China. It remains one of the most quoted sources in academic and non-academic writings on the subject, despite its sensationalist subtitle, which reads 'How Christianity is transforming China and changing the global balance of power'. The impact of the book was far reaching. It put the spotlight on a social and potentially political phenomenon in China which up until then had received very little attention from the West. It led to an increased academic study of contemporary Chinese Christianity which greatly aided our more nuanced understanding of its growth and impact. The consequences were also far reaching for some of the individuals featured in Aikman's account, who were subsequently visited by China's Public Security Bureau. My own study, which began in earnest in 2006, can be understood as a somewhat incredulous 'really?' in response to Aikman's subtitle. Once religious zeal (a regular feature in studies on contemporary Chinese Christianity, and not always well disguised) and headline grabbing language are stripped away, what really is the social and political impact of Christianity in China today?

Number of Christians in China

The PRC is officially an atheist state well known for its persecution and destruction of religion and its material manifestations during the Cultural Revolution. Since the beginning of the reform era, China has seen the rapid revival and growth of all religions. According to the most detailed and comprehensive survey carried out into the number of religious believers in China so far, conducted in 2007 by the Beijing Horizon Research Consultancy group, of Chinese people over 16, 85 per cent believe in a certain supernatural existence or engage in certain types of religious activities. Real atheists, namely those who do not believe in anything supernatural or engage in any religious activity, therefore only seem to account for 15 per cent of the population (Yang F. 2012b).

As far as Christianity is concerned, until recently – and certainly in the West – the entrenched paradigm was that Christianity was considered a foreign religion which was tightly controlled by the government; that the majority of Christians worshipped in 'house churches', which uniformly stood in opposition to the official churches and the government; and that Christians were persecuted by an atheistic party, which considers religion the opium of the people and a potential tool for foreign interference in Chinese affairs. In recent years, some academics have started to question this entrenched paradigm. Ashiwa and Wank (2009) reject the state-control frameworks which view the state–religion interaction as inherently antagonistic in favour of seeing multiple processes, including competition, adaptation, and cooperation, as well as conflict, carried out through interaction by multiple actors in the state and religions. Ryan Dunch (2008) also maps out the developments regarding the mutual adaptation of religion and socialist society in reform era China. While the state has clearly shaped the parameters within which religious believers operate, Dunch says that the metaphor of 'conversation' between the state and religious organizations is far more apt than the domination/response paradigm. Where Christianity in particular is concerned, Nanlai Cao (2007) warns that it is problematic to juxtapose Christianity and China as two mutually distinguishable moral universes. It is after all mainly local Chinese believers who have revived the faith, and an upwardly mobile stratum of society is beginning to join the urban churches in ever greater numbers. Daniel Bays (2012) and Lian Xi (2010) vividly portray the rich and diverse history of Chinese Christianity in its many orientations. Both authors present a clear case of a Chinese Christianity, that may have been influenced by missionaries from outside China, but whose most popular and rapidly growing groups are built on indigenous Chinese Christian leaders' work.

The significant efforts since the reform era of Chinese Protestant leaders within the Three Self Patriotic Movement (TSPM) and of academic theologians, who have worked at the development of a Chinese Christian theology and at making Christianity not just acceptable, but respectable in the eyes of the leaders, also cannot be ignored, although they are often viewed critically and derided as 'non-believers' by some Christian groups outside the official church. On the other hand, the fact that some of the most outspoken critics of the Chinese government today are Christians, has done little to quell the government's suspicion of Christianity, nor has the coverage of the resulting harassment and imprisonment of some individuals outside China contributed much to arrive at a more balanced picture of the role of Christianity in China today.

It appears that the polarized view has also led to an inflated estimated figure of the actual number of Christians in China today; foreign estimates and estimates coming from within the 'house churches' tend to be particularly high and speak of up to 100 million Christians in China today. Of the 23.2 per cent who identified themselves as believers in a religion in the above mentioned survey, only 3.2 per cent identified themselves as Christian (as compared to 18 per cent as Buddhist); after extrapolation this leads to a figure of about 32 million Christians in China today, of whom only 3.5 million are Catholic.[1] In addition, there are another 43 million people, who said they believed in the existence of Jesus Christ or had attended Christian meetings in the past years but did not identify themselves as Christians. Regardless of the actual number of Chinese Christians, which may well never be ascertained, more attention seems to be paid to the growth and potential influence of Christianity in China today than to the growth of other religions. Even a *Southern Weekly*'s 2009 issue listed the fact that 'more and more people are becoming Christians' as one of the ten most surprising social changes of the first decade of the twenty-first century (Yang F. 2012b).

The foreign factor

There is little dispute about the fact that Christianity was first introduced to China by foreigners, although in order to better understand the situation today, this statement may require slight refinement. Christianity in the form of different denominations has been introduced to China by different foreign missionaries since the Nestorians in the seventh century, and more forcefully so since the middle of the nineteenth century. It is the Protestant missionaries who benefited from the terms of the unjust treaties following the Opium Wars, who were associated with 'foreign aggression and imperialism' by official historiography after 1949, but who also had a long established track record of advocacy and competence, in particular in areas such as education and health care. Most Christians in the early twentieth century lived away from the big urban centres, but with the missionary schools also came a degree of upward mobility. Christians were also active in social and political reform activities, leading anti-foot binding or opium suppression societies and holding office in provincial legislatures. In the early twentieth century, the American mission in China was dominated by groups promoting the 'social gospel' whose work in China seemed to go hand in hand with other efforts in China's modernization. It led to ground-breaking projects by the Chinese YMCA and YWCA, an aspect that will be discussed in more detail in Chapter 4.

Discussions over the role of the foreign mission in China and movements towards more independence of the Chinese churches date back to the early twentieth century when the Chinese Christian Union was formed to encourage more self-support and autonomy. The Edinburgh Missionary Conference in 1910 in turn led to the establishment of 'The Church of Christ in China', whose participants did not want to create a 'federation', implying different denominations, but who wanted to create a new church organization which would be a non-denominational, single Chinese church. Instrumental in the debates over Chinese or foreign leadership of the churches was a group which Daniel Bays (2012: 100–2) calls the 'Sino-Foreign Protestant Establishment', which consisted of a group of men who constituted an elite policy-making and decision-making 'establishment' among the great variety of missionaries and missionary organizations in China at the time. Despite its name, this group was initially entirely foreign, but Chinese leaders started to be incorporated from 1910 onwards and included a number of YMCA veterans as well as leading theologian Zhao Zichen (T.C. Chao) and intellectuals from Yanjing University.

The foreign missionary scene however went far beyond this group of well-educated and well-connected intellectuals. There was a great influx of missionaries of a variety of different creeds and denominations, often not part of any wider missionary organization but driven by their own personal vision and zeal. Historical studies show that by the 1920s one must broadly distinguish between 'liberal' elements on the one hand who tended to accept the higher criticism of the Bible and the importance of social action over preaching, and conservative groups on the other, usually referred to as 'fundamentalists'. China's own edition of the world-wide controversy between modernism and fundamentalism started in the 1920s, too, and in some form continues to this day. Into this mix one needs to add the 'Pentecostal' groups, which proved (and continue to prove) very attractive in China and which embody the 'irrational' and 'non-intellectual' spectrum of Chinese Christianity with a strong emphasis on the bodily experience of Christ. In Diarmaid MacCulloch's words, equally appropriate for the Chinese context

> liberal Protestantism was inclined to find the spontaneity of the Holy Spirit rather unnerving [...] as so often in the history of Christianity, at first the mainstream Churches scarcely noticed what was happening beyond them, or if they did notice, they hardly took seriously what they saw among what seemed liked small groups of eccentrics.
> (MacCulloch 2009: 989)

The 1920s also saw the first beginnings of indigenous Christian groups which grew out of orthodox Christian belief and Chinese popular religion. It is quite difficult to keep track of these groups and movements with their varied and colourful names. Bays reckons that by 1929 as many as a quarter of all Chinese Christians fell into these independent groups (Bays 2012: 115). Finally, the 1920s also saw the creation of the National Christian Council and the Church of Christ in China, a further attempt at establishing a Chinese organization across denominations, but it was criticized for being 'shot through with modernist theology and to be avoided at all cost' (Bays 2012: 111) and many mission groups never joined.

Therefore, early attempts at establishing a non-denominational Chinese church were unsuccessful for much the same reasons as the official church project in China today seems beset with troubles, that is, the existence of multiple denominations and sub-denominations, which did not agree to or could not relate to the intellectual efforts at establishing an overarching church organization based on liberal theology. Efforts by the National Christian Council and the Church of Christ in China to contribute to the improvement of working and living conditions of peasants and workers were also hampered by a lack of funds resulting from the Great Depression (which impacted on the YMCAs) and the resistance of the local elites, who saw their positions threatened by the social activism as embodied in a number of projects. While these two organizations grew very little during the 1930s, independent evangelical Chinese leaders like Wang Mingdao and Watchman Nee managed to attract big numbers (see Lian 2010). In the view of contemporary critics, they all emphasized the spiritual salvation of the individual, downplayed the importance of church structure and did not consider the role and responsibility of the church in relation to society (Liu and Wang 2012: 342). During the war years, for example, independent churches called people not to works of mercy but to repent their sins and be regenerated before God in preparation for the second coming (Bays 2012:144), quite possibly a more comforting and more pragmatic approach considering the scale of suffering witnessed in those years.

After the end of the Second World War, the 'Chinese Christian Movement' was set up by the National Christian Council, which constituted a link between university centres and the YMCAs and YWCAs. Members were students, who were liberal and sympathetic to the Communists and who loosely identified themselves as Christians; one of the movement's main proponents was Wu Yaozong. It was this group, which became the launching pad for the so called 'Three Self Patriotic Movement' (TSPM), which was created in the summer of 1950. At its core was a 'Christian Manifesto', drafted by Wu Yaozong with input from Zhou Enlai, which signalled the end of the foreign mission in China and articulated the link between the foreign mission and imperialism. The National Christian Council ceased to exist once the TSPM was formed, but had voted to support the TSPM and signed the manifesto. However, the differences in outlook between the great variety of Protestant groups and leaders had not diminished and many refused to sign the manifesto, most famously Wang Mingdao, although Watchman Nee did, whose 'Little Flock' constituted a large proportion of the final number of signatures.

Like the NCC, the TSPM was (and is) not a church. It was placed under the direct supervision of the Religious Affairs Bureau (a state agency under the State Council), which in turn came under the authority of the United Front Work Department, which supervised and directed all relations with non-party groups. This structure exists until today (RAB has been renamed State Administration of Religious Affairs, SARA), but was interrupted (dissolved) during the Cultural Revolution. 'Three self' refers to 'self-governing, self-supporting and self-propagating', a concept first mooted as early as the nineteenth century and not a Communist invention;[2] but from 1950 'three self' signalled a clear stand in relation to the 'foreign element' in the Chinese church and resulted in the expulsion of all foreign missionaries still in China. As a result of the various political campaigns, which affected China's Christian population and leadership much in the same way as it did the rest of the population, no constructive thinking (and certainly no writing or publishing) went into what this Chinese church, free from 'foreign elements', should really constitute, beyond a somewhat vague notion of an all-encompassing, non-denominational structure. At the same time, many Chinese, who had received theological training in the decades before 1949 and who could therefore have contributed to the formation of a Chinese theology, were lost together with millions of other Chinese in the political struggles during the years from 1958–1976.

Chinese theological thinking and publishing only started again in the 1980s (see next section); the same decade also saw the resumption of foreign missionary endeavours in China, much of it through the teaching of English on campus. Almost every single one of the intellectuals I interviewed for this study encountered Christianity through their English teacher, who would also run Bible study classes. But following 1989 a new and arguably much more influential type of 'foreign element' than the English teacher has emerged. A number of democracy activists who fled China after the crackdown converted to Christianity in exile; the best known among them are Yuan Zhiming, Han Dongfang and Chai Ling. Many academics followed in the early 1990s, not motivated by political reasons or necessity but taking advantage of opportunities to study abroad. They converted to Christianity while studying in places like Yale or Princeton and stayed on to study theology and to devote their life to the church and the mission. A number of them regularly return to China, sometimes in the guise of business ventures. They form networks with Chinese Christians in Taiwan and Southeast Asia and in my view can be considered a contemporary incarnation of the 'Sino-Foreign Protestant Elite', to appropriate Bays' term: a male elite of Chinese ethnic origin – and often originally from mainland China – who play a significant part in the direction of the Chinese mission through publications, theological training and the provision of funds. They are closely connected to the two most influential 'sub-cultures' in Chinese Christianity today, urban intellectual 'house churches' and Wenzhou churches, through publication and training projects and through strong personal ties. The question of theological orientation, denominations and church building are central to their endeavours.

This new Protestant elite, who trained overseas, were among the first to take advantage of opportunities to study abroad. Since then the number of Chinese students abroad has risen exponentially, mostly in English speaking countries like the United States and the UK. They constitute another important 'foreign element' in Chinese Christianity today. Many young Chinese will encounter Christianity as part of these studies abroad, where the desire to learn about western culture and the search for companionship and a social life often leads them to Chinese churches. Mission work on campus overseas specifically targeted at Chinese students is well structured and its organization based on Chinese cultural understanding (Rawson 1999). It is more developed in the United States than in the UK, where the period of study tends to be shorter and the percentage of students returning to China straight after graduation is higher.[3] Those who become themselves active in the mission are a minority and tend to stay abroad for a longer period of time or indefinitely, but many of the returned graduates contribute to the rising numbers of urban Christians in China.

Lukas Zhang has observed the following main changes in the Chinese churches over the last decade, some of which are directly linked to this greater integration of Chinese Christianity on a global scale (but mostly across the Pacific). All congregations, including TSPM churches, are younger, better educated and livelier than in the past. No longer are churches dominated by one (lower) sector of society. The crucial role played in the development of urban churches by intellectuals, white-collar workers and overseas Chinese has also led to a theologically more pluralistic landscape. Churches have also moved from being at the receiving end of charity to the active involvement in charitable work and towards an increasing orientation to countries outside China in missionary activities. Finally, he sees a clear trend towards cooperation between different churches in the realm of theological training, missionary work and other projects, often co-ordinated by overseas Chinese 'pastor-intellectuals' (a term analysed in more detail in Chapter 6) (Zhang, L. 2010).

Theology

To the student of Chinese intellectual history the different trajectories in Chinese theology and their relative popularity and success mirror the intellectual debates in practically all fields and disciplines over the twentieth century. There is the familiar dichotomy between traditional and modern(ist) thinking, the relative influence of foreign thought and education on the formation of different 'schools of thought' or strands of theology, and the different degrees to which individuals representing these 'strands' were willing to actively engage with the politics of the day. These differing attitudes which – as in other intellectual fields – led to different roles and fates of the various individuals involved as the historical events of the twentieth century unfolded. These events in turn exacerbated the intellectual (or in this case theological) differences and turned them into deeply held misgivings and animosities between individuals and groups, which are still prevalent and palpable among many Christian intellectuals today.

Generally speaking, the theological landscape of the twentieth century tends to be roughly divided into liberal or modernist theology on the one hand and conservative or fundamentalist theology on the other. The former stands for a 'liberal' interpretation of the Bible, without presupposing its inerrancy, and applying the same hermeneutical methods to the Bible as to any other text. Liberal or modernist theology is also associated with social reform and the role of the Christian/church in society. 'Fundamentalist' theology on the other hand upholds the inerrancy of the Bible, Jesus Christ's divinity, the virgin birth, penal substitution and the resurrection of Christ. The TSPM leadership is universally associated with liberal or modernist theology and in recent decades with Chinese 'theological reconstruction' as developed by Bishop K.H. Ting (hereafter Ding Guangxun, to follow the pinyin transcription of his name) since 1998. The top priority in this campaign to 'build up theological thinking' is to make sure that faith accords with the Bible, to 'pay attention to individual spiritual development', and 'to promote Christian ethics'. Its key characteristics lie in its emphasis on love (leading his critics to conclude that he promotes justification by love rather than faith), an emphasis on the cosmic Christ and an understanding that what it means to be Christian differs depending on the historical and social context. ('Theological Reconstruction' and its emphasis on love will be discussed in more detail in Chapter 3.) Ding argues that not everything in the Bible is God's word, hence denying the unchanging inerrant truth of the Bible which is a core belief for the majority of Christians in China. Instead, Ding wants to change the Chinese church into something new, 'a church that conforms with the historical tide and to the needs of the people' (Fällman 2008: 52). For the majority of Chinese Christians, this view of the Bible is unacceptable and one of the reasons why Ding and the TSPM are considered 'non-believers'. It is however not entirely without currency; TSPM churches are popular and Ding is widely revered among many of their followers.

Theological training is an important issue pertaining to the development of Chinese churches. More and more urban pastors in unregistered churches have now received formal theological training, sometimes abroad. But in recent years, small theological seminaries outside the TSPM have become an important feature in the development of Chinese theology and have contributed to the training of pastors in the unregistered churches. Their establishment and theological orientation is driven by Christian intellectuals cum house church leaders and is broadly defined as 'Calvinist' or 'New-Calvinist'. According to Fredrik Fällman (Fällman 2013: 155–7), cultural openness and social involvement paired with political criticism is a feature of this 'New Calvinism'. 'New Calvinism' is a term used in the United States which denotes the recent revival of strict Calvinist principles within traditionally evangelical or Pentecostal denominations. In China most academic interest on Calvin arose in the 2000s albeit outside the TSPM context. *Jiaohui* magazine, which is discussed in more detail in Chapter 6, is one of the important organs of this theological orientation, which is labelled 'fundamentalist' in the TSPM discourse. The 'foreign factor', which is the involvement of overseas Chinese or mainland exiles as mentioned in the previous section, is key in its development. Its influence, while dominant among the best known and most politicized churches in China today, appears to extend beyond urban intellectual churches. Nanlai Cao, too, reports that since the 1990s Calvinist-based reformed theology is predominant in the Wenzhou church community (Cao N. 2011: 103).[4]

Calvinist reformed theology demands 'correct' biblical exegesis, but it also provides guidelines for the organization and management of churches, as well as the church's role and responsibility towards society and culture. It appeals to intellectuals and fits very well a scholarly community, as logical explanations and reason can be an integral part of theological investigation. Fällman (2013) argues that many 'New Calvinists' 'share a relentless criticism of the Chinese government that can also be a tool for self-promotion and for overseas support'. He speaks of an

> imagined community of "Chinese Puritans" that sees itself separate from other denominations, from "liberal" ethics and depraved political thought and who shares the vision of the creation of another China, a democracy on constitutional ground with rule of law, with full religious freedom and based on Puritan ethics.
>
> (Fällman 2013: 160)

While this is an apt description of a very small group of individuals, it does not capture the entirety of this theological movement. There are ambitious plans among the 'New Calvinists' for the establishment of a church organization based on Calvinist principles to counterbalance what they see as the patriarchal, even dictatorial tendencies among Chinese 'house churches' on the one hand, and to provide an alternative organization to the TSPM based on a clear theological foundation on the other. In this context good relations between the government and the church are key (see Sun Yi's contribution in Liu and Wang 2012: 342–6).

Cultural Christians

As a result of the historical 'foreign element', Christianity, perhaps more than any other religion/thought, was viewed with a great degree of ambivalence in China of the reform era. New perspectives towards Christianity were adopted in the 1980s, when emphasis was put on Christianity as a culture rather than a religion. Instead of being viewed as the ideology at the heart of imperialism, Christianity was increasingly considered as the source of Western success and Christianity became an object of intense academic study. Those involved in the academic study of Christianity were called Cultural Christians, although there were differences among them, which Frederik Fällman (2004) categorized in his study of Liu Xiaofeng, usually considered to be China's first and foremost Cultural Christian. What distinguishes the different Cultural Christians is their personal attitude towards the faith, that is whether they themselves are believers, and if so, how they live this faith. While the earlier generation of Cultural Christians often converted to Christianity, they regarded their faith as a private matter and did not attend churches. Bays (2012: 203) argues that this was partly for fear of the consequences were there to be a crackdown on religion, and partly because of the low intellectual quality of official church congregations and their leadership. Cultural Christians had a strong motivation to change society morally and to lay a foundation for a new modernity on Chinese and Christian ground.

According to Lian Xi (2013), the term 'Cultural Christians' was first coined by Ding Guangxun in 1998, although Danny Yu argues that Ding never used the term as 'he would never give the name "Christian" to anyone outside the church' (Wang F. 2006: 261). This comment may have been influenced by a general disappointment Ding felt with the lack of involvement in the TSPM churches by Cultural Christians. Today much work on Christianity, including theology, is done outside theological seminaries in university based centres which focus on the study of Christianity and within the Institute of World Religion at CASS. They are often called centres for the study of religion, but often focus on Christianity. These centres are mostly found within departments of history or philosophy, but also in departments of Western literature and culture, where the Bible is often studied as a literary text. The accumulative effect of these studies, at the heart of which lay attempts at a re-evaluation of Christianity in China, was that at the end of the last century Christianity was considered to be 'one of the five major strands of contemporary Chinese culture' and 'the most powerful influence on and competitor to

Chinese culture' (Chen K. 1998). While it is true that Christianity is presented as an alternative belief system or superior set of values to guide China through the social challenges it experiences, most Christians, whether 'cultural' or not, would see Christianity as complementary rather than competitive to Chinese culture.

Yang Fenggang (Yang F. 2012a: 64) argues that religious research has emerged as the third force in China, besides that of the religious believers and the authorities, playing complicated, but increasingly important roles in China's religious scene. At times the role of researchers and believers is not easy to distinguish. (At the time of writing, Wang Yi and Yu Jie, possibly the most politically active and most devout Chinese Christians were taking part in an academic discussion held at Purdue University organized by Yang.) In the literature the term Cultural Christian is sometimes used interchangeably with 'culture Christians' or 'Christian intellectuals' to describe the same phenomenon. Some scholars put the term into quotation marks to signal the problematic nature of the term. Lian Xi (2013), for example, refers to the younger generation of Christian intellectuals, who take a leading role in the most politicized churches in China today as 'Cultural Christians', although they themselves would strongly reject this term.

Christianity and the party

The early focus on Christianity as an academic discipline has now somewhat shifted and many Chinese academics researching religion today as well as officials have recognized the role of Christianity and Christians in social ethics, vocational virtues and family morality. It has become quite clear that Christianity (as well as other religions, notably Buddhism) has a lot to offer in the context of China's latest state building project, the 'harmonious society', in particular when it comes to moral education and social values. This was officially endorsed in 2001 when the Chinese Central Government convened the National Religious Work Meeting, which emphasized 'the development of the positive content of religious doctrines'.[5]

While many social spheres have undergone profound changes, religious policy has remained the most ideologically driven sphere. As Yang Fenggang puts it 'The superstructure has become incompatible with the economic basis today. As far as religion is concerned, we are still stuck in 1957' (Yang F. 2012a: 84). Following the end of the Cultural Revolution, the government reinstated the old control bodies in the form of the TSPM as they had existed before. In addition the China Christian Council (CCC) was formed in 1980 to deal with issues of congregational life, pastoral issues and nurturing (instead of politics). The two organizations are commonly referred to as *lianghui*. Ding Guangxun was instated as chair of the TSPM as well as of the China Christian Council. He was also President of the Nanjing (Jinling) Theological Seminary and a vice chair of the National Chinese People's Political Consultative Conference. Thus Ding, who died in November 2012, dominated all the official Protestant organizations during his lifetime and yielded considerable political influence in his role as vice chair of the NCPPCC.

A document passed on 31 March 1982, commonly referred to as Document 19, remains the most detailed description and explanation of government religious policy to this day. It makes a vague distinction between 'normal' religious activity and those that are not deemed normal and therefore subject to suppression. The question of religion is referred to as 'contradictions among the people', thereby relying on a terminology first coined by Mao in a seminal document in 1956, and to be dealt with using administrative measures. To date, China does not have a law on religion. Despite the constitutional safeguard of religion, no law has been drafted to protect this freedom. Instead, all religious matters are dealt with on an administrative level. As Yang Fenggang argues, the result is that the outdated religious policy has rendered itself ineffective in controlling religion, all the while antagonizing the Chinese populace and the world community. In his view the religious policy has become one of the liabilities in China's stride for modernization and for entering the global stage. 'If the restrictive regulation persists in the current form of constraints and suppression, I would not be surprised if the religious policy becomes the last straw that breaks the camel's back' (Yang F. 2012a: 84).

It is therefore perhaps not surprising that the establishment of a comprehensive law on religion to replace Document 19 has become the main focus of the work of some Christian intellectuals today, while for others the question of the freedom of religion in China has become the core issue on which all associated rights and freedoms hinge. These nexus are analysed in detail in Chapter 7 of this book.

Christian values are invoked in the context of building the 'harmonious society', in particular where charity, social justice and a generally 'moral' way of living is concerned. And Christian values are also seen to lie behind the economic success of countries in the West. While the party remains officially atheist, there are Communist Party members and leading government advisers, who are Christians and overseas (UK and US) churches are full of young Chinese students, who are often also members of the Communist youth league. The requirement to be an atheist in order to be able to join (or remain within) the party is no longer stringently enforced. According to one rather astonishing estimate, as many as 3 to 4 million party members had become Christians by 2004 (Zhengming Magazine, September 2004, as quoted in Lambert 2006: 156). All people interviewed for this study reported party members as part of their congregation; sometimes they themselves were party members. According to one pastor of an unregistered church in Chengdu, party members join the churches as the party cannot provide answers for the fundamental questions in life, like the meaning of life or the question of life after death. Party members are welcome in the unregistered churches. For the open churches like Early Rain Reformed Church[6] in Chengdu, having party members as part of the congregation is one way to increase the understanding of their activities on the side of officialdom. There are, however, limits to the degree to which party members can be involved, at least in the more formally regulated churches like Early Rain. According to the statutes of Early Rain, party members are barred from holding any office or leading role within the church. Their continued party membership is seen as equivalent to a person still using drugs or gambling; while the church is open to them to help them with their struggle to overcome these vices, individuals first have to 'come clean' and complete their transformation before they can take on certain roles.[7]

While this particular church clearly expects the ultimate renunciation of party membership of converts, this is not a generally accepted view. Others argue that the return of party membership, especially of more high profile individuals, creates unnecessary antagonism. China's most prominent Christian party member is the economist Zhao Xiao, who seems to have no trouble combining his role as economist and close advisor to the government with involvement in evangelical work and rousing visions of a growing Chinese Christian population. But perhaps the most puzzling statement on the party and the church has come from one of my interviewees in Chengdu. A married academic and Communist party member in her late thirties, Rong was attending Bible study groups and had found great solace and encouragement in Christian teachings which helped her in dealing with the marital problems she had been experiencing. Asked whether she was contemplating being baptized, she said that she had thought about it, but that she probably would not, as she didn't like the 'regulatory confines of an organization' preferring to remain free and independent. She did not seem to see any apparent irony or contradiction considering her continuing membership of the party.

While Western media tend to focus on the persecution of the church in China and emphasize the seeming paradox of its astonishing growth despite the repressive measures, the relationship between suppression and the growth of Protestantism is rather more complex. Although commonly associated with the destruction of all religion, Daniel Bays (2012) argues that the turmoil of the Cultural Revolution actually gave Christianity an opportunity to grow five to six fold in the years from 1966–78. The controlling organizations like the TSPM and the Religious Affairs Bureau were dissolved and the security forces and the police were largely absent too. 'House churches' were very adept at adjusting to the new situation. Talented and charismatic leaders emerged, who preached a theologically conservative salvationist and revivalist gospel, and who proved to be effective evangelists. The fact that Protestants did not require ordained clergy to conduct services further contributed to their relative growth (as opposed to Catholics, for example). Protestantism therefore emerged in a dynamic mode in 1978. Even people inside the mission say that the suppression appears to be one major factor influencing the growth. Tony Lambert writes that the suppression of the 'house churches' aids their growth. Indeed some pastors have said to him that they did not look forward to the day when 'house churches' were open, as the periodic crackdowns were more conducive to producing true disciples from the ranks of the millions of new converts. These church leaders were aware of and resented the shallowness of spiritual life and churches in the West and did not want this or the effects of Eastern Europe post-communist societies replicated in China (Lambert 2006: 209).

Rationality vs. spirituality

Religion is a difficult subject to broach in conversations and interviews. It is very personal and people have so much invested in it, in particular in China, where the subject often evokes emotional responses or a heated discussion, especially when outside observers are involved. Ultimately, a study of religion is an attempt to rationalize what is arguably an irrational experience; reason, by virtue of the nature of religious belief, must be suspended regardless of the intellectual standing or rigour of the individual. This may be one of the reasons why the past decade has seen an increase in sociological studies conducted in the field of Chinese religion. These studies have added greatly to our understanding of the practice of religion, including Christianity, and its socio-cultural implications in China today. Numerical data presented from surveys interpreted with the use of sociological frameworks are difficult to dispute from any interest group's point of view, be it the Chinese government or the Christian mission. They rely firmly on scientific and rationalistic methods, sticking to Hu Jintao's 'scientific view of development'. Even the most ardent proponents of a new spirituality and the most devout believers cannot escape the lure of the survey to bring within grasp and rationalize contemporary Christian practice. As Wang Yi and Liu Tongsu put it in the preamble to the surveys they present in one of their most recent publications 'In an age of rationalism, people require data to speak for themselves' (Liu and Wang 2012: 271).

However, it is precisely the fact that religion goes beyond reason and lies outside the field of human rationality that it is considered of value and importance in China today. Official discourse appeals to emotions (love) and political reformers invoke the importance of 'transcendental values' derived from a source outside the human realm as a basis for civil society. Yet, the concept of religion itself and its rational utility in China's future is an elite concept, which dates back to the early twentieth century. At a popular level the world then and now was 'enchanted' with ghosts and spirits and a myriad of gods and goddesses (Madsen 2013: 22). Indigenous Chinese Christianity, too, was and in some areas continues to be a highly charged, emotional, irrational and often bodily experience of God. Early theologians (who of course belonged to the intellectual elite) referred to the members of some of the Christian groups in the 1930s as 'half insane'. Today terms like 'heretic' or 'low *suzhi*' are used to demarcate the invisible borders between the relatively rational and the outright irrational in the wide spectrum of Christian belief. In this context the question of who are the arbiters of this relative rationality, becomes key. In 1983 the government created an official list of 'evil cults' with the approval of the TSPM. The key criterion for this label is whether a religious group engages in criminal activity or constitutes a health or security risk, either to its own members, to members of the public, or to the government.

Chinese Christians do not tend to question the concept of 'evil cult'; in fact it is readily used in Christian literature to refer to certain sects as well as Falungong. Indeed the suppression by the government of what are deemed cults is considered a success, even though the suppression may have relied on the same methods as used when suppressing 'true Christians'. But one also detects attempts at defining one's own practice of belief as more rational than others' in China's very diverse and eclectic religious landscape. 'Rational' voices are keen to distance themselves from practices that are too closely associated with superstition, for example speaking in tongues, dreams and visions. Tales of miraculous healing seem to be accepted when presented in a more 'scientific' way, or when the healing is ostensibly proven by medical tests or expressed in medical terminology, while they will be rejected when considered to be steeped in 'superstition', as this passage from Lambert illustrates.

> In the West, many stories of healings and miracles in China have been circulated with little attempt at verification. Some frankly incredible stories have been used to boost fund-raising. A degree of healthy scepticism is in order, particularly concerning very second hand reports from the Chinese countryside. Chinese peasants in many areas are still steeped in much superstition [...]. In Daoist and Buddhist folk religion, it is common for people to have remarkable dreams, see visions and be taken up into heaven and to converse with immortals, perhaps even the Jade Emperor himself.
> (Lambert 2006: 121)

Therefore the question arises as to who is qualified to judge which is real and which is fake. To this author, it seems that only a 'true' Christian is allowed to judge (thus disqualifying the TSPM, commonly considered as too 'rational' and worldly in the eyes of many Chinese Christians), or that miraculous accounts will only be accepted if they are perceived to come from 'true' Christians, but will otherwise be relegated to the zone of cult or superstition (and possibly considered deserving of suppression). 'True Christian' is rarely defined by those who use the term, but its understanding seems closely linked to a 'proper' understanding of the Bible, a high level of education, an urban identity and a (relatively) rational, often male view of the world.

The evangelists who entered the countryside following agricultural reform in the 1980s often preached a message that tied in with Chinese folk religion and may have had female saviour figures. In their preaching, Christianity was often considered for its efficaciousness rather than for its 'truth'. Quasi-Pentecostalism also became the feature of rural churches (from the 1990s also in some urban churches) and featured a belief in miracles, divine intervention in people's lives for physical and spiritual healing, and special direct communications with God and Jesus including the speaking in tongues, dreams and vision. The positioning of one's own belief, or one's own church in the case of intellectual church leaders, as relatively 'rational' – and hence 'credible' or 'legitimate' – coupled with close doctrinal monitoring is therefore an important element of the various pronouncement and declarations from within the sector of unregistered churches in recent years.

This relative rationality is closely tied to the male domination one observes in many urban churches as far as theological and more general direction of the church is concerned and will be analysed more closely in Chapters 5 and 6. It is also closely tied up with the concept of *suzhi*, perhaps best translated as cultural or educational quality of an individual. According to Ann Anagnost, the discourse of '*suzhi*', which was originally linked with the one-child policy, circulates in reform era China as a form of common sense adhering to bodies as a measure of their worth as human capital. It seems impossible to anchor '*suzhi*' with any kind of fixed meaning; Anagnost calls it a '"floating signifier" [which] traverses the complex terrain of economic, social and political relationships' (Anagnost 2004). What is meant by '*suzhi*' tends to be determined by the cultural context and the particular agenda of the speaker. In Christian writings the term '*suzhi*' features heavily. Raising the '*suzhi*' of congregations, of the pastor, of theological training, of the cultural level, of particular missionary objects, etc., is central to the concerns expressed in the publications analysed in Chapter 5. In this discourse low *suzhi* seems to be associated with the rural, the female, the migrant, the 'outsider', the overly spiritual, the irrational and thus corresponds to similar forms of differentiation (some may say discrimination) in other sectors of Chinese society (see Jacka 2009).

'House churches'

This study avoids the use of the term 'house churches' but prefers to use the more general term churches instead. Where the context requires a distinction between officially registered churches and others, I refer to 'three-self' or TSPM churches and to 'house churches' or unregistered churches to make the distinction clear. Chinese academic sources very rarely use the term 'house church'. If they do, they usually do so by putting the term in quotation marks. It is important to take note of this, as it reflects the rapidly changing situation as far as the various different types of Christian congregations in China are concerned and how the government as well as society in general view them. Western media's emphasis and use of the term 'house churches' as well as the politically even more charged 'underground churches' is the result of disproportionate media influence of one particular sector of Chinese Christians abroad, for whom the term has become a political marker and who use it consistently. It is worth spending some time on the following on presenting more mainstream thinking on this question.

In her sociological study of Beijing Christians, Gao Shining (Gao S. 2005) rejects both the term 'three-self church' and 'house churches'. Instead she speaks of 'established churches' and 'congregations yet awaiting legal status'. Established churches are defined by her as 'government approved non-profit, popular-type non-popular' organizations (*minjianxing de fei minjian zuzhi*). She considers them 'popular', because they are attended by a diverse range of population drawing from all sectors of society who come of their own free will; but they are also non-popular as their self-determination is very limited. Congregations, on the other hand, are defined by Gao as non-profit, Christian organizations with undetermined status. She considers the term 'house church' inappropriate, as most do not meet in people's homes. Nor is it correct, in her view, to refer to 'three-self' churches, as other congregations, too, adhere to the principles of three-self as they are all effectively self-governing, self-funding and self-propagating. Gao on her part proposes the term 'spontaneous churches' (*zifa jiaohui*), but I have not come across this term in any other literature, nor does she herself use this term in her study. Yu Jianrong consistently puts the term 'house churches' in quotation marks, while many writings emanating from within this sector simply refer to *jiaohui* without the preceding qualifying noun. The term 'privately set up Christian meeting points' is also in use, in particular by sources on government policy on the issue of registration. Daniel Bays also shuns the term 'house churches', referring to 'unregistered churches' instead. Wang Aiming of the Nanjiing (Jinling) Seminary has been referring to the 'magesterial church' versus 'free church'.

The common terminological dichotomy of 'official churches' and 'house churches' implies clearly drawn lines between the two, when in reality the sector is diverse and varied. There are many reasons why people worship in one or the other type of church; often the reasons are practical rather than theological let alone political, although the emergence of the phenomenon of 'house churches' is usually linked to political developments. Some stress theological differences which became more apparent in the early 1950s as an important factor in the development of 'house churches', others see the radical politics of the late 1950s and 1960s in which Chinese Christians – like all other Chinese people – got caught up, as key to the emergence of 'house churches' (see Gao S. 2005 and Bays 2012).

Today, there are mostly new and different reasons why people do not attend the 'three-self' churches, some mundane, others more spiritual. Following the growth of the city, the distance to the (few) TSPM churches can be too far; others cannot make the Sunday service for work related reasons, so are attending mid-week services at unregistered churches . For many of the increasingly educated urban Christians, the quality of the TSPM pastors is simply not high enough. Some believers, who are educated and were baptized abroad, may have theological differences with TSPM churches, and 'house churches' can offer a more communal and more intimate experience than their TSPM counterparts (Gao and He 2011).

A survey conducted among Beijing 'house churches' provides very interesting data on a number of aspects related to urban churches. It was conducted from within the sector with the aim to aid strategic planning, to describe a development model that other cities can follow, to identify areas of support where overseas churches can step in, and to provide data to counter wrong assertions about 'house churches'. According to the data presented (which are based on a survey conducted in 2007), the average size of a Beijing house church was about 50 people, although the average size of a Sunday worship was 76 people. Forty to fifty people per congregation was considered ideal by the authors of the survey, as it enabled full support for all members and was a relatively safe size that did not attract too much attention (Liu and Wang 2012).

My own interviews in 2006 showed that in their daily practice the congregations, like many other religious groups, had become very adept at working with and around the regulations and restrictions governing social groups. As any gathering of more than 25 people was considered unlawful, congregations larger than this number came together in smaller groups at different times, thus preventing breaking the law, but also putting enormous strain on the resources of the congregation, in particular the pastor's energy. Events that did involve the whole congregation were often held at karaoke halls or hotels; training sessions for new pastors were often disguised as business meetings without any visible religious paraphernalia, using professional posters and PowerPoint presentations instead.

Regulations were most easily negotiated around where congregations were associated with private businesses as the use of these facilities lends greater security to the congregation.[8]

Of the 46 churches surveyed by Liu Tongsu in 2007, five were founded in the 1990s, the remaining 41 between 2000 and 2007. According to Liu, active church planting with the aid of teams, existing churches and theological seminaries is the main form of church building in Beijing today and by far surpasses the spontaneous emergence of churches or the transformation of fellowships and Bible study groups into churches (Liu and Wang 2012: 281). Most congregations are young; in the majority of cases surveyed, more than half of the congregation were under 35 years old. Even those, who are older than 35, are often young Christians in the sense that their conversion occurred only in the last few years. The initial enthusiasm often wears off; hence continuity and sustainability are an important issue in church work. At the same time, those who have grown up with Christianity and have attended churches with their parents, are now uninterested and are leaving the faith behind, being lured by the pleasures and entertainment offered by the secular world. The disenchantment with and lack of interest in the faith is a key problem recognized among the churches, who are aware that they need to step up their attention to this particular generation. Generally speaking, secularization is a big issue for Christian churches, and some go so far as considering this a bigger challenge to church development than government restriction.[9]

Churches (as opposed to 'meeting points', *juhui*) tend to have full-time pastors, the vast majority of whom had received formal theological training, often through theological seminaries set up by 'house churches'. The pay of full time pastors is low and does not cover living expenses. Various strategies are employed to deal with this situation, including living on church premises, living with parents or using accommodation provided by the previous employer (*danwei*). The lowest paid or unpaid full-time pastors are all female and rely on their partner's income (Liu and Wang 2012: 288).

More than 80 per cent of 'house churches' meet in rented accommodation rather than in somebody's home. Therefore the most effective mechanism of disruption by the government is to prevent the renewal of leases. It means that new premises have to be found on a regular basis, which always results in an (at least temporary) shrinking of the congregation as practical matters (like distance to the new location) impact on attendance. Since this survey was conducted, a small number of churches, notably Shouwang Church in Beijing and Early Rain Reformed Church in Chengdu, decided to make this issue public by meeting in public open spaces to highlight the disruption of their meeting points as a result of government interference with their leases. This resulted in a number of confrontations well documented by overseas organizations (for example China Aid). Early Rain Reformed Church in Chengdu has since resolved this issue by buying their own property.

Purchasing one's own property is not straightforward even where the funds may be available, as unregistered churches are not legal bodies. In fact what unites all 'house churches' is their legal status, that is any congregation that is not officially registered with the government is in theory illegal, although this standpoint has softened enormously in the last few years. There is no longer an a priori assumption that churches, just because they are not registered, are illegal, and all sources agree that the situation is greatly improved. Despite the well-publicized experiences of Shouwang and Early Rain, most congregations are no longer bothered by the authorities as far as their worship activities are concerned. But the lack of legal status continues to have other implications, and the general aim of the churches is to obtain legal status, that is, to register. However, there are serious disagreements among churches, between the churches and the government, as well as within the government over the modus of registration. While churches wish to be registered as religious bodies in their own right and ask for a registration process that reflects the constitutional safe-guards of freedom of religion and freedom of assembly (Yu Jianrong 2008), the government continues to opt for a 'divide and rule tactic'. The CCP continues to classify the conflict with Christian churches as 'contradictions among the people' and has divided churches into four sub-categories, each with their own management approach (Yang K. 2012). But not all churches are in agreement over the general benefit or rationality of registration. Those who disagree, do so for different reasons. On the one hand there are those, who deny the issue altogether. They are only concerned with the development of their faith and reject the importance of the world around them. They do not even wish to engage in the discussions over registration. On the other hand, there are churches, who reject the necessity of registration in principle. Their point is that no religious group should be required to register at all and that the requirement to register in and of itself constitutes a violation of the constitution (Yu Jianrong 2008).

Christian sub-cultures

The general use of the term 'house churches' and the disproportionate influence of a small number of intellectual congregations on the discourse related to them, can give the impression that all 'house churches' follow a similar pattern or share certain characteristics. In fact the variety of different Christian groups, especially among rural Christians, remains huge. This variety is mostly the result of individual evangelists since the reform era, partly of the continued thriving existence of indigenous Christian groups that date back to the first half of the twentieth century. They are mostly disregarded in the intellectual literature emerging from the urban churches. Apart from the obvious distinction between 'evil cults' and recognized Christians, and within the latter the common distinction between official churches (be they Protestant or Catholic) and 'house churches', scholars are starting to identify further 'sub-cultures'. The tendency is to identify different Christian 'sub-cultures' according to the social profile or the geographical background of their members. Katrin Fiedler identifies the most important as the Wenzhou 'boss Christians', the 'healing Christians' and urban 'culture Christians' (Fiedler 2013: 138). Lukas Zhang speaks of a Beijing model, a Wenzhou model and a Pearl River Delta model (Zhang L. 2010). They are probably all inadequate systems of categorization as they inevitably disregard the myriads of local practices; it is also very difficult to categorize a field as dynamic as contemporary Chinese Christianity.

For example, most of the characteristics of the 'healing Christians' that Fiedler, referring to research dating back to 2001, cites as being deeply entwined with economic poverty, are equally relevant to the urban female intellectuals I interviewed for this study. For them, too, Christian belief constituted a form of liberation (from their own anxieties), empowerment (by feeling that they have God on their side), encouragement (for others to believe) and tangibility (tangible proof of God's power by way of their renewed psychological and often physical health).

As far as the degree of influence on current developments, including the key question of relations with the government and the legal status of churches is concerned, urban intellectual churches and business/entrepreneur churches (originally emanating from the Wenzhou region but increasingly 'exported' to other areas) are the most important as they have ways and means to communicate with the government and networks overseas, both missionary and academic. The written primary sources used in this study all emanate from these two sectors of Chinese Christians. In addition there have been initiatives to create 'house church' alliances or federations in recent decades. One initiative originated from Anhui and Henan provinces as reported by David Aikman (2003: 295); another alliance was formed in 2005 in a Beijing suburb (Wielander 2009a). These initiatives show the intent to establish some form of common voice and cooperation between different churches. Perhaps these different 'sub-cultures' and federations are early signs of what a number of my interviewees see as the future of Christianity: a landscape of different denominations – including TSPM which may evolve into its own denomination – freely competing in today's 'religious market'.

Methodology and aims

This book is called Christian Values in Communist China; it aims to provide insights into the way Christian values impact on social and political change in China today, but also how the many changes that have taken place in China have shaped Chinese Christian values. Christian values may not only have an influence on China's transformation; their more notable existence in China today is in itself a symptom of China's transformation. But what evidence is there, ten years after the publication of Aikman's book, that Chinese Christians will change the 'global balance of power'? More pertinently, what evidence can we find that Chinese Christians and their values have a transformative impact on contemporary Chinese society and politics?

This book is firmly rooted in the sinological tradition of text study complemented by data from extensive interviews in China and the UK. It is the result of an attempt to try to understand what people, most of them Chinese, have been thinking, writing and saying to each other about Christianity in the last decade or so. This includes academic studies conducted by academics of individual local or regional case studies (by sociologists, anthropologists, historians and sinologists); theoretical writings of intellectuals in Christian publications; online journals and reports aiming to provide information for the wider Christian community as well as Chinese theological writings. These include online publications, published letters to congregations, scholarly articles from 'Cultural Christians' collated on a number of different websites including http://blog.boxun.com (maintained by the Independent Chinese Pen), and www.pacilution.com (maintained by the Pushi Institute for Social Science, an independent think tank in Beijing whose work focuses on law and religion in China). Semi-structured interviews, perhaps more aptly described as extensive conversations, were conducted in Chinese over a period of six years starting in 2006. The subjects were Chinese Christians from all walks of life and all age groups; many, but certainly not all of them, are best described as intellectuals or academics. They included some of the leading 'Cultural Christians' as well as Protestant intellectuals with their own relatively well-known churches, whose writings also constitute an important part of this study. In total about 70 individuals engaged in prolonged and sometimes very personal conversations with me on the significance of Christian belief in their own lives. They included Catholics and Protestants, attending all types of churches. All names have been changed unless the person's views are also in the public domain through their writings.

This book takes a distinctly China-centred approach, that is using Chinese sources to present the Chinese 'side' in charting the development of Christianity in China, in the spirit advocated by Peter Tze Ming Ng.

> We may be thinking that Christianity could become a transforming social force in China, which would help in modernizing China or move it towards a Westernized civil society; but then we are surprised to find that Chinese Christianity is not moving towards the same kind of civil society in the Western sense. We may also be thinking that the house churches are merely demonstrating their resistance to the control of the Chinese government, but then we are surprised to find that there are more to be seen and these house churches have turned out to be a new kind of indigenous Christianity in China.
>
> (Ng 2012)

This study approaches the influence of Christianity in China today as intellectual history rather than as religious or theological history. It is not a book about religious practices, but it is a book about values and ideas, including how the practice of a particular faith influences the way people think and act in a wider social and political setting. The question of theology will be addressed insofar as it is a key area of differences and disagreement between individuals and groups of Christians, both historically and today, but it is not the main concern of this book. Despite the great differences that exist between different Christian groups, which are well documented in ethnographic and anthropological literature (and on which a short synopsis was provided above), the word Christian is used in this study to denote all individuals and groups, who believe in a Christian God, whether Protestant or Catholic. They all broadly share a basic understanding of the individual's relation to God and the state, a concept of good and evil, the notion of justice and the importance of love, the notion of charity and God as a transcendental source of values; they all base their faith on the Bible. Beyond that, however, there exist huge differences. While most of the political activity by Christians, which has seen media coverage in the West, emanates from Protestant churches, this study does not restrict itself to this particular group of Christians, in particular where the more theoretical chapters in this book are concerned.

The following six chapters are broadly organized around six key themes in whose context the possible impact of Christianity has been mentioned. These are morality, love, charity, online mission, intellectuals and transcendence (as a political concept). Chapter 2 on morality analyses the main tenets of China's newest ideological project, the 'harmonious society', and the contribution Christian ethics and values may be able to make to China's moral reconstruction, a required aspect of the 'harmonious society'. But it also looks at Christian values at the individual level to see how Christians negotiate their own values and the values and behavioural norms in society. Drawing in its analysis on theoretical thinking by Ci Jiwei, Fei Xiaotong and Yan Yunxiang, the chapter concludes that at an official level Christian ethics are seen as conducive to improving the moral standards of Chinese society and as compatible with the new state ideology. Individual Christians are in principle happy to contribute and respond in a positive way to the calls and appeals made to them by the party-state to put their superior ethics to good use. But they are also wary of their faith being reduced to a convenient set of ethics. Striking a balance between the demands of their God and the party state and between the expectations of their church and society at large demands daily negotiation and creates an inner conflict.

Chapter 3 continues within the framework of state ideology with particular focus on the term and concept of love (*ai*) in official Chinese discourse today. It argues that its use has strong Christian overtones, most likely derivative of Chinese Christian theology that emphasizes love as its central concept. Through references to this core value in Chinese Christian theology, the government signals to the growing Christian population that their values are compatible, indeed shared, with Communist ideology. References to Michael Hardt and Alain Badiou show that this emphasis on love as a new term to re-invigorate Communist philosophy is not confined to China. The private and personal aspect of love becomes part of and aligned with China's newest ideological project; it is lived out in actual relationships between non-Christian men and Christian women, in which both parts seem to benefit psychologically and spiritually without causing great upset to established gender roles and societal expectation. On a national scale the Chinese government hopes to replicate this relationship as a 'loving relationship' between the party and Christians in order to build a 'harmonious society'.

Charity is often understood as 'love in action', and Chapter 4 analyses Christian charity in China today by taking two NGOs, Amity Foundation and Huiling, as case studies to illustrate the very complex relationship between Christian caritas and socialist concerns on the one hand, and the varying appeal of the social gospel and government control mechanisms on the other, all of which shape the reality of 'Christian love in action'. The Chinese government is signalling its recognition of the importance of the social gospel and acknowledging the positive contributions it can make to Chinese society today, but at the same time it is also continuing its control over charitable activity as introduced in 1950. Despite the official rhetoric, engaging in charitable work that goes beyond well-meaning efforts of the individual remains difficult, if not impossible, for religious organizations.

Chapter 5 focuses on the Chinese 'online mission' by analysing some of the most professionally produced web-based publications. Following a brief outline of their main characteristics and features, this chapter presents an analysis of these publications in the wider context of the church agenda, church-state relations, and the Chinese mission. The analysis results in a complex and diverse picture catering for a varied Christian readership. But it also shows the importance of global networks in the production of these publications as part of the international Chinese mission, and the dominance of male 'pastor-intellectuals' in this endeavour.

The role of overlapping networks of mostly male intellectuals, some of whom reside overseas, is developed further in Chapter 6, which hypothesizes that Chinese Christian intellectuals may be able to fulfil a special 'bridge-function' or act as unifying force in Chinese society in a period of political change. After a critical examination of the term intellectual and the theoretical link between Christian belief and political action with particular attention to the Chinese context, the hypothesis of the bridge-function provides the framework for the analysis of developments over the last decade in order to determine, what evidence there is that Christian intellectuals are the 'missing link' that will lead China to democracy, as has been claimed.

Chapter 7 continues the theme of the previous chapter by focusing on Chinese Christian liberals and the way faith and politics are linked in their theoretical writings. It investigates the links between Christian liberals and other liberal groups showing that Christian liberal thinking has had a profound influence on and representatives in all the categories of liberals over the last decade. This chapter also introduces the nascent attempts at formulating a political theology in China, which stipulates the importance of a transcendental source of values in the construction of a polity as well as in the emergence of a true civil society in China. Finally it explores the likelihood of the emergence of a wider political consensus based on the notion of 'transcendental values', and 'conscience' in contemporary China.

Chapter 8, by way of conclusion, sums up the main findings with additional observations by the author linked to recent events and an outlook on future studies.

Unlike most studies on Chinese Christianity, this book is not written by a Christian, at least not in the sense this term is understood by the people in the mission, the individuals I interviewed and/or whose writings I studied. The author is a central European lapsed Catholic, whose sober-mindedness has been honed by nearly two decades of exposure to British understatement. The disputes over the degree of evangelism or how to prepare the world for the second coming of Christ, the cheer-leader like atmosphere of Haidian Church in Beijing or the quiet sincerity with which professional women in Chengdu submit to the patriarchal doctrine of the new urban 'reformed churches' are all equally fascinating as well as different from my own experience of the Christian faith as a young person and my relation to it today. The purpose of this study is emphatically not to determine who is 'right' or who holds the 'correct' belief among the many different voices analysed in the subsequent pages, but to demonstrate the diversity and complexity of Christian thinking today, the many factors influencing it, and the ways it may and indeed may not play a role in China's social and political transformation.

Notes

1. This surprising number is even lower than the official figure of 4 million. Yang Fenggang provides three possible reasons for this: that Catholics are less inclined to self-disclose their faith; that the survey which covered all provinces and regions did not adequately capture regional concentration of Catholics; that Catholicism has actually declined in recent years as a combined result of the passing of the older generation and the effects of the 'one child policy' on a faith that was primarily passed on from generation to generation (Yang F. 2012b: 20).
2. The 'Three Self' principle dates back to the nineteenth century and was first formally drafted during an 1892 conference of Christian missions in Shanghai. It originated from the foreign mission and signalled almost unequivocal agreement that the future of the Chinese church depended on Chinese leadership and Chinese modes of worship.
3. Discussions with members of the Chinese Pastor Association in London, December 2012.
4. There are reservations from theological scholars like Alexander Chow regarding the term 'New-Calvinist', which in his view does not appropriately describe the main focus of this group, but as no new term has yet been coined, this study continues to use 'New Calvinist' in line with Fällman.
5. This is seen as a positive development by most people involved in religious work in China; however, it also makes it very clear that whatever contribution any one religion can make to the 'harmonious society' will be strictly controlled.
6. The church's Chinese name is *Qiuyu zhi fu guizheng jiaohui*. Early Rain Reformed Church is its official English name.
7. Author interview with Wang Yi, Chengdu, November 2012.
8. All of this information was obtained during fieldwork in Beijing in September 2006.
9. This topic frequently occurs in the publications analysed in Chapter 6. Conversations with Chinese pastors in London also confirmed the importance of this issue in their own work.

2 Christianity and China's moral reconstruction

In the 1980s a small side street in Sanlitun a few blocks east of the Friendship Store was a magnet for those with aspirations to be trendy. There individual stallholders sold items of clothing that contrasted radically and favourably with the standard fare sold in the government stores. The market's clientele was mostly young and of course urban, including students – many of them foreign – , the odd tourist, and what popular culture referred to as 'hooligans' (*liumang*), individuals existing on the grey margins of legality and morality, who often ran the stalls and profited most from the market's success. While things were cheap, they were mostly out of the Chinese students' reach. Initially just a few stalls, the market grew over the years and increasingly moved to the sale of counterfeit designer goods. It drew hordes of tourists and started to attract the local authorities' attention. A few years ago, in a move ostensibly designed to put a stop to the sale of illegal copies, 'Silk Street Market', as it became known, was moved from the small side street into a five-storey purpose-built block nearby. The upper floors sell traditional handicraft items, Chinese souvenirs and T-shirts, but the biggest pull factor remains the vast array of counterfeit goods, which is confined to the basement. Instead of putting a stop to it, the move seems to have resulted in the institutionalization of the sale of fake goods.

Such quasi-official sale of fakes is emblematic for what is generally referred to as China's moral crisis and is not confined to a few fake designer handbags. It extends to food products, medicine, educational diplomas, certificates and building components. Immoral business ethics have also led to contaminated blood transfusions, poisoned drinking water and faulty constructions leading to avoidable death tolls. Investigations into large-scale health problems and accidents often reveal the underlying causes as negligence, cutting corners, wilful and often commonly known deceit and other immoral behaviour. Yan Yunxiang (2011) defines immorality as an intentional violation of the prevailing ethical values and doing purposeful damage to other people's interest. He argues that the lowering of the moral bottom line, as observed in China , is worrying and potentially a most dangerous social problem, especially when these acts of immorality are carried out by groups of individuals in semi-open or open cooperation. In China organized immoral behaviour tends to involve institutions at various levels (including some government institutions) and has thus developed into a kind of institutionalized immorality. The now officially promoted Silk Street market, whose main success is built on the production and sale of fake products, therefore neatly encapsulates what is one of China's biggest problems and greatest challenges for its leadership.

Addressing China's moral crisis by attempting to establish a new moral code and a revamped ideology has been a major undertaking in Chinese politics over the last decade, which has seen the conception of the newest ideological project, the construction of the 'harmonious society'. This chapter analyses the main tenets of this new project and the contribution Christian ethics and values may be able to make to China's moral reconstruction, considered a required aspect of the 'harmonious society'. The analysis draws on a number of different theoretical models including Ci Jiwei's philosophical explanation of China's ideological transition in the early reform era (Ci 1994) as a development from 'utopianism to hedonism', which provides a useful framework to understand the development of the 'harmonious society' as well as the appeal of Christianity to intellectuals post 1989. But this chapter also looks at Christian values at the personal and individual level to see how Christians negotiate their own values and the values and behavioural norms in society. It borrows Yan Yunxiang's concepts of 'unbound individuals' and the 'divided self' (Kleinman *et al.* 2011b) in this analysis. In addition, Fei Xiaotong's model of concentric circles (Fei 1992 [1947]) is employed to illustrate the new social relations of individuals 'unbound' by traditional social structures and the influence Christian belief has had on the relative moral distance of strangers in China's changing moral landscape.

Hedonism and a new utopia

In his *Dialectic of the Chinese Revolution*, written in 1994, Ci Jiwei explains Chinese history since 1949 in philosophical terms as a movement from Marxist inspired utopianism under Mao to a period of nihilism and hedonism under Deng, where hedonism is understood as a 'sublimated form of utopianism and a sequel to nihilism'. Nihilism, in Ci's terms, refers to a situation in which reality and meaning have become so separated that the gap between them no longer seems to offer the possibility either for the meaningful interpretation of present reality or for hope-inspired action with a view to the future. For Ci, nihilism is not just the absence of meaning, but the fall from a previous condition of meaningfulness. The fall from idealism into meaninglessness is a dynamic process, which will only calm down when some new meaning has been found, he argues.

In their early stages Deng's reforms represented a continuation of utopianism by more pragmatic means, in Ci's terms, but as they continued they showed an increasing readiness to compromise with nihilism, even participated in its very progress. Hedonism emerged as a way of filling the void of nihilism without going through the ordeal of a new search for meaning. Deng's reform, indeed, was in part an attempt to overcome nihilism through hedonism. But the reforms in the 1980s did not go far enough and resulted in the sublimation of hedonism into a new ideology, political liberalism, which reached a climax in the democracy movement of 1989. After its crackdown, there was a widespread sense – registered in the rampant growth of cynicism and apathy – that all worthwhile collective goals had been tried and found either wanting or beyond reach. After the crackdown, the party-state's response was to widen the reforms in order to 'desublimate political liberalism into more widespread hedonism' in Ci's words (Ci 1994: 1–15).

In political terms this seemed to work well enough in the 1990s (in as much as the political status quote was not challenged), but the rise of a variety of spiritual movements and the rapid growth of religion also signalled that hedonism could not replace the search for meaning. In response, as Ci predicted, traditional values from the pre-communist past were brought back 'in a duly domesticated and non-subversive form for the sake of cultural pride and distinctiveness in an otherwise homogenous global culture of hedonism' (Ci 1994: 241). While Deng Xiaoping spoke in negative terms of the necessary wiping out of 'spiritual pollution' (often associated with western culture), Jiang Zemin's reconfiguring of the same concept into a positive, constructive notion of the 'civilized society' or 'spiritual civilization', tying in with a nationalistic agenda, created a larger role for the promotion of key Chinese cultural values. Most recently this has been expressed in the construction of the 'harmonious society', the newest incarnation of China's socialist utopia. Ideologically, the 'harmonious society' is a further descendant on the ideological lineage in which individual party leaders aim to position their political platform and thereby maintain the moral legitimacy of the party. The emphasis on harmony in this latest evolution as formulated by Hu is a response to existent conflict and competition within a society starkly transformed by three decades of reform (see Dynon 2008).

To understand the collapse of moral authority as experienced in China today, Ci Jiwei's understanding of the traditional Confucian morality system as a three level structure is very helpful. In this model Ci speaks of a code of conduct (*li*), a code of virtue (*ren*) and a code of belief (*tian*). The main purpose of the code of virtue and the code of belief was to ensure that the code of conduct was followed, or in other words, if for the purposes of maintaining civic order a code of conduct alone sufficed, there would be no need for either a code of virtue or a code of belief. This three level structure is modelled on Dong Zhongshu's formulation of Confucian morality. Dong moved the foundation of moral order beyond *ren*, the code of virtue, and located it in the idea of *tian*, bringing into the moral order elements of coercion and prudence. However, over the course of the Confucian tradition, the code of belief was seldom allowed to take precedence over the code of virtue. For most of the history of Confucian China, the centre of gravity was firmly situated between the code of conduct and the code of virtue (Ci 1994: 105–7).

In stark contrast to this, the main feature of morality in Mao's China was the subordination of virtue to an entirely politicized belief where moral goodness was a function of holding certain beliefs that were openly part of a political program. Virtue was what promoted the political program, vice was what hindered it. No new code of virtue developed under Mao, as Ci argues. Instead vague notions of collectivism and altruism took its place, which dictated a code of conduct depending on the political campaigns as manifestations of the code of belief. As Mao's code of belief, his utopia, was tightly connected to his own person, his death was followed by a worsening of the moral climate (Ci 1994:113–5). Therefore, in Ci's analysis, the traditional system of morality was already destroyed under Mao. What had replaced it was a code of belief dependent on one person rather than a comprehensive system of morality. Since the collapse of this code of belief with the demise of the person who embodied it, Chinese leaders have been unable to replace Mao's utopia with any credible alternative, yet the traditional moral structure is also no longer available to act as universal framework. In this space, new ideas and ideals inform the actions of individuals and lead to the constant negotiations about their appropriateness in what Yan Yunxiang calls the new 'moral landscape'.

Approaching the problematic from the psychological perspective of the individual rather than the level of ethical discourse, it is difficult to imagine that moral principles, however all encompassing, are ever applied entirely and consistently. Nor is it possible to imagine the complete eradication of moral standards by which one grew up (to avoid the term traditional) and their replacement by either something entirely new or indeed nothing at all, as the discourse on the 'moral vacuum' in China would imply. Ellen Oxfeld's (2010) study of a village in Southeast China shows that 'traditional' notions of moral obligations and reciprocity form part of the villagers' moral landscape and seem to be reasonably intact at village level. At their most basic, even if villagers did not agree on what obligated them, they did seem to agree on the concept of obligation itself and the responsibility of the individual to fulfil their 'moral debts' (Oxfeld 2010: 51).

As Yan Yunxiang (2011) tries to unpack the public perception of moral crisis in China, he speaks of three different approaches. The perceived loss of traditional values and an alleged lost paradise are a classical (and global) reaction. So is the unfavourable comparison, which in the Chinese context tends to hinge upon the lack of civility and public morality in China compared to other parts of the world.[1] Finally, the diversification of values from collective ethics to individualistic ethics plays a crucial role in constituting a public perception of a moral decline or crisis. As the dominance of a single version of collective ethics has ended, the national panic about a 'moral vacuum' has emerged. It is easy to agree with Yan, who argues that in reality there is no moral vacuum in China, but what is missing is one all-encompassing collective ethical system that all subscribe to; in short there is no longer one absolute moral authority. Its place has been taken by a plurality of values, of which religious values form an important part. The party's latest ideological project is an attempt to square this circle by trying to provide an umbrella ideology for this increasing plurality of values; a holdall for different utopian visions of a better society loosely referred to as 'socialist'.

The 'harmonious society'

The construction of a 'harmonious society' has been the central theme of China's economic, social and political activities since October 2006 when the party passed a strategic document entitled 'Chinese Communist Party Central Committee's Resolution on Major Issues of Building a Socialist Harmonious Society'. This was reaffirmed by Hu Jintao at the Seventeenth National Congress of the CCP in October 2007 (Ai G. 2008: 13). According to Hu Jintao, a 'harmonious society' is one with democracy and rule of law, equality and justice, honour and love,[2] a society, which is full of vitality, stability and order, and is environmentally friendly. In theoretical terms, the concept of the 'harmonious society' is said to constitute a merging of Confucianism and the Chinese interpretations of Marxism as they evolved over the course of the twentieth century. Confucius, who in the discussions on the 'harmonious society', has been raised to the status of 'socialist utoparian' plays a significant part not just in providing the central theoretical concepts like '*xiaokang*' ('Small Tranquillity', often translated as 'being relatively comfortable') and '*datong*' ('Grand Union', 'Great Commonwealth of Harmony' or in Maoist terms simply 'communism'), but also provides the essential Chinese cultural anchor, the all-important 'Chinese characteristics', to this new model of society. More importantly, the 'harmonious society' constitutes a further development in Chinese Marxist thinking since the reform era. Hu Jintao's 'harmonious society' is a direct development of Jiang Zemin's '*wenming shehui*' (civilized society), which dominated the discussions of the 1990s. It is a more evolved and more sophisticated model and an attempt to address the stark inequalities that have arisen from China's economic reform and which have been acknowledged since the early 1990s.

For Gilley and Holbig (2010) the ideological project of the 'harmonious society' shows an 'agile, responsive and creative party effort' away from the previous economic-nationalistic approach towards an ideological-institutional approach as a response to the party's fear that different combinations of factors with different critical values might interact to suddenly and radically alter the overall level of legitimacy, causing system-threatening events (Holbig and Gilley 2010: 398). It constitutes recognition of China's new social complexity, acknowledging the 'appearance of all sorts of thoughts and cultures' in Chinese society and the fact that 'people's mental activities have become noticeably more independent, selective, changeable and different'. The party also recognizes 'people's heightening awareness of democracy and the law and growing enthusiasm for political participation' (Holbig 2009: 51) and shows readiness to adapt the dominant ideology (socialism) from within in order to sustain the party's legitimacy in the face of growing diversity and uncertainty. To put it in Ci Jiwei's terms, the party is trying to present another utopia as hedonism appears to have failed to suppress liberal political values.

Qin Zhiyong writes, 'the harmonious culture is a culture that embraces pluralistic unity, open-mindedness, tolerance, collaborative order, and mutual benefit for all' (Qin Z. 2008: 62). The building of a 'harmonious society' is ostensibly firmly rooted in traditional Chinese culture and rests upon a particular interpretation of Confucianism by focusing on its innovative and open-minded side, much in the same way as early twentieth-century reformers like Kang Youwei and Liang Qichao have done. While this reference to traditional Chinese culture is generally accepted, a close examination of key speeches on the 'harmonious society' and its conceptual forerunners, as carried out by Josef Gregory Mahoney, reveals that there is far less reference to Confucius than to Marx, Mao and Deng in the speeches of Jiang Zemin and Hu Jintao on the subject. Mahoney convincingly argues that there is a clear and discernible thread of continuity between Mao, Deng, Jiang and Hu. Confucius is important only insofar as he was a key influence on the formation of Chinese Marxism in the first place, but the building of the 'harmonious society' does not constitute a re-evaluation or re-discovery of Confucianism per se (see Mahoney 2008). Nicholas Dynon (2008) also delineates the progressive development of the party ideological discourse from Deng to Hu; while he clearly identifies Jiang Zemin's repositioning of the discourse as a constructive, nationalist project focusing on Chinese cultural values, to which Hu's notion of social harmony has been added in recent years, there is no specific mention of Confucianism in Dynon's analysis.

As Holbig and Gilley (2010) tell us, Hu Jintao originally engaged in the academic discussion on the role of Confucianism in Chinese society, but decided to draw back from it and to 'neutralize' this contested element of traditional by reconfiguring it in the larger context of 'traditional Chinese culture'. Key Confucian slogans are retained (for example *xiaokang shehui*), but these notions are 'reduced to sterile clichés representing an amorphous imaginaire of historical achievements and future greatness that is referred to as Chinese culture' (Holbig and Gilley 2010: 410). For Ai Jiawen (2008), the project of the 'harmonious society' constitutes a refunctioning of Confucianism, by lifting tradition out of its original context and reconceptualizing it. This means choosing elements that are compatible with Marxism like love of order, stability, strong leadership and harmony and investing it with new meaning, while ignoring other concepts that criticize Marxism. As we will see in the next chapter, the same has been attempted with core Christian values like love.

The 'harmonious society' is a recasting of socialist ideals in the context of a new social reality, with the hope that it may capture people's imagination, perhaps even turn into a new code of belief, to use Ci Jiwei's terminology. Accompanying it has been an attempt at formulating a more concrete code of ethics to inform people's behaviour (Ci's code of conduct). The so called 'Eight Honours and Eight Shames' (*barong baru*) launched by Hu Jintao in 2006 presented an eight point moral code consisting of a positive and a negative each. Initially designed as a yardstick for Communist party officials, the code has been propagated more widely in the population as guidelines for 'right and wrong' behaviour. Their English version reads as follows:

> Love the country; do it no harm. Serve the people; never betray them. Follow science; discard ignorance. Be diligent; not indolent. Be united; help each other; make no gain at others' expenses. Be honest and trustworthy; do not sacrifice ethics for profit. Be disciplined and law abiding; not chaotic and lawless. Live plainly, work hard; do not wallow in luxuries and pleasures.
>
> (Xinhua Net 2006)

While the first three points reinforce the message of patriotism and the importance of a 'scientific approach' – long-time staples of Chinese socialist propaganda – the following five are difficult to argue with from the point of view of any established ethical framework, be it religious or secular, Chinese or foreign. Nanlai Cao reports that the 'Eight Honors and Eight Shames' almost immediately became an idiom in the church circles of Wenzhou Christians. They used this official phrase to celebrate their superior Christian morality and identity claiming that the Eight Honours and Eight Shames just showed the progressiveness of Christianity, 'since Christians had already achieved them' (Cao N. 2011: 68). The following examines examples of the discourse on moral reconstruction and the importance of value systems other than 'Confucian' ethics in this process.

Reconstructing moral culture

In the early 1980s, when China had just embarked upon 'Reform and Opening up', the leadership's main concern was how to prevent negative foreign influences from penetrating into China while at the same time allowing the positive influences into the country that were necessary to achieve the goals of economic development and modernization. The development of communication technology, and in particular the internet, have made it increasingly difficult for the Chinese leadership to control the flow of information into China, but the intention has remained the same, that is to take on board whatever is useful and beneficial, while at the same time trying to disallow what is deemed harmful in terms of foreign ideology and thought. Or in the words of Qin Gang 'only by learning from other cultures in the process of cultural integration and blending, and by sublimating what is useful or healthy and discarding what is not in the cultural collision can we enrich and develop our harmonious culture' (quoted in Qin 2008: 67). The 'harmonious society' requires cultural construction, which refers to the improvement of the cultural quality of both individuals and the whole society. The question that poses itself for the leadership then is what sources to draw on in order to formulate a new code of virtue in an increasingly pluralistic landscape. For some academics the answer seems to point in one direction.

Xiaoying Wang (2002) has described the degeneration of public social mores in her conceptualization of the 'post-communist personality'. According to Wang, the official encouragement of wealth by Deng has given rise to a type of mentality that is bent on getting rich without any set of values whatsoever to guide or regulate it except as a negative reaction to all moral values. The 'post-communist personality' as described by Wang is characterized by a ferocious response to the ethos of consumerism and the unprecedented opportunities for wealth and pleasure, by hedonism and egotism, by a lack of moral code or sense of self, and a lack of guidance and inhibition. Furthermore, the 'post-communist personality' shows no interest in a new ideology but retains resentment for the old ideology which leads to social disruption, free-riding in every possible way and has contributed to a great extent to the social and environmental problems China is facing today (Wang X. Y. 2002: 6–8).

Xiaoying Wang continues that the 'leftist' values that would be needed in order to address the catalogue of social issues that have arisen in over two decades of reform are associated with the old Maoist order and instil cynicism and resentment. However, the fact that the party has held onto the monopoly of state ideological apparatuses has made it very difficult for other social forces to contribute effectively to the development of a new, nationwide moral culture. The party's 'Spiritual Civilization' project of the late 1990s has relied on socialist and communist values, which have long been discredited by the public, and has been not more than a campaign of political slogans calling for a healthy lifestyle and a polite and law-abiding citizenry (not unlike the KMT's New Life Movement of the 1940s) at best, and as an ideological justification to eliminate political dissent at worst (Wang X.Y. 2002: 17).

In a recent interview on the question why Chinese society 'has turned bad', Shanghai University's Wang Xiaoming (Wang X. 2011) sees the root problem in China's education system and the lack of positive experiences (like a loving relationship) outside the utilitarian and material as adults. Because of the pressures in China's current education system, the child learns that, in order to obtain a 'beautiful life' he or she needs to suppress their own true human nature. As a consequence the child feels small, constantly needing to bend his or her own nature in the interest of 'working hard' rather than playing. Parents and educational authorities destroy the child's sense of self-determination, a situation that is perpetuated at university. However, upon graduation the individual realizes that actually, in a society where jobs and resources are unevenly allocated on the basis of *guanxi* or other games, not everything depends on how hard he or she works. This leads to a profound sense of powerlessness, first in the face of school and parental authority and later in the face of an unjust society. Not only do individuals realize that there is no way to protest, but their sense of powerlessness also makes it very difficult for the individual to become proactive. But to be an upright and honest person requires a proactive and conscious choice by the individual, as Wang Xiaoming argues. Quoting Jing Jun, Kleinman *et al.* (2011: 28) also emphasizes the importance of self-respect, self-confidence and self-determination as the basis of cultural awareness required to instigate moral action.

To Wang Xiaoming (Wang X. 2011) there are three diagnostic questions to determine a society's moral state. Does society make a young person's sense of self-determination stronger or weaker? Is this young person's sense that society is just getting stronger or weaker? Does the same person experience increasingly more or increasingly less aesthetic value apart from the monetary? If the answer to all three questions is weaker or less, then the moral state of society will deteriorate. In such an environment, the individual would require some form of emotional support in order not to lose their balance and to remain upright and sane. In Wang's view the emotional support received through love would be one way to withstand the powerlessness and to remain honest. Wang's points are reminiscent of one of China's most eminent theologians in the Republican period. Echoing Lu Xun, Zhao Zichen (T.C. Chao) argued that the greatest problem of China was the Chinese people, who needed to change from inside out in order for the nation to achieve political unity and social stability. Zhao believed that the danger to China lay in its weakness as manifested in the general rejection of *renge*, or moral character. To him

> The entire meaning of moral character lies in self-consciousness, self-determination, self-revelation, self-control, autonomy, freedom, self-creation, and self-determination of the direction of one's own life. [...] Moral character is a renewal of the organic life by the individual through love. Moral character is love, the will to good; moral character is the constant effort of the will to good.
>
> (Zhao as quoted in Lin M. M. 2010: 128)

It is this constant and conscious effort that Wang Xiaoming has diagnosed as beyond the individual's capacity in the current Chinese social environment, unless he or she enjoys the support of love. For Zhao Zichen universal love and moral excellence were two central principles of Christianity; two aspects which continue to be emphasized by Chinese Christians today including the Chinese Protestant leadership.

Zou Xingming (2008) a researcher at the Haidian Institute of Social Sciences, explains the lack of social values in contemporary society with an inadequacy of the Confucian values, which do not serve contemporary, modern society well. While 'traditional Chinese culture' – Confucianism in the widest sense – is held up as example for 'good' behaviour in the official discourse, Zou identifies the limitations in the Confucian concept of social love. These limitations centre around what Zou refers to as the 'hierarchy of love' (*ai de dengcha*) in Confucian thought. This hierarchy was primarily a hierarchy based on blood relationships and meant that love for the family was greater than love for the person next to one in the street. According to Zou Xingming, the 'hierarchy of love' in terms of Confucius was a result of recognizing human nature and necessity, and was a useful moral basis in a feudal hierarchical system. He acknowledges various Confucian concepts that were intended to counterbalance the social effects of the 'hierarchy of love', but argues that the 'hierarchy of love' was and remains stronger than these other concepts and forms the greatest obstacle in the building of the 'harmonious society'.

Fei Xiaotong ([1947]1992) used the metaphor of the concentric circles appearing on the surface of the lake when a rock is thrown in to describe how the individual related to society in traditional China. According to Fei, each individual was at the heart of their own circle, each circle representing a layer of social relationships, the distance from the centre in turn representing an emotional and moral distance. He furthers states that with a loosely organized society such as China's, it was not easy to find an all-encompassing ethical concept. Fei Xiaotong states very clearly that in the traditional Chinese system of morality, there was no concept of 'love' comparable to the one in Christianity, namely a universal love without distinctions.

In the contemporary context, Zou Xingming (2008) detects this hierarchy of love in four main manifestations. First, the hierarchy of blood is still deeply entrenched in Chinese thinking. Social networks based on blood relationships still dominate modern Chinese life. Whatever benefits 'oneself' still tends to be first and foremost protected. Second, there is the hierarchy of place, which is related to the strong feelings people harbour for their place of birth. In social terms this hierarchical love for place coupled with local power, at worst, can lead to local protectionism. Third, Zou speaks of the hierarchy of identity. Here he refers to labels people put on each other which lead to rampant discrimination by the rich of the poor, by the urban population of the rural population, by white-collar workers of blue-collar workers. And finally, Zou speaks of the hierarchy between the public and the private, which he considers an extension of blood hierarchy to the degree that a conflict is reached between public and private interest. People have no regard for what is public; when it comes to the public they only think in terms of their rights, but never in terms of duties.

Xiaoying Wang has similar concerns when it comes to traditional Chinese values. While a problematic social and moral order was also a characteristic of Western early stages of capitalism, Wang is concerned whether post-communist China has the moral and cultural resources to cope with such problems in the way the West clearly did in the form of Christianity in general and Protestant ethics in particular. She does not consider Confucianism to be an adequate equivalent (Wang X.Y. 2002: 11). The new morality that China urgently needs according to Wang must be capable of giving meaning and discipline to the pursuit of goals by individuals. While individualism is rejected by the party as a bourgeois trait ('bourgeois individualism') and equated with selfishness, Wang defines individualism as 'ideas and practices [...] in which a person is treated as a moral agent capable of choosing and carrying out his or her own life plan while respecting the same capacity on the part of others' (Wang X.Y. 2002: 8). As Wang says:

> Some such morality, containing some form of individualism and some corresponding conception of justice is necessary, if a society that allows and encourages the pursuit of individual interests, as post-Mao China does, is not to degenerate into individual shapelessness and social chaos and injustice. Neither Marxism nor the Chinese tradition provides sufficient resources for such a morality.
>
> (Wang X.Y. 2002: 17)

Writing about the Good Samaritan, Yan Yunxiang seems to detect these traits in the contemporary Good Samaritans of China.

> Unlike Lei Feng and other selfless socialist role models promoted by the government, the contemporary Good Samaritans act entirely of their free will and do not expect any official recognition or reward. [...] In the reform era, this collective morality of responsibility and self-sacrifice has been replaced by a new individual morality of rights and self-realisation.
>
> (Yan Y. 2009: 22)

Writing after the Sichuan Earthquake, Yan detects a rise of universalistic moral values which in his view reflect the individualization of Chinese society, much in the sense of Xiaoying Wang. Commenting on the compassion towards strangers displayed by the many thousand volunteers involved in relief work after Wenchuan, he observes that it was very different from the compassion in traditional China but resembled more the moral of the Good Samaritan in the Bible, where bonds of brotherhood transcend geographical, racial, economic, and social boundaries (Yan Y. 2009: 20).

Christian ethics

Chinese Christians quite happily agree with the suggestion that their values are conducive to harmonious social relations, although the degree to which they are willing to be enlisted in this newest socialist state building project varies significantly depending on their background. TSPM leadership has responded (or has been enlisted) to contribute to formidable tomes like *Religious Theory of the Harmonious Society* (*Hexie shehui de zongjiao lun*) in which the importance of Christian ethics in the construction of the 'harmonious society' is emphasized, with particular focus on charity work, an aspect that will be critically examined in Chapter 4. As a religion, the social function of Christianity is considered to lie in the field of ethics and morality.

For Melissa Lin (Lin M.M. 2010) it is the loss of *chengxin* (honesty and credibility) in Chinese society which lies at the heart of social immorality; to her the sale of fake products – undertaken for the short-term benefit of the individual and at the expense of the interest of the larger community – is symbolic of it. Moral construction needs to teach a new balance between the interests of individuals, society and the state, which can lead to a new code of conduct informed by a code of virtue and a code of belief, to use Ci Jiwei's terms. She sees this as one of the main areas where Christian ethics can make a contribution in Chinese society today.

Where business ethics are concerned, Christian values are considered necessary to rein in the excesses of a market economy, which, as a model, is understood to have been built on Christian foundations. Christianity allegedly provides the necessary ethical constraint to counterbalance the dynamics of the market. 'Even if more wealth is created, without a spiritual factor, society will not become any more peaceful and stable', states an article – echoing Xiaoying Wang – in the *China Youth Journal* entitled 'China Needs a Market Economy with Churches'.[3] Here the contemporary Christian message on ethics and morality is considered to be the outcome of the West's modernization process and therefore an important element to be incorporated into the totality of ethics of a China that itself is in the process of modernization. Therefore, approving and incorporating the positive Christian ethics and morality and strengthening the social function of Christian ethics can be a positive boost to socialist ethics and morality, according to the same source.

The article was written in 2002 by a prominent economist, Zhao Xiao, a Communist party member who later converted to Christianity. He is known for promoting the incorporation of Christian values into Chinese culture, a message that appears to be supported within the elite circles he frequents. Zhao considers love and the spirit of contracts as essential for the development of a positive business culture in China. Zhao sees no basis for contracts between equals, a key element of business culture, in traditional Chinese ethics while for Christians a contract in the form of the covenant is the basis of God's relationship with humanity (an aspect which is also key for Chinese Christian liberals and their formulation of a 'political theology' as discussed in Chapter 7). Love, on the other hand, is a key ingredient for harmonious relations among people, Zhao states. The prevalent hierarchy of love in Chinese culture and the commonly used phrased (as coined by Mao) 'there is no love without reasons and no hate without reason' are counterproductive in his view. Generally, faith can serve as a common basis for trust, the most important ingredient for cooperation, but which is crucially lacking in Chinese society today. In terms of business ethics, faith can provide a transcendental motivation that goes beyond mere profit seeking, as if one's purpose is to do business 'for the glory of God', then the ways and means by which business is conducted must also conform to this ideal (Zhao X. 2011b).

In terms of business culture, Zhao Xiao sees great value in the Christian concept of original sin which has led to the importance of structures and frameworks in order to mitigate against people's fundamental sinfulness. The belief in a person's innate goodness in Chinese culture, on the other hand, has led to the importance of personal relationships over the creation of structures and frameworks within which to operate. Zhao sees no problem incorporating these positive aspects of Christianity into Chinese culture, which has already proven flexible and adaptable over the centuries.

In fact, Christian entrepreneurs are considered pioneers in the post-Mao 'socialist market economy' and an important partner of the state development project. In his study of Wenzhou Christians, Nanlai Cao (2007) has observed that Christian entrepreneurs have earned much recognition and respect for their economic success by the state, which in turn has translated into the state's acceptance of local unregistered churches to which these entrepreneurs belong. Not only are the Christian entrepreneurs seen as models of economic success, but in some cases they have become actual partners of the state in governing the local community. This way the local government makes pragmatic use of the social standing and proven managerial ability of certain (Christian) individuals, thereby enhancing its legitimacy, while the benefit of such cooperation with the state on the side of the Christian entrepreneurs lies in social stability (achieved through good governance) which is necessary for economic success. As Nanlai Cao says

> Although it is too early to say whether the state and the church have co-opted each other in their common pursuit of social stability and economic development, Christianity certainly has gained recognition from the state as a useful source in local governance.
>
> (Cao N. 2007: 55)

But Christian belief is not only seen as a moral asset for local governance and the secret of economic success, it is also plays an important role in disciplining and motivating the workforce – another important factor in ensuring the success of a business.

The positive influence of Christian values is not regarded as confined to the field of business. Decades earlier, Zhao Zichen identified a complementary role of Christianity and Chinese culture. He wanted to encourage the spiritual transformation of the individual so that it would have an impact on social reconstruction. Zhao subscribed to the notion that 'moral character could save the nation' (*renge jiuguo*), the concept of love was the starting point for this transformation. Zhao Zichen held that apart from the love of God there was no tenable meaning of life. Decades later, Zhuo Xinping (2006a) of CASS discerns three aspects where Christian influences have had an impact on the spiritual cultivation of the Chinese. First, he says, the Christian concept of original sin has improved the Chinese estimation and evaluation of the possibility and ability in the human self, leading to improved mental cultivation and meditation on the significance of human life by many Chinese Christians. Second, the Christian concept of transcendence has brought a new dimension to the Chinese understanding of transcendence in the Confucian and Daoist traditions as it points out transcendence outside oneself and outside the bounds of human beings. In Zhuo's words

> This transcendence, as a means of ultimate concern and ultimate transformation, is an important guiding principle for the human pursuit of truth, goodness and beauty in this world. In this 'transcendence'…we can understand the basis of 'harmony' as interpreted by Confucius or others.
> (Zhuo 2006a: 162)

Third, Zhuo says that the Christian concept of agape (which he renders as 'universal love') has sublimated the human love or benevolence in Chinese tradition.

Gao and He (2011) argue that religion is a harmonizing force between the individual person's faith and the value system(s) of society. As society has become increasingly complex and alienating offering ever more choices, religion gains added significance, and in particular for disaffected people. Religion no longer guides politics, as was the case in Western societies, but religion can become an independent ethical force and a monitor of social moral life. Christianity will only be able to fulfil its positive social potential, if its influence is no longer viewed in political terms. In their view, Christianity's implications for society, culture and morals need to be considered in an objective way, if it is to realize its potential to make a significant contribution to the 'harmonious society' (Gao and He 2011).

Christian faith, morality and the individual

Religion is one important element in the new plurality of values we see in China today. This plurality is characterized by the rise of new ethics of individual rights and self-development on the one hand (which draw on a variety of influences) and the continuing expectation of collective ethics like self-sacrifice and duty on the other. It leads to a phenomenon, which Yan Yunxiang calls the 'divided self', where the individual has to negotiate different moral codes which will impact on his or her decisions in different ways depending on the concrete situation (Yan Y. 2011: 41–51). This stands in contrast to Ai Guohan's claim that in the interactions of individuals with the society and its structure harmony is realized, and that it is harmony that is evoked by interactions between the structure and the selected values and judgment of an individual at a particular moment (Ai G. 2008).[4]

Yan Yunxiang approaches China's moral crisis from the perspective of the individual, whose identity previously was defined not only by family and kinship networks, but also by the collective – either the commune or the work unit – and ultimately the socialist state. A number of changes in the reform era have led to the increasing importance of the individual as a moral actor, who now has to assume more responsibility, experiences greater uncertainty and risk and overall has to work harder. The dissolution of agricultural communes and the work unit in urban society and the migration of millions of people for work have unbound the individual; the latter in particular has to negotiate life in the cities as individuals rather than from within the structure of the family. Economic reforms have also brought new life aspirations and social mobility; a new generation of migrants has aspirations to move into white-collar, professional jobs (Kleinman *et al.* 2011a). There are also new patterns of social inequality, as the recently published Gini coefficient figures testify;[5] but new social inequality also includes an increase in gender inequality. And the reforms have also brought new social relations. More and more individuals find themselves interacting in public life with other individuals, who are either unrelated or total strangers. These new social relations necessitate high social trust and a morality that is based on universal values (Yan 2011). However, social trust in China is at an all-time low,[6] and new universally accepted values have yet to emerge.

China's newly 'unbound individuals' have to contend with the challenges of privatized housing, a strained or inadequate education system, expensive medical care, environmental pollution and corruption, leading to a whole catalogue of worries and anxieties. According to most recent research by the Pew Global Attitudes Project (Pew Research 2012), 81 per cent of respondents either completely agree or mostly agree that 'the rich are just getting richer while the poor get poorer'. The majority agree that their living conditions have improved, but this more general satisfaction is accompanied by a sharp rise in the concerns about the safety of food and medicine as well as corruption and the above mentioned income gap. Fifty-two per cent of Chinese like American ideas about democracy. But according to the same survey, 57 per cent of people are worried about a loss of traditional culture and as many as 71 per cent feel that their way of life needs to be protected from foreign influence. The latter figures tie in with the different ways people perceive a moral crisis as mentioned above.

According to Haiyan Lee, the post-Mao reaction was the withdrawal to the private and the elevation of personal fulfilment above public service. She concedes that the refusal to participate in an oppressively politicized public world is a potent form of resistance, but it has also had the consequence of rendering everyone without a civic arena in which to affirm one public political existence (Lee 2007:

307). Guobin Yang argues that against this background the internet, more specifically online communities have become 'spatial havens' where citizens, acting out of an utopian impulse, construct new identities, imagine new worlds, and nurture moral sentiments. The case studies he presents expose the badly damaged condition of trust in Chinese society, yet at the same time seem to show that members of online communities still had faith in a society threatened by the collapse of morality and trust (Yang G. 2009: Chapter 7).

The distrust felt by Chinese individuals is not confined to certain other individuals, but extends to all major elements of the economy and the government. It includes a mistrust of the market as a result of fake products and bad service as well as a mistrust of service providers and strangers. It may extend to friends and even relatives and most certainly includes distrust in law enforcement officers and the law and legal institutions. It is underscored by a distrust of basic moral values (Yan Y. 2011: 60). Such distrust is confirmed by cases like the one involving an attractive young woman working for the Chinese Red Cross, who boasted online about her wealth and luxurious lifestyle. The case exposed deeply entrenched problems and unethical behaviour in one of China's very few large charity organizations allowed to collect donations from the wider public (Wong E. 2011). Most recently trust in high level leadership has also been undermined by the scandal surrounding Bo Xilai and the private wealth accumulated by Wen Jiabao's immediate family, as exposed by the *New York Times* (Barboza 2012).

Against this background of social distrust a quiet consensus seems to have emerged that Christians are trustworthy and reliable. Nanlai Cao (2009) notes that Christianity has assumed a moral high ground in many urban localities due to its emphasis on spiritual ideology and ethical principles. For many – Christians and non-Christians alike – being Christian means being good. Lambert (2006: 43) argues that Christians are seen as moral examples and model citizens whose self-sacrificing care often shines out in painful contrast to venal officials who mouth empty slogans about 'serving the people'. An assumption – justified or not – that Christians are 'trustworthy' is also reflected in the advice given to Chinese students by a contact in their embassy when arriving in the United Kingdom, that they should befriend Christians, as they are honest.[7] For some, Christian charitable service is considered a perfect example of mutual adaptation between Christianity and Chinese society (Liu Xutong 2004).

It is true that many individuals display a higher level of morality after joining the Christina faith, which has led others, including officials, to conclude that Christianity is useful in combating family and marital problems, poor interpersonal relations, as well as social ills like drug abuse. The statement 'he/she must be a Christian' has become a phrase to praise the moral standing of a person, implying a 'good person, who is different from others'. There is a general agreement among Christians and non-Christians that faith and morality go hand in hand (Gao S. 2005: 290). Christians themselves overwhelmingly think that their influence on society is positive, with 92.8 per cent of respondents in a Beijing survey stating that they have a positive impact on the moral construction of society (Gao S. 2005: 313).

For Gao Shining, the ability to trust somebody and consider somebody else as an example is a great achievement in China after the Cultural Revolution, where mutual trust has been essentially eroded. She quotes Sartre's famous statement 'hell is other people' as an appropriate description of people's experiences during the Cultural Revolution and thereafter. In this 'hell' that is other people, Chinese Christians, despite their relatively small number, stand out by virtue of their high quality of character and hence exert a disproportionately high influence in society, argues Gao (Gao S. 2005: 125–6). In this context it is important to point out that the studies quoted above and the apparent importance of Christian belief as a signifier of social trustworthiness are based on an urban context, in which social relations need to be built among strangers. In a village community like the one described in Oxfeld's study (2010) different factors come into play. Insofar as religion is one of these factors, it may well be shared by the whole village community as is the case in Catholic villages, for example.

Fei Xiaotong's metaphor of the concentric circles on water developed on the basis of traditional rural society helps to illustrate the shift of the individual's social relations in urban China. In Fei's model the relative distance from the centre – the individual – to each circle represents an emotional and moral distance, which was based on family and kinship ties in traditional society. Following the destruction of the Confucian moral system, the fact that for China's 'unbound individuals' strangers have replaced family and kinship ties and the levels of distrust felt by individuals sometimes even towards their families, these circles now represent new layers of social relationships. In the absence of an all-encompassing moral authority, individuals have to rely on their own benchmarks to guide them through their daily negotiations of relations with other people and institutions. The resulting actions and behaviour will differ depending on the person's background and aspirations. Playing the system, including cheating, can be perceived as a legitimate path, if it brings better status, more money and in turn also benefits for the family or personal 'in-group', whose interests one has at heart. For others it may result in the pursuit of moral studies, trying to become a 'nicer person'.

Faith plays an important role in this context. The universal values based on a common faith which Zhao Xiao evokes in the context of business ethics are an important factor in the building of social trust among strangers. All Christians believe in an external moral authority that demands obedience to its code of virtue. This is recognized in fellow Christians, leading to higher levels of trust between two strangers, who are both Christians, than between strangers, where only one or no person is Christian. Using Fei's model, a fellow Christian will be represented in a circle that is closer to the individual at the centre than a non-believer. The social distance between the self of a believer and all related persons – where relation does not necessarily refer to family relation, but to relation in faith – is closer than the social distance between the self of a believer and other strangers. In a culture where family relations used to determine levels of trust, morality and responsibility, the fact that Christians refer to one another as 'brothers and sisters' gains added significance here. Therefore, while faith leads to increased social trust, at the same time, shared faith also leads to the creation of new in-groups and out-groups.

Yet, not all Christians are socially equidistant from the individual self of a believer. Additional factors, like whether a person is a member of the same church (which are often socially stratified), whether they have the same educational background or whether they are from the same locale, influence how close and thus how bound by a shared code of virtue the individual feels. Chinese Christians have not entirely overcome the 'hierarchy of love' as described by Zou, leading to new meaning attached to the boundaries of the concentric circles in Fei Xiaotong's model. A fellow Christian of the same church and the same background will be closer to the centre than a fellow Christian of a different social background or from a different area in China. But while a non-Christian stranger will be felt to be most distant, the individual believer's behaviour and conduct towards this distant stranger will nonetheless have to follow the basic code of virtue as prescribed by their faith. Hence the public perception of Christians as trustworthy, which leads to the paradox that for the non-Christian individual self, a Christian stranger is perceived to be closer in terms of trustworthiness (but not necessarily in terms of required moral responsibility) than a fellow non-believer.

Divided or whole?

How bound the individual Christian feels by the code of virtue prescribed by his or her faith depends on a variety of factors including the depth of their faith and the duration since their conversion. Some people have little problem 'compartmentalizing', but are not considered 'true Christians' in the eyes of those, for whom compartmentalizing is not an option. In her study of Beijing Christians, Gao Shining (2005) identified a number of different types of believers when it comes to their relation between Christian faith and morality. First there are those, whose morality is entirely guided by faith. They have lived a life of hardship, often including a prison sentence. Only a very small number fell into this category on the basis of Gao's case studies, but I argue that they have since been joined by a younger generation of intellectual church leaders, who entirely live by their faith and expect a similar commitment from the members of their congregation. By far the biggest number in Gao's study fell into the second category for whom there was a certain distance between faith and value direction. To this group, faith was a habit, a practice reserved for one day a week. Increasingly, however, individuals in this group, too, experienced a conflict between their faith and the conduct it demands and the values in society at large. The case of the lawyer, who, as a result of his professional environment regularly has to act in ways which go against his Christian values, represents a classic case of the 'divided self'. This particular individual bridges this division by praying morning and evening, asking for forgiveness, a system which he thinks works quite well (Gao S. 2005: 211).

For some individuals, the Christian moral code is stronger than their faith. Even though their faith is not profound, certain generally accepted social practices are no longer considered acceptable (for example taking financial handouts in the workplace when knowing that the provenance of the money is dubious), leading to decisions that go against the grain and identify the individual as 'Christian'. In some cases the new faith leads to a complete value change; they include the familiar (but nonetheless rare) cases frequently referred to in evangelistic literature of the good for nothing criminal, who completely turns his or her life around as a result of a key experience. More common is a slow change in values, as observed by Gao in business men, who no longer seek immediate gain from a relationship.

Regardless of the strength of their faith, for Christians morality is the starting point as well as the end result of their faith. Christian values are often in contrast to what is common and hence stand out and get commented on. This can be in a positive way, but it can also lead to ridicule. It also leads to expectations of a certain kind of behaviour from Christians, who will be reprimanded (by non-Christians), if they fail to conform to this expectation. Christians are also seen as admirable or useful by officials and Christianity holds appeal for the educated middle class. Many individuals of this stratum of society initially attend TSPM churches, but leave them, because their clergy are not well trained enough to deal with their more complex psychological dilemmas (Gao S. 2005: 215–17). Instead they find unregistered churches which have become more mature in outlook and more open in recent years. They have names, fixed places, Sunday schools, choirs, and publications. Their clergy, who often have postgraduate degrees, are well trained and underwent formal theological training. In these churches, debates take place in earnest how Christianity and Chinese culture can come together; they also get actively involved in society (Gao and He 2011). These churches also place high moral and spiritual demands on their members, who are expected to engage in constant self-examination and dialogue with their God.

The individuals, who lead these churches, often identify 1989 as a key date in their journey towards the Christian faith. They were students at China's elite institutions during the 1980s and early 1990s, if not active participants in the events of 1989 then closely interested and deeply affected by the outcome. They were devouring books on Western culture and civilization like all students during that decade and usually encountered the Bible in the same process. The academic studies by 'Cultural Christians' played an important role in their initial encounter with Christianity. They were individual examples of Ci Jiwei's nihilists, but were untempted by the promises of hedonism. The party no longer offered them any satisfactory ideological answers; its emphasis on business and consumerism did not provide any opportunities to contribute for these uncompromising, idealistic elite intellectuals in search for a new moral order. Christianity with its long intellectual tradition, all-encompassing belief structure and associational manifestations provided a credible alternative to the party's pathway that was either blocked off or no longer promised to lead anywhere other than a shopping mall.

The leading intellectual figures in Chinese Christianity today, whether they have founded their own churches inside China or have made a life in the Christian mission outside China, were all students or academic staff at leading Chinese universities in the 1980s. Many of them had been party members or were aspiring to be party members before the ultimate disillusionment with the dominant ideology post-1989. Following the destruction of the Confucian scholarly tradition (which emphasized moral and intellectual values over material values) and the instrumentalization of education in the post-Mao period as a means to obtain material rewards, there no longer existed any significant indigenous cultural resources for the negation of hedonism (Ci 1994: 241). Christianity presented an answer to all their searches; it provided an all-encompassing moral system, valued intellectual leadership, and constituted a utopianism that will never disappoint (as its promise does not lie in this life).

Relating the story of one's conversion is an important feature of contemporary Chinese Christianity. Interviewees usually start a conversation with this account, whether prompted or not.[8] Peng Qiang, now a church leader and independent publisher in Chengdu, was a student at the China Youth College for Politics (Zhongguo qingnian zhengzhi xueyuan) in the early 1990s. Born in 1973 he had still caught the tail end of the political hopes of the 1980s and encountered Christianity while a student at a college, which prepared its students for a political career and party membership. He was introduced to the Bible during a class on Western culture and found ways to explore it further through the Bible study group offered by his English teacher. His interest was not an isolated one. Professors at his college at the time included Wang Dongcheng and Ai Xiaoming, who all converted to Christianity in due course. In 1993 Peng was baptized in the bathtub of a Beijing hotel room, wearing ripped jeans, a black shirt and an oversized army coat (the fashionable look of a rebel in China of the late 1980s and early 1990s) complemented by the ultimate hallmark of the non-conformist, long hair (Yu and Wang 2010a: 49–56; also personal interview November 2012). Zha Changping's wife evoked a similar image of her husband as the leather trousered, hard drinking disillusioned intellectual rebel in search for meaning (personal conversation, November 2012).

The churches these and other men have founded have become relatively well known in recent years. Although in a minority, they are well connected to each other within China and are closely linked to Christian networks outside China, which are led by individuals, who have found the Christian faith in a similar search for meaning as described above. Some of them are post-1989 exiles, but others have discovered faith as postgraduate students abroad; a number of them used to be party members enjoying high level connections. They now dedicate their whole life to the work with their churches; many of them have been ordained ministers, thus assuming intellectual, moral and spiritual leadership in one person. They place high demands on the individuals in their congregation and do not condone a 'divided self' or an approach which allows the individual to compartmentalize their faith as something reserved for Sunday worship. They offer spiritual support through small groups and regular (written) communications with their congregations and provide an important voice of moral guidance for their members. Although their churches whose theology can broadly be described as 'New-Calvinist' (see Chapter 1) place importance on Christian engagement with society, they do not accept the reduction of Christianity to a set of social ethics in the service of society and ultimately the state project of the 'harmonious society', as promoted by the TSPM leadership.

This emphasis on the nexus between Christian faith and morality constitutes a core issue that divides Chinese Christians. TSPM theology stresses Christian ethics, or more precisely and in Ci Jiwei's terms, it puts relatively more emphasis on Christianity's code of ethics summarized as love and its corresponding code of conduct where this love is put into practice, and downplays the importance of the code of belief (faith). (For an in-depth analysis of the role of love in Chinese Christian theology see Chapter 3.) But even moderate critics like Gao Shining caution that one must not forget that faith does not equal ethics. In reality, many Christians themselves are not quite clear about the difference and there is a strong tendency to 'moralize' faith, by believers and non-believers alike.

For the majority of Chinese Christians, their faith leads to a constant negotiation of the moral demands of their belief and the extent to which they can follow these demands in a wider society without putting themselves at risk. What they consider a risk will depend on their individual situation, their own moral benchmark, which in turn is determined by the strength of their convictions. What I mean by risk here is not necessarily the risk to their own personal safety, as the discourse on Christianity from certain quarters will make us believe, but the risk of ridicule by others, the risk of losing out on opportunities to gain wealth (by refusing to take part in certain practices), or simply the risk of being considered 'different'. The obvious answer to this is to keep their faith a private matter, to confine its expression to the safe environment of Bible study groups, student fellowships and churches and to restrict all meaningful personal interaction to members of the same group in order to limit as much as possible the degree of conflict between their own inner moral universe, which is shared by fellow Christians in their church, and the pluralistic moral practices that make up the contemporary Chinese moral landscape. But increasingly, there are individuals for whom this division of the self is not an option and whose faith influences their behaviour in wider social relations, as not doing so would compromise their belief and result in a conflict with their conscience and their God. Crucially, their faith provides an empowering sense of self, which enables them to follow its corresponding moral code and guidance.

Conclusion

Unashamedly dedicated to a nascent consumerism, the small independent market in Silk Street embodied the first stages of what Ci Jiwei called a move from utopianism to hedonism in Chinese society. Students and young intellectuals were too poor and too idealistic to partake in this shift at that time. Instead of frequenting the market, they attended the many 'salons' and discussion groups that sprang up in the 1980s. These shaped the young generation leading the demonstrations in 1989, whose disillusionment with utopianism expressed itself in demands for political liberalism. Post 1989 the 'crude hedonism' encouraged by the party's new reform strategy only demanded respect for the political status quo in return; as Ci Jiwei put it, hedonism represented one way of undergoing nihilism without raising it to the level of conscious reflection (Ci 1994: 6). But many of those, who through intellectual effort were able to raise the condition of nihilism to the level of conscious reflection, consciously resisted the path of hedonism. In their continued search for meaning they found a new ideology in the form of Christianity, providing an all- encompassing code of belief, virtue and conduct.

Hedonism may have replaced politics for about two decades following 1989, but it has not been able to provide any answers for people's spiritual questions. As Gao Shining's survey and interviews as well as my own research have shown, Christianity was one belief system, which offered answers for many young and educated Chinese (the demographic with the fastest growth in Christian faith after the 1990s) looking for the meaning of life, who were searching for knowledge and an explanation for biological mysteries, or who were looking for spirituality and transcendentalism (Gao S. 2005: 126). Depending on the strength of their new found faith, this new belief system (code of belief) with its corresponding code of ethics and code of conduct may result in the 'divided self', an individual negotiating contradictory emotions, torn between the demands of their faith and the behavioural norms of society, the desire to contribute positively and constructively to the common good and a newly formed Christian conscience that prevents the individual from partaking in commonly expected behaviour. Despite this conflict, faith does lead to a stronger sense of self-determination in individuals and provides an important aesthetic value beyond the monetary. It also provides a strong sense of empowerment, partly through membership of a circle of like-minded people, and partly through the comforting notion of God's love which helps the individual to make a 'proactive and conscious choice to be an upright and honest person', to refer back to Wang Xiaoming. Faith provides a 'moral backbone' for the individual, which helps in the daily navigation through an uncertain social environment. This 'moral backbone' is strengthened through social contact in the churches and the guiding voice of the pastor and other mentors in small study and discussion groups.

Christian interviewees always point out that they are good, law-abiding citizens, but in the context of widespread scandal and distrust, even the most docile and compliant Christian will expect others, including the government, to respect a moral bottom line. Experiences of a lack of this moral bottom line lead to frustration in dealings with others in society, ranging from such mundane instances as people not keeping their word or not showing up for meetings to far more serious examples. The result is often to try to keep meaningful social contact and cooperation to fellow Christians, and to restrict contact with non-Christians to a minimum. This includes romantic relationships (see next chapter), but also applies to leisure activities and business activities, thus forming important new 'in-groups' of trust in an untrustworthy environment. The social relations and their resulting moral obligations still follow Fei Xiaotong's pattern, which place the Christian individual at the heart of concentric circles, each layer of which represents the relative distance in terms of moral obligations. But the different layers no longer represent family or kinship. Instead, Christian faith has become an important factor in determining the relative distance of a stranger to the self at the centre.

At an official level Christian ethics are seen as conducive to improving the moral standards of Chinese society and as compatible with the new state ideology. Individual Christians, who believe in this new utopia of the 'harmonious society' (and they are more numerous than one might think), are in principle happy to contribute and respond in a positive way to the calls and appeals made to them by the party-state to put their superior ethics to good use. But they are also wary of their faith being reduced to a convenient set of ethics for political purpose. For true believers, faith, not ethics, is key to their moral existence. Striking a balance between the demands of their God and the party-state and between the expectations of their church and society at large demands daily negotiation and creates an inner conflict. The example of the former nihilists turned Christian leaders, who now play a crucial role in the moral and spiritual direction and support of urban churches and their members, suggests that this conflict will result in a strengthening of the faith the more credibility the party state loses. After all Silk Market, too, has long lost its appeal; it is the genuine that now holds appeal with the trendy, the avant-garde and the idealistic.

Notes

1 An unfavourable comparison between the state of public toilets in China and America seems to lend itself as ready metaphor in this context. See for example Fan Xuede *Meiguo cesuo yinxiangji* (Impressions of American Toilets, Fan X. 2012: 112–4).
2 The Chinese term used in the original is *you'ai*, which has also been translated as 'fraternity' by a different author (Mahoney 2008: 115).
3 An English translation of this much quoted article by Zhao Xiao can be found at www.danwei.org/business/churches_and_the_market_econom.php (last accessed 15 March 2013).
4 Ai Guohan is professor of Writing at Rowan University and President of the Association of Chinese Professors of Social Science and Humanities in the United States.
5 In January 2013 the Chinese government released the Gini coefficient figures for the first time after a 12-year break. The figures show a wealth gap of 0.474, marking a slight improvement to the figures of 2008 released at the same time. The index measures wealth distribution on a scale of 0 to 1, where 0 indicates absolute equality and 1 the concentration of all wealth in the hands of one person. Readings above 0.4 are considered to mark a high degree of inequality. However, the government's figures do not correspond to figures produced by academics, which state an index of 0.61 for the year 2010 (Li Y. 2013). Accurate figures on anything are notoriously difficult to come by; therefore what matters more than the question as to which figure is accurate, is that the official numbers do not match what ordinary people are experiencing.
6 A study conducted by the Institute of Sociology under the Chinese Academy of Social Sciences concluded that social trust had fallen from 62.9 points in 2010 to 59.7 in 2012. Only 30 per cent of urban residents (on which the survey focused) trusted strangers; family members remain the most trusted people (see He D. 2013).
7 Information obtained in conversation with Chinese university students in London; it has not been possible to verify whether this advice was given in an official or unofficial capacity.
8 For the personal story of a number of key figures in the urban intellectual churches and overseas churches, see the two edited volumes by Yu Jie and Wang Yi (2010a and b).

3 Christian love and China's 'harmonious society'

In *Civilization and its Discontents* Sigmund Freud argues that there is a fundamental 'antithesis' between civilization and man's most primal urges.

> The existence of this inclination to aggression, which we can detect in ourselves and justly assume to be present in others, is the factor which disturbs our relations with our neighbour and which forces civilization into such a high expenditure. In consequence […] civilized society is perpetually threatened with disintegration. The interest of work in common would not hold it together; instinctual passions are stronger than reasonable interests. […]. Hence […] the commandment to love one's neighbour as oneself – a commandment which is really justified by the fact that nothing else runs so strongly counter to the original nature of man […]
>
> (Freud 1961: 55–69)[1]

While Sigmund Freud's theories and model of the unconscious mind remain controversial in China, the passage above must nonetheless resonate with those concerned with the stability and harmony of China's civilization. 'Love thy neighbour' has essentially become part of China's latest ideology project, the building of the 'harmonious society', which tries to address China's huge social problems and differences on an ideological level. Love has found its way into local government websites, charitable organizations and Marxist philosophical writings. It seems that not only popular culture but also official discourse has discovered love in China today.

This chapter examines the role love plays in the official discourse on the 'harmonious society'. Through analysis of official ideological writings and Chinese Christian theology it suggests that the use of the term in the discourse on the 'harmonious society', despite the official emphasis on Confucian values, has strong Christian roots and constitutes an acknowledgement of the growing importance of Christian values in contemporary China. The use of the word is an attempt to re-appropriate a popular, inherently positive value and attach an ideological meaning to it. Reference to non-Chinese communist philosophers demonstrates that this tendency is not confined to the Chinese context. The 'love' this chapter is concerned with is perhaps best represented in the Greek terms of *agape*, the Latin

Love and the harmonious society 47

term *caritas* or the German term *Nächstenliebe,* although the final section of the chapter does take into account the role of Christian love in romantic/marital relationships.² These relationships are informed by a complementarian view of the role of men and women as common among evangelical Christians, who see the Bible as the infallible word of God. The conclusion argues that the government is hoping for a similarly harmonious relationship with Christianity based on a complementarian interpretation of the relations between Christians and the party.

The Chinese texts I have been analysing invariably use the monosyllabic term *ai* as a noun to express these notions. The use of this monosyllabic term is relatively recent, as is the use of the term outside a romantic context. It belongs to a group of affective terms, which also include the monosyllabic *qing*, as well as the bisyllabic *aiqing*, *qinggan*, *tongqing*, and *aixin*. While the use of the term *ai* outside the romantic context may be relatively recent, Haiyan Lee shows that love already became an important concept in the discourse of modernity in the early twentieth century, when it was declared that love should be the sole principle underscoring all social relationships. This included relationships with people outside the immediate family and as such was tied up with the rebellion against the traditional Confucian family and hierarchies. But love also played a contradictory role in the project of modernity. One the one hand, it heralded the rise of the private and personal, on the other hand it was an important aspect of nationalism and nation building, which called upon an emotion – to love the country – that transcended the private (Lee 2007: 6–10).

Zhang Jie was one of the first post-Mao writers to take up the subject of love and desire 'as weapons of exposé, encoding emotional and bodily experiences as symbolic of human resilience' as Haiyan Lee argues (Lee 2007: 301). Love as a literary theme recurs in post-Mao literature, spanning an arch from the idealized, platonic lover of Zhang Jie's story in the late 1970s to the hedonistic sexual exploits of Wei Hui's *Shanghai Baby* in 1999, a literary development that in and of itself is perceived by some as symbolic of China's moral and intellectual decay in the reform era (Zhou B. 2007). One year before the publication of Wei Hui's book in China, another young writer named Yu Jie burst onto the scene with a collection of essays full of social and political criticism, which made him another literary sensation. He Qinglian, whose *The Pitfalls of Modernization* was published in China in the same year as Yu Jie's first book *Fire and Ice*, has commented that, although her book was recommended reading by many university lecturers, the students at the time were only interested in Yu Jie's writings.³ In 2001 another collection of his essays (the seventh since *Fire and Ice*) called *The Verge of Love and Pain* was published. In the last entry in the collection, Yu Jie explains that while the title of the book was borrowed from a love song by Wang Fei, who sings about the critical condition of being eternally caught between love and pain in a romantic relationship, he used it in a completely different context. He felt the same critical condition not because of (romantic) love (*aiqing*) for one person, but in response to the vast masses of people around him. 'Only because of love (ai), I can feel pain; only because of deep-rooted pain, can I produce even stronger love' (Yu Jie 2001: 351). We are given to understand that it is this love for the ordinary people around him, which fuels his motivation and constitutes the raison d'être of his writings. Yu Jie, who converted to Christianity a few years later, has been one of the most outspoken critics of the Chinese government. His books stopped being available in China and his Beijing congregation *Fangzhou* was subject to close scrutiny and repeated raids by the police. Yu Jie was closely involved with the drafting of Charter 08 and has been in exile in the United States since 2012, where he is at the heart of a campaign to free Liu Xiaobo and promote his writings.

Christianity – a religion of love

Love is a central aspect of all Christianity; in the Chinese theological context it is of even more importance. It is in this context that the use of the monosyllabic noun '*ai*' is most prevalent. The studies undertaken by religious scholars in the 1980s and 1990s led to a slow paradigm shift in regards to the role of religion in society away from 'religion as opium' to 'religion as culture'. This in turn enabled the academic study of religion, which through the prolonged close involvement with their subject, led to the recasting of religion, in particular Christianity, as a positive rather than negative element of culture. The many studies and translations that resulted from the endeavours of these scholars often were the first encounter with Christianity for many of the young, urban Christians (like Yu Jie), who have contributed to the growth of Christianity in recent years (He G. 2011).

These endeavours at re-evaluation continue today. Zhuo Xinping (2006a), Director of the Institute of World Religions at the Chinese Academy of Social Sciences, argues that in the era of globalization China should be ready to look anew at the endeavours of the Christian mission in China; a more positive evaluation will provide a more solid base for cultural interaction and understanding in this new era of peaceful co-existence and harmonious development. For Zhuo Xinping the Christian concept of agape (which he renders as 'universal love') has lifted the human love or benevolence in Chinese tradition to a different level where rather than being based on human relationships and being conditional, Christian love transcends the human realm and is unconditional. By emphasizing this love, Christianity, according to Zhuo, is regarded as a 'religion of love'.

This particular emphasis on love in Chinese Christian theology is largely due to the efforts of one man. Ding Guangxun, who died in November 2012, was perhaps in equal measure revered and reviled by the Chinese Christian population (see Wickeri 2007). Since the early 1980s, the Three-Self Patriotic Movement (TSPM) and the Chinese Christian Council (CCC) have stepped up their work to develop a Chinese Christian theology 'rooted in the Chinese soil'. In Western media and academia, the Chinese official church is sometimes viewed with criticism, which echoes the often very harsh criticism and hostility that emanates from the Chinese 'house church' community. The reality in China is much more complex; the rise in Christianity has been marked and official churches are overflowing. While many criticize the official Church for 'selling out', for being too secular and too accommodating of party policy, its success and appeal to all strata of society is undeniable. It would be simplistic, warns Nanlai Cao, to regard the official church as a tool of the Chinese state and treat those who worship or minister 'above ground' as state collaborationists. It would be equally unsophisticated to interpret all other churches as a form of resistance (Cao N. 2007). As shown in Chapter 1, the lines are much more blurred and have become more so in recent years.

According to Cao Shengjie, President of the China Christian Council, there is a cordial relationship between church and society in China today, which is underpinned by consultation through constitutional channels. Hundreds of representatives in the official Christian church participate at varying levels within the National Chinese People's Political Consultative Conference; Ding Guangxun was one of the vice presidents of the conference for almost two decades (Cao S. 2006: 150). Love is the central tenet of the 'Reconstruction of Theological Thinking' in China and is built upon Ding Guangxun's theology that stresses that love is the supreme attribute of God. In his words 'Only by acquiring a Chinese selfhood, a Chinese identity, can the Church of Jesus Christ in China live down its colonial past history and its image as something Western' (Ting 2004: 57). The central tenet of his theology was the move to a non-denominational Chinese church built on the core message that God is Love (*shangdi shi ai*).

> To know God as love is to say that the supreme attribute of God is not his power and might, nor his omniscience, nor his deity, nor his majesty and dominion and righteousness. Transcendence signifies the inexhaustibility of the cosmic love and immanence, the unfailing presence of that love in the whole creation.
>
> (Ting 2004: 88)

Hand in hand with the importance of God's immanence in Ding's formulation goes his emphasis on the Christ-like God. The (official) Chinese Christian God is the God of the New Testament as embodied in Christ's attributes; it is the 'Cosmic Christ'. We will revisit the significance of this particular definition of God and transcendence later, as it provides a key link between the communist understanding of love and a Christian understanding of God's love as influenced by a modernist interpretation of divine presence.

Ding's theology is a direct result of the political and religious developments in China since 1949 and reflects the positive impression that many Chinese Christians had of the early revolutionaries, whose moral goodness, self-sacrifice and honesty for many stood in stark contrast to the old regime and which for Christians posed the question as to how to interpret good deeds outside the Christian faith. Herein lies the starting point for Ding's theology. He focuses on Christ, the Christ-like nature of God and the universal extent of God's work, which is not limited to those who declare faith in God. The cosmic Christ as drawn by Ding shows God as the cosmic lover, not as cosmic tyrant or punisher. He works by education and persuasion rather than coercion and forced obedience. Ding rejects the standard metaphor of God as a father as unhelpful in the Chinese context, as the father figure in traditional Chinese culture is not associated with love and kindness. His theology also puts less emphasis on the original sin as orthodox Christian theology does.

This conception of God not only makes it possible to co-exist with or even embrace the ideals of communism, but is also sensitive to traditional Chinese culture, in particular Mencius, who posits that human nature is essentially good.

Although it is liberation theology that is most commonly associated with Marxism, it is not an important influence on Ding. He has expressed his appreciation of liberation theology in the struggle for independence, democracy and a more humane socio-economic system and its emphasis on context and practice. However, he disagrees with liberation theology, which makes liberation rather than the reconciliation of God and humankind central to theology. Ding cites the example of China where despite having been liberated for several decades, and despite the significant improvement in people's livelihood since liberation, liberation in itself cannot address and even less resolve the fundamental issue of God's reconciliation with humankind (Ding 1998b: 198; Ting 2004: 70–2). He also cautions against the idealization of the poor, as 'poverty is no virtue, unless voluntary, and does not always bring with it wisdom' (Ting 2004: 71). And in what can only be read as a direct reflection of the Cultural Revolution, Ding asserts that while the poor may be poor, their thinking will usually have been influenced by the ruling class. Correct theory, Ding says, never emerged by itself from the poor; progressive theory has always been produced by intellectuals from relatively well-off families during peaceful and stable conditions (Ding 1998b: 196).

The key point of Ding's theology is also the point on which there is greatest disagreement with him from within evangelical circles in and outside China. According to the TSPM/CCC campaign 'to build up theological thinking', justification by faith should be 'played down' or *danhua* (literally 'diluted') in Chinese. From this has come the impression that Ding has replaced justification by faith with justification by love, although this is refuted from within TSPM theological circles. Ding also argues that the Bible was inspired by God, but that not all in the Bible was God's word, which, according to Fällman (2008: 52) led him to conclude that the parts whose message is not that 'God is love' are not God's words. This, again, is anathema to the evangelical belief in the inerrancy of the Bible.

Lambert's criticism of Ding is unequivocal. He implies arrogance on Ding's part, who apparently bemoaned the fact that the vast majority of Christians, even within the TSPM/CCC churches, were evangelical or fundamentalist in a pejorative sense. Lambert calls Ding's 'theological construction' a 'thinly disguised aim to cut the church's conservative evangelical moorings and guide it down a theological cul de sac.' Ding's 'new theology' is apparently a 'turgid blend of Marxism, liberal Christianity and process theology' as well as 'surprisingly close to dangerous trends such as "openness theology"' (Lambert 2006: 22). It is not the purpose of this chapter to delve deeper into these accusations. What they do highlight, however, is the way in which theological disputes as they take place outside China, impact on the evaluation of Chinese Christianity, in particular the theological direction of the TSPM leadership. To an outsider they are all too reminiscent of other ideological and intellectual disputes that have played out in China over the last hundred years. What seems to add further fuel to the criticism of Ding is that he belonged to a generation of left-wing intellectuals, who purposefully returned to China from abroad in the early 1950s hopeful that the new state would bring a real, positive change to which they wanted to contribute. Most of them suffered during the political campaigns of the 1950s and certainly during the Cultural Revolution, hence their early support of the regime has rarely been questioned. Ding's fate during those years was relatively mild, a fact that is held against him as further proof of his collaboration and his lack of faith.

While Ding's theology is influenced by communist ideals, in the context of the reform era, this Chinese Christian theology gains new significance. The ideals of socialism and communism no longer serve as inspiration for individual and social behaviour; Lei Feng no longer serves as an effective role model. The social ills and divisions that run through all levels of contemporary Chinese society and which form the main obstacle to the building of the 'harmonious society' require new answers. While in the 1950s Chinese Christians could not help but be impressed by the heroism and selflessness of early communist revolutionaries, contemporary Chinese communists, almost despite themselves, cannot help but be impressed by Christian witness. While Ding formulated his theology in the light of a new atheist reality, the Chinese Communist Party today appears ready to inject new life into its ideology by incorporating central elements of Chinese Christianity, like the importance of love, into its doctrine.

The vitriolic voices which demonize Ding and the TSPM leadership are largely confined to certain groups of American Christians and are not as universally shared as these groups claim (see Bays 2009). Ding's emphasis on love (*ai*) as a central tenet of Christian faith has found a ready audience, not only in the Chinese Christian population but also in international church organizations. Through Ding's profile in Chinese political organizations, his influence has also contributed, as I argue, to the proliferation of the monosyllabic term *ai* in official literature, which has started to appear in the first decade of this millennium. His attempts at creating a theology 'rooted in the Chinese soil' may not ultimately be successful (the jury is still out, I think), but his endeavours, together with the academic studies of 'Cultural Christians', are partly responsible for bringing Christian concepts into mainstream thinking and as such constitute an interesting example of the way political discourse is formed in today's China.

Christian love and the 'harmonious society'

There are a number of additional signs that indicate an influence of Christian philosophy on the emergence of love in the discourse on and the practical steps of building the 'harmonious society'.

One important element in building the 'harmonious society' is, in Qin Zhiyong's words,

> the best achievements of the world civilizations…The building of the harmonious society will not work out without cultural exchanges and dialogue among world cultures…to actively learn with a broad vision and

open minds the achievements of civilizations in the world to assimilate their useful elements and integrate them into the harmonious culture to be built.

(Qin Z. 2008: 66)

This echoes Wang Hui who has urged Chinese intellectuals to 'break their time-honoured dependence on binary paradigms, to pay more attention to the factors that might contribute to institutional innovation within society' (Huters and Wang 2003: 186). While both writers above refer to world civilizations, many speak more concretely of Western civilization, but refrain from becoming more specific.

One of the many official publications on the construction of the 'harmonious society' lists Western thinking as one of five ideological reference points. (The other four in this particular source published in Yunnan are Confucianism, Daoism, Chinese Minority Thought, and Marxism.) The Christian concepts of paradise, universal love, and equality are listed as beneficial to the maintaining of stability and harmony (Hu and Shi 2008: 23–5). In contrast to many local religions and 'superstitions', Christianity is viewed as a rational belief system and a modern religion. According to Nanlai Cao (2009: 56; also Yang M.M.-H. 2004), the social stigma attached to popular religion contrasts sharply with a sense of cultural legitimacy and superiority associated with Christianity in today's China. While popular religion and 'superstition' has been associated with 'backwardness', Christianity, has been associated with science and modernity, and many local officials hold a favourable attitude towards Christianity for this same reason. At the same time, Christianity is slowly starting to lose its stigma as a 'foreign' religion. The combined efforts of Ding Guangxun and other religious leaders as well as academics at CASS[4] have resulted in the increasingly accepted notion that Christianity too forms part of Chinese tradition and can therefore safely be included when referring to the all-important 'Chinese characteristics'. The formulation of a specifically Chinese Christian theology as developed by Ding Guangxun has made it possible to refer to all the culturally positive aspects perceived to be contained in Christian thought and belief as part of a Chinese cultural heritage and development. Repositioning Christianity in this way also constitutes one aspect of what Nicholas Dynon (2008) calls the appropriation of *wenming* (a term referring largely to non-Chinese notions of progress) as a Chinese rather than a foreign concept through the formulation of a distinctly Chinese notion of civilization supported by aspects of foreign civilization.

Zhuo Xinping sees many opportunities for the Christian church to play a positive role in the reconstruction of wider society. He sees no difficulty for Chinese Christians to bring 'faith, love and hope' to China. In so doing, in Zhuo's words, they can avoid the 'disenchantment' with Christianity that is prevalent in the West today. Christians in Asia would then initiate a process of 'desecularization of the world' in place of the secularization processes that are taking place in the West (Zhuo 2006a: 197–9). Rather than being subject to Western, imperialist influence, Chinese Christians in this official vision become the incarnation of the good, nationalist Chinese citizen, representing and taking an idealist image of China to the rest of the world.

For Zhao Xiao, professor of economics, communist party member and close advisor to the Wen Jiaobao's government,

> there is no culture that can match Christianity's degree of prizing love, because what it emphasizes is a form of unconditional love, a love for everyone, including those who are not lovable, including those who have hurt you or oppressed you. You have to love them, regardless of whether they are good or bad to you, regardless of whoever they are, you must love them. So this kind of love is a sign of the openness of modern society and modern civilization. [...] if Chinese society wants more openness, more harmony, then it needs the spirit of universal love.
>
> (Osnos: no date)

In his blog Zhao Xiao (2010a) establishes a direct link between concepts propagated by Hu Jintao and Wen Jiabao in the 'harmonious society' discourse and key Christian values like faith, hope and love. For Zhao this implies that China's modernization does not just include economic modernization and political culture, but also a modernization of ethics and values. Specifically he understands the modernization of ethics as a mix of traditional Chinese values and Christian faith, which will put China in good stead to become a globally leading nation, an idea he also expanded on in a speech at the Chinese Theological Forum in Korea, in 2010 (Zhao X. 2011a).

The panacea of love

The term 'love' appears in a variety of official and semi-official writings on the 'harmonious society', of which a number of examples are presented in the following. Qin Zhiyong, for instance, states that, 'the ethical outlook centred on the premise that the humane person loves others is the cornerstone of the harmonious culture' (Qin Z. 2008: 63). A researcher at the Zhengzhou Research Centre for Marxism Philosophy named Liu Taiheng (2005) claims that the spirit of love is the most prominent among China's universal traditional values. In his article entitled 'The Harmonious Society and The Traditional Ethical Spirit of "love"' Liu equals the traditional virtue of *ren*, often translated as benevolence, with '*airen*', loving people. In a rather radical departure from the Analects,[5] Liu considers 'love' the fundamental spirit of traditional Chinese culture, which formed a central part in the philosophy of all of Confucianism and Daoism. According to Liu, it is this spirit of love that lies at the heart of all of China's achievements as a civilization; 'love' affirms that 'nature and humanity are in harmony' (*tian ren he yi*) and its ultimate idealist aim is to establish a '*xiaokang*' society and a world in great harmony (*datong shijie*). Love, according to Liu Taiheng, is therefore the essential ingredient to building the 'harmonious society' in China. Love will solve contradictions on a social level and promote world peace on an international level.

Another author writing 'Under the Banyan Tree' considers Mo Zi's 'universal love' (*jian'ai*) and its function for the 'harmonious society'. Mo Zi's concept of *jian'ai*, which in this article is explained as a love that is not restricted by blood lines or hierarchical differences, is considered to be of great importance in the building of the 'harmonious society' in China. According to this writer, *jian'ai* can train people 'of high quality' (*gao suzhi de remin*) and a loyal workforce, it can lead to harmony between people and nature, is the key to a good and virtuous government and can create a 'cleaner' social atmosphere with less corruption, fewer self-serving officials and a population that is therefore safe and at ease (Zhu Y.: no date).

According to the Beijing Review (Tang Y. 2007), a small town in Henan has achieved national and international fame through its education in 'love'. According to the teachers, 'love' is the central motivational force in people's lives; to love and being loved are considered strong social forces. They reckon that love is the source of all happiness and kind heartedness. It is the ability to sense the need of others; it is unconditional and in this case compared to motherly love. Central to the efforts at Lujiang is the traditional Chinese belief in education as the source of all things; in this case, it is an education in love.[6]

Early discourse on socialist morality in the PRC was also expressed through the use of 'love'. Mao Zedong's foreword to the first release of the Xinhua Daily on 29 September 1949 spoke of the 'four love principle' to enforce public morality. All Chinese citizens were exhorted 'to love the motherland, to love the people, to love labour and to love public property'. In case this love did not come naturally, Mao proposed three ways in which it could be implemented. One was the setting up of inspiring examples of public morality so that revolutionary values like unselfishness and altruism could be inherited and fostered. Another was the publicizing and punishment of bad examples for the purpose of exhortation and admonition and finally, launching a mass movement with the result that officials who abuse power would be severely punished and honest government would be encouraged. 'Love' here was in part a continuation of the Confucian *ren*, although it also differed greatly from it because of the strong political connotations and limitations imposed by the way all the objects one was obliged to love were very strictly defined (Wu Y. 2003: 101 as quoted in Lin M.M. 2010: 20). For example, the term 'people' (*renmin*) was restricted to certain social classes in Maoist terminology and excluded all 'enemies of the people', a category whose definition varied as political campaigns unfolded, and whose interpretation was often down to local cadres. While this provides some evidence that 'love' (as a verb) was used in the early years of the PRC, by 1963 Mao is quoted as saying that 'Communism is not love. Communism is a hammer, which we use to crush the enemy.'[7]

More recent examples of Marxist ideology disagree strongly with Mao on this. *The Spirit of Love and the Construction of Socialist Harmonious Culture* published in 2009 understands the spirit of love as firmly grounded in Marxism and socialism. It argues that the concept of love belongs to the system of ethics in any given society and is determined by the nature of the economic relations in this society. Systems of public and private ownership of the means of production each have their own moral system, which develops according to the logic of historic materialism, so that, for example, the seeds of socialist love are found in the capitalist system. But ethics also have a class nature, meaning that each social class has its own moral system. In a society in which no common benefit has been established, no unified ethical principle of love can be found. Specifically, in the capitalist class the meaning of love is restricted to blood relations, family and friends. Strife and competition in turn give rise to the desire for a universal love, which finds expression in religious doctrine like the Christian 'Love your neighbour like yourself' (Wang and Zhou 2009: 1–8). The authors identify different areas of harmonious culture (including the 'loving and harmonious culture' of the ruling power, of the professional world, family and marriage, charity, etc.) on each of which they present the most recent policies, regulations and official pronouncements. In the foreword to this rather dry (and I suspect little loved) volume, Yan Shuhan of the central party school writes that people underestimated the loving aspect of Marxism. Indeed, love was an important aspect of Marxism and to propagate this would increase its appeal. Seeing that love was a familiar word and concept and part of the consciousness of national mass culture, Marxist theoreticians and propaganda workers needed to 'use scientific methods to research and use this already commonly accepted, positive concept so that it can become a meaningful carrier to promote socialist harmonious culture' (see foreword to Wang and Zhou 2009).

A volume called *Ai Yu Lun* (On Education in Love) goes one step further by outlining a detailed plan of how to implement an education in love. After a detailed explanation of the etymology of the character *ai* and its meanings in the Chinese language as well as an overview of the Western equivalent terms and their roots in Greek philosophy, the author adopts a definition which distinguishes between the spirit of love (*ai de jingshen*) and the practice of love (*ai de shijian*). He further refines his definition of love as 'ideological sentiment' leading to 'corresponding action'. What he means is corresponding action that benefits the collective, that is, society (Cui D. 2011: 11). Love, to him, is a basic psychological need in every human's spiritual life. Philosophically, his proposed education in love is rooted in Marxism and in 'historical cultures', including love in Chinese traditional culture, love in religion, in romanticism and in rationalism. Education in love should include lessons on loving people (oneself and others), nature, and society, which includes education in collectivism, patriotism, socialism and internationalism. This kind of education should take place in a variety of contexts. In addition to special classes on love, an education in love should be included in the context of the established *suzhi* education process (which currently focuses on patriotic events), in the teaching of the humanities and sciences as well as in other work done by schools. The aim is that love should become internalized by turning into a faith, a moral quality, a norm of behaviour, a responsibility and promise to others, and a habit. It thus unites the individual and the collective, the human and physical environment, sections of society with the whole of society and today's mankind with the mankind of the future. By loving oneself, a harmony of mind and body will be realized; by loving each other, harmony between people will be realized; by loving nature, harmony between man and nature will be realized; and by loving society, harmony between man and society will be realized, claims this source.

A comment on a story on education in Ningbo run by Xinhua net seems to agree: 'the power of love [...] will have a miraculous effect on resolving contradictions, removing misunderstandings, reducing conflict, all of which will ultimately move society towards harmony' (Lu Yongjian 2005). And finally, during a schoolchildren's visit to Zhongnanhai in 2009, Wen Jiabao said to the pupils 'Everything depends on love (Zhi you ai cai you yiqie). We hope that [you] children understand love, cherish love, learn and master love. You must turn love into practical action' (Wang and Zhou 2009: 3).

Love and communism

Wen Jiabao's words echo Michael Hardt's understanding of love as a social and political force.[8] In a talk entitled *About Love* delivered at the European Graduate School in 2007,[9] Michael Hardt argues that love could be a process or even field of training for the self-transformation of humankind in order to construct a democratic society. Hardt rejects the more traditional communist notion of solidarity which in his words is limited by standard conceptions of rationality and people's rational calculus of interest. He considers solidarity to be a calculation of interest in the way we ally with each other, while love is a passion and thus goes beyond the confines of rationality. Love, in his view, develops a different relationship between reason and the passions; unlike solidarity or friendship, love has transformative power, and, according to Hardt, requires training (Hardt 2007).

Zou Xingming's (2008) criticism of the 'hierarchy of love' in the Chinese moral landscape (introduced in the preceding chapter) in turn echoes Hardt's criticism of the modern restriction of love to the couple and family as a result of which one should love most those who are closest, both socially and geographically, and should love those the least who are furthest away. In their book *Multitude, War and Democracy in the Age of Empire*, Hardt and Negri say that 'the concept of love is almost exclusively limited to the bourgeois couple and the claustrophobic confines of the nuclear family. Love has become a strictly private affair. We need a more generous and more unrestrained conception of love' (Hardt and Negri 2004: 351).

Hardt – a left-wing intellectual who by his own account believes neither in God nor the unconscious – frequently refers to Christian theology to support his argument for love as a political concept. Hardt advocates a reinterpretation of the Christian notion 'love thy neighbour' as the basis for an open social contract. Instead of understanding this to mean that one should love those closest and most familiar, he suggests that the 'neighbour' is turned into a placeholder, an open space, that potentially extends to all others and thus 'love thy neighbour' becomes an expression not of love of the familiar (or 'love of the same' in Hardt's words), but the love of difference, leading to 'harmony in diversity' (*he er bu tong*), to borrow a Chinese phrase (Hardt 2007).

Both Wen and Hardt are searching for new concepts and, perhaps more pertinently, a new terminology to inspire and motivate people to take part in the building of a new society. While Wen's 'harmonious society' may not be exactly Hardt's vision of a democratic society (which in turn is very different from the established liberal democratic model), they both have left traditional Marxist terminology behind and are searching for a new term untainted by the history of communism and Maoism that appeals to the individual's capacity to act in the collective interest, in the same way as 'old' notions like solidarity have done. They have both centred on love as a signifier meaningful – or indeed meaningless – enough to serve as a hold-all for a variety of different notions individuals may identify with as they relate to other members of society. There is perhaps no other term that transcends religious, political, and cultural boundaries quite in the same way as 'love'; it is core not only to Western and many Eastern schools of philosophy but also part of global popular culture, the latter owing more to John Lennon than to the Bible. Michael Hardt certainly draws liberally on a variety of interpretations of love (ranging from St Paul to St Augustine, Lacan to Pasolini), but returns most frequently to Christian understandings of love, searching for a new interpretation of these.

In his *In Praise of Love*, Alain Badiou, declares that the 'politics of love' is a meaningless expression. To him, love is about two people being able to handle difference and make it creative. Politics, on the other hand, is about finding out whether a number of people, a mass of people in fact, can create equality (Badiou 2012: 54). In love, differences can be transformed into creative existence, but 'nothing of the sort can happen in politics in terms of the basic contradictions, the upshot being that in effect there are clearly designated enemies' (Badiou 2012: 57). Nonetheless, there are philosophical-political notions one can compare to the dialectics present within love, according to Badiou. The word 'communism' encompasses the idea that collectivity is capable of integrating all extrapolitical differences; a person's identity can't prevent them from participating in a political process of a communist type. The communist idea, to which Badiou subscribes, is the 'idea of a world that isn't given over to the avarice of private property, a world of free association and equality [in which] it will be easier to re-invent love.' By 'communist' Badiou understands that which makes the held-in-common prevail over selfishness, the collective achievement over private self-interest. Love is communist in that sense, he says. Love is minimal communism (Badiou 2012: 90).

We can therefore see that the invocation of love to inject new appeal into communist philosophy and theory is not unique to the Chinese context; neither is the inspiration by (and ultimate rejection of) Christian thinking in this endeavour. But while Hardt and Badiou expand on their theories in the select circles of American and European intelligentsia, the Chinese population is affected by China's discourse on the 'harmonious society' through constant exposure thanks to the party's millions of propaganda workers, which according to one recent official claim may amount to as many as 10 per cent of the population (China Digital Times 2013).

All their endeavours are of course only effective, if the official discourse is noticed and taken seriously by those it wants to speak to. Signs are that certainly within TSPM circles there are keen responses to the invocation of love. Books such as *He zai ai zhong* (Harmony Lies in Love; Pan 2007) or *Ai zai xingdong* (Love Lies in Action; Pan 2012) stress the positive role of churches and Christians in the 'harmonious society'. This role lies primarily in good relations with non-Christians, positive family and marital relationships, a message of peace and the active involvement in social service through the application of the Christian commandment 'love your neighbour like yourself'. While referring to the Bible and Confucian ethics instead of Marx, these works are not dissimilar in nature to the dry volumes referred to above and it is difficult to gauge how widely read they are (although they came warmly recommended by an academic friend active in Haidian Church).

I discussed the use of 'love' in the official discourse with a small group of Catholics of very different backgrounds without suggesting that it may be Christian inspired. Mr Chen, the owner of the small stall, was born into a Catholic family in 1969 and was in Beijing in 1989, a key event in his life which led to a profound disillusionment on his part, as he said. His godson, Juyi, a young music student at one of Chengdu's universities, had been only recently baptized. He found his way to Catholicism through the study of Gregorian chant and now proudly inhabits his new identity by wearing a chain with a big, artistic cross over his shirt for all to see. In attendance was also Ms Zhang, a woman of similar age to Mr Chen, and her daughter. Ms Zhang was originally from Qinghai, where she grew up in a Catholic family; her grandmother had been baptized by a French missionary. She said she had had no idea of the Bible or the Ten Commandments when she grew up. There was no mass or church they could attend; only occasionally a priest would drop by. She later moved to a village in Shandong, which also did not have a church, but where it was possible to attend unregistered congregations from time to time. In her own words she only started to properly understand her faith once she moved to Chengdu and started to attend the Catholic church in the city. Her daughter was in her late teens and had Tibetan features. Mrs Bai, a woman in her sixties, had only started to attend the church a year ago, but had found faith through a miraculous healing experience after a grave illness (from the symptoms she described it might have been a stroke).

Juyi, the young student, was not aware that the monosyllabic term '*ai*' was used in government discourse and 'shocked to hear it' as he put it. Upon reflection, he considered it empty and devoid of meaning like all the other propaganda. To him and his friends all of this was part of the same 'white noise' that one had to put up with, but which was meaningless in their lives. Mr Chen on his part was convinced that the 'love' used in the discourse on the 'harmonious society' was borrowed from Christianity. He considered it a good thing; it meant that at least the broad direction was the same. Despite his first-hand experience of the student protests and their outcome in 1989, Mr Chen was the most sympathetic to the government of all those present. He was generally appreciative of the broad direction the reforms have taken, acknowledging that in the 1980s it would have been very difficult to sit together in this formation and discuss these issues as we did on this November afternoon in 2012. He was also appreciative of the many material improvements the last 20-odd years had brought. Mrs Zhang, was less generous in her approval stating categorically that the food she ate hadn't been put on the table by the party but by God. The three women, although of different generations, all agreed that the 'love' referred to by the government was 'similar but not the same' as the Christian love they could relate to, although they struggled to elaborate in what way.

For He Guanghu the use of love in the official discourse was not directly related to Christianity or Ding Guangxun. In his view, the party was looking for a new terminology as all the old expressions were associated with lies. The main reason 'love' was adopted was that it was an attractive word with plenty of positive connotations and hence easily embraced. At the same time, it was generally understood that love was what was most obviously lacking in contemporary Chinese society. Additionally, it did appeal to students and intellectuals that were drawn in by Christianity. He thought that the use of the word love in official discourse was a good thing, a viewpoint others around him criticized him for.[10] A well-known, openly gay, Catholic film-maker in his thirties also conceded that the use of the word love by the party was 'very clever'. He was quite certain that it was borrowed from Christianity and granted that it had universal appeal, but its use by government propaganda rendered it 'meaningless and empty', 'merely another lie' and 'window dressing'.[11]

One aspect in which the socialist use of love and love in Christian theology are 'similar, but not the same', as the three Catholic women put it, is the absence in socialist rhetoric of any reference to the source of love or why indeed one should be propelled to love one's neighbour beyond the assertion that love is a core meaning of socialism. In socialism, to love one's neighbour remains a mere commandment, born out of necessity as the interest of work in common does not hold society together, as Freud argued. Socialist rhetoric demands love of the people, and offers to educate people in 'love' without offering much in return in terms of motivation and inspiration. The Chinese ideological works cited above take the orthodox view on religion as a temporary phenomenon connected with the current stage of development. On the other hand, the Christian God – Ding's 'cosmic lover' – is the eternal source of all love. In Badiou's words, Christianity is the finest example of the use of love's intensity towards a transcendental conception of the universal. It grasped perfectly that there is an element in the apparent contingency of love that can't be reduced to that contingency and raised it to the level of transcendence. Badiou, however, does not recognize this universal element as transcendent, but sees it, too, as immanent. In his view, the power of love must be brought back to earth.

> We must demonstrate that love really does have universal power, but that it is simply the opportunity we are given to enjoy a positive, creative, affirmative experience of difference. The Other, no doubt, but without the 'Great Other' of transcendence.
>
> (Badiou 2012: 64–5)

It is here where we revisit Ding Guanxun's earlier definition of God in which he says that 'transcendence signifies the inexhaustibility of the cosmic love and immanence, the unfailing presence of that love in the whole creation'. By emphasizing God's immanence in all creation and by focusing on his physical embodiment through Jesus Christ, Ding is emphasizing an immanence (over transcendence) that was also central to historical communism and which continues to be a central element to contemporary communist philosophy as articulated by Hardt and Badiou, for example. It also stands in contrast to the evangelical notion of God as transcendent source of all values, emphasized so strongly by Christian intellectuals like Wang Yi and Yu Jie.

But Badiou also reminds us that political difference with the enemy is 'irreconcilable' as Marx said; a postulation whose Maoist interpretation impacted directly on the lives of millions of Chinese. The division of the Chinese population into 'people' and 'the enemy' – goalposts that also shifted as campaign after campaign unfolded – had a long lasting and far reaching effect on the individuals categorized as enemies, which they often did not survive. The notion that God loves all men equally including all those who are not lovable provides a great source of comfort and solace to Christians and is hugely empowering. Its healing effect for Chinese Christians – be it for physical or emotional wounds – cannot be underestimated especially in the context of China's recent history, and thus delivers a far more powerful message than party exhortations.

Romantic love and harmonious relationships

In the previous chapter we have seen that churches, congregations and small groups devoted to Bible study form small moral universes which are largely separate from mainstream society. Christians try to be among themselves and engage in activities with like-minded people who share the same values, where they can choose to do so. Contact with non-Christians is mostly sought in the context of evangelizing and, increasingly, charitable activities, both of which tend to take place as structured, collective activity. On an individual level, the most important nexus between these small universes and non-Christian society are romantic relationships, where only one half of the couple is Christian.

In Zhang Jie's famous novella *Love must not be forgotten* the female protagonist is torn between settling for a handsome, perfectly adequate suitor or staying single in the absence of 'true love' as experienced between her mother and her secret, idealized lover. Part of what had made this communist cadre, who was killed during the Cultural Revolution, so desirable to her mother, was his unwavering idealism and spirit of sacrifice, even though it meant that the love between them could not be realized. The newly created youth fellowship of one of Chengdu's earliest intellectual churches debated similar issues during their second Sunday afternoon gathering in November 2012. The topic of the discussion was 'Can you be in a relationship with a non-believer?' The group consisted of nine young people in their mid-twenties to early thirties, although they appeared considerably younger than that. The group was moderated by a church elder, an academic at Chengdu University, and his wife, both in their mid-forties. It soon became apparent that the discussion topic appeared to have been chosen for the benefit of one female member of the fellowship, who was in a relationship with a non-Christian. The two had been talking about marriage, but she was not sure whether he would be able to accept her faith, let alone convert to the faith himself. She considered him a 'good person'; much 'better' even than some Christians she knew. The discussion carried on for almost three hours, although there was little disagreement among the other ten people present. It was very clear to all of them – none of whom had had a similar experience, or indeed any experience of a romantic relationship apart from teacher Chen and his wife – that it was much better to have a Christian partner, as shared values based on a shared faith were the only way to overcome the problems and difficulties one naturally encounters in the course of a marriage. Among the concerns raised with the young woman were whether her partner would accept her Sunday commitments to church service, and whether she would be able to accept his non-Christian values and behaviours. It was suggested more than once that she would be well advised to break it off now and try to find a new, Christian boyfriend. (To her credit, she did not yield under this considerable peer pressure, at least not in the discussion that afternoon. She remained adamant until the end, that he was a good person and that they could make it work.)

In reality many Christian women are in relationships, usually marriages, with men, who are not Christians. Judging from lengthy conversations with some of them, this seems to work quite well for both sides. Of three professional women in their late thirties and early forties, who shared their experiences with me, one had been baptized two years ago, while the other two were still undecided, but had attended regular Bible study groups for up to a year. Both of them were truly impressed by the physical and psychological transformation the conversion to Christianity had brought about in their friend, Chang, who used to suffer from anxiety, chronic ailments and depression. The Chang I met was a radiant woman and a model of serenity, calm and warmth towards others – a living advertisement for the healing powers of the Bible and true inspiration to her friends. Part of Chang's unhappiness had been caused by her marital problems, which the other two were also experiencing. Without going into too much detail, it was clear that these problems were partly the result of common practices in the male professional world and included heavy drinking and other women, be they 'hostesses' at business banquets or other extra-marital relationships.

But by the women's own accounts, these difficulties had been exacerbated by their reaction to these issues as headstrong and assertive wives. Studying the Bible had made them realize that nobody was without sin; that they, too, were fallible and that instead of constantly fighting with their husbands they needed to concentrate on their own spiritual improvement and had to learn to love those that were 'unlovable' as the Bible taught them and to become 'good wives'. In practice this meant that they tried not to question their husbands' behaviour or nag them for their shortcomings. As one of them put it 'Now I just bring him his slippers when he comes home, pick up his socks and attend to his needs.' All of them reported improved relationships with their husbands, who appreciated the better atmosphere at home. Perhaps not surprisingly, all reported active encouragement from their husbands to continue to study the Bible and possibly convert to Christianity. Not only had their home life improved, but as a result of this, they also observed small changes in their husbands' behaviours. Chang said that her husband would now often prefer to stay at home rather than join in social activities that did not involve her; another said that her husband, too, was starting to have an interest in the Bible.

The women reported not only encouragement from their husbands, but also from the party secretary at their university. Chang was once reprimanded for allegedly evangelizing in class following the complaint by a student. But once her (male) superior had reminded her to stay clear of the subject of her own belief in class, he did express great interest in her beliefs and general support of her faith as a useful attribute in society.

Christian women often mention that their husbands consider them to be 'better wives' since their conversion to Christianity. Christianity played an important role in early women's liberation in China, partly through campaigns against footbinding as well as education and healthcare, but mostly through the living example of the female missionary. Today all churches, including urban intellectual churches, have a high proportion of female church members. Only five of 44 churches surveyed by Liu Tongsu had a female membership of less than 50 per cent; in the remaining 39, women were in the majority. In more than half of the churches (52 per cent) women made up between 60–70 per cent of the whole congregation. On the basis of these figures, Beijing churches are still considered to have a relatively higher proportion of male members than churches in other parts of the country (Liu and Wang 2012: 291). The vast majority of Chinese Christians today, including those, who attend TSPM churches, are evangelical, and subscribe to a very conservative worldview. In terms of male–female relations, this means a complementarian view of the role men and women play in society, and specifically in church. Leading roles within churches are mostly held by men, a situation largely accepted by women, who consider this to be 'how God wanted it', even though they may be equally educated.

In an English sermon at Haidian Church in Beijing, Cathy Zhang speaks of three qualities necessary to be a 'helper' (the role of a woman in the relationship) as understood in the Bible. Starting with her own experience of marriage, her sermon presents a comparatively feminist interpretation of the role women play in relationships. A woman has to be humble, compassionate and transformative; only through change in oneself can one expect change in others (a view most Western psychotherapy would also subscribe to). A young male preacher in Wenzhou puts it in less feminist words. 'Women tend to be emotional and first committed to sin. Brothers are rational because men were the first created by God. Women are the hands and legs of men, while men are the head' (Cao N. 2011: 99).

Both men and women are considered to be of equal value, but the emphasis on the spiritual nature of women and the rational nature of men, as well as the complementary roles they play in society, where women tend to be in a supportive role to men, seems naturally to lead to a situation where it is the role of men to lead, and the role of women to love. Relationships, where only the woman is a Christian believer, then become the locus where the ideal relationship between Christian belief and Chinese business and political culture is lived out. Churches or Bible study groups satisfy the women's psychological and spiritual needs by providing regular like-minded company, opportunity to reflect and take comfort as well as guidelines on how to be a better person (wife) through the power of love. They bring this new calm and sense of empowerment to the relationship, where, in an ideal scenario, the man, in the privacy of his own home, can enjoy the benefits of the improved relationship while making adjustments to his own behaviour in his marriage, which may or may not translate into changed behaviour outside the home in his dealings with colleagues, business partners and superiors. They are happy to accept their wives' Christian values, which they consider a 'good thing'; through their wives' faith they also experience a vicarious spirituality which brings private benefits to them without compromising their public, rational persona.

Conclusion

This chapter has argued that the use of love in the discourse on the 'harmonious society' has strong Christian roots due to the centrality of love in Chinese Christian theology as associated with Ding Guangxun. Those involved in ideological work have recognized the importance and popularity of love as a term and have been keen to adopt it. In the process of adoption, the government is also attempting to control the discourse; recognizing the importance of the concept and adopting it, allows it to shape its definition.[12] This is evident from the sources cited above, which try to locate love firmly within Marxist discourse.

This is a very clever way of recognizing and trying to enlist the ideological support of a potentially very critical and growing social group, and has a number of advantages for the government. Not only does it mean that the energies and resources of this sector of society can be channelled into a (from the government's perspective) constructive project, but it also potentially enables the government to pass on certain duties to the community (like charitable work) while at the same time re-establishing its legitimacy. Therefore, by acknowledging core values of Christianity, the government is primarily acting in its own interest. Not only is it perceived to be more liberal and more 'embracing' of society's diversity and hence enhances its image, but it also allows the government to have certain expectations of this group.

The majority of people I spoke to over the course of this study were broadly supportive of the government and recognized the role they as Christians may be able to play in China's 'harmonious society' on the basis of their core values. Chinese Christian individuals uniformly stress that their belief makes them good, law-abiding citizens, who have positive social relationships and superior work and business ethics. But as we will see in the next chapter, attempts to turn the rather woolly 'love thy neighbour' into Christian love in action in the form of real charitable projects on a bigger scale are hampered by a variety of obstacles presented by the government.

Through references to this core value in Chinese Christian theology, the government also gives a signal to the growing Christian population that their values are compatible, indeed shared, with communist ideology. Thus the national project of building the 'harmonious society' seems to invite the Chinese Christian population to enter into a relationship with the party based on love. The private and personal aspect of love here becomes part of and aligned with China's newest ideological project; it is lived out in actual relationships between non-Christian men and

Christian women, in which both parts seem to benefit psychologically and spiritually without causing great upset to established gender roles and societal expectation. On a national scale the Chinese government hopes to define love (here for the country) as a relationship between two social groups, the party and Christians, on similar terms in order to build a 'harmonious society'. Mirroring the marital relationship, the party wants to take on the male, rational role of ideological leader, while Christians should take on the female, spiritual role of supportive lover, resulting in a happier marriage where relations are improved, but where the hierarchy remains clearly defined.

Chinese Christians across denominations and generations are not easily tempted by these overtures, taking little interest in the 'love' emanating from official discourse, which, they grant, is 'clever', but 'meaningless' 'white noise' and 'window dressing' that has got 'nothing to do' with their own lives. One of my interviewees in Beijing perhaps put it most poignantly and most pessimistically when he said 'The idea that religion can play a role in the harmonious society is just garbage.[13] What they really want is to improve the relations between religion and the government.'

Notes

1. I am indebted to Niall Ferguson's *Civilization. The West and the Rest* (London, Allen Lane 2011) which has brought this particular quote by Sigmund Freud to my attention.
2. There is no place here to get into the great philosophical discussions about the distinction and segregation of eros and agape as well as attempts to bring them together and to explain the relation between them which has been of great importance in Western Christian philosophy. It is a topic that has, for example, been addressed again in Pope Benedict XVI's encyclical 'Deus Caritas Est'.
3. He Qinglian on Twitter, 12 January 2013 https://twitter.com/HeQinglian.
4. For a detailed discussion on these efforts see Dunch 2008.
5. Fei Xiaotong in his analysis of *ren* as expressed in the Analects says that whenever Confucius tried to define *ren* he had to return to the ethical principles of individual relationships.
6. On the Lujiang experiment see also Duitournier and Ji (2009).
7. Time Magazine, 13 September 1963.
8. Michael Hardt is an American literary theorist and political philosopher based at Duke University. He is the author (together with Antonio Negri) of *Empire* (2000) and the sequel to this book called *Multitude: War and Democracy in the Age of Empire* (2004).
9. There is so far no published article on Michael Hardt's thoughts on 'love'. The idea of love as a political concept is briefly introduced in Hardt and Negri's book *Multitude: War and Democracy in the Age of Empire*, and Hardt has given a variety of talks on the subject since the publication of the book and most recently at the conference 'The Politics of Love' held at Syracuse University from 16–18 April 2009. See http://pcr.syr.edu (last accessed 8 July 2009). A full recording of his talk at the European Graduate School can be found on youTube at www.youtube.com/watch?v=ioopkoppabI (last accessed 12 April 2010). My summary of his points is based on this recording.
10. Author's conversation with He Guanghu, Beijing, November 2012.
11. Telephone interview with Cui Zi'en, November 2012.
12. Wang and Zhou's book (2009) is a case in point.
13. He used this English expression.

4 Charity

Christian love in action?

In September 2012 SARA (China's State Administration of Religious Affairs) launched the first nationwide week of religious charity in China. Over 200 representatives from government recognized religious organizations were present at its opening ceremony in Wuhan, which signalled the support for religious groups' involvement in charitable services, provided this involvement was 'long-term, institutionalized, and provided in a standardized manner' (UCA News 2012). After decades of changing attitudes towards this sector, the 'charity week' marked another step towards the government's acceptance and now promotion of religious charity in China. It also seems to mark a return, at least in ideological discourse, to the happy marriage of religious social service and socialist ideals as first encountered in the decades prior to 1949.

This chapter will cast an eye back to the decades of the Republic, the promulgation of the social gospel through the YMCA and its influence on early Christian thinkers. It will also look at the understanding of charity in contemporary China before analysing two case studies of ostensibly Christian organizations. The two case studies highlight the challenges and complex environment within which all charities (subsumed under the term 'social organizations', *shehui zuzhi* in Chinese) have to operate. They also provide a frame of reference to better understand charitable activity by churches outside this organizational realm. In addition to the regulatory pitfalls and restrictions imposed on religious charity, the social gospel is not a doctrine that all churches subscribe to today.

Minsheng and the social gospel

Sun Yatsen's political doctrine was encapsulated in the 'Three People's Principles', *sanmin zhuyi*, a term he first used in 1905 and to which he returned in 1919, revising and reflecting upon it until his death in 1925. *Minsheng*, most commonly translated as 'people's livelihood', is one of the three pillars of his ideology. It is the least well defined of the three and related to a social utopia in Kang Youwei's sense (see Bergère 1998: 352–87 and Myers 1989). For Sun, the mainspring of social evolution was harmony, and the principal force in human evolution cooperation, not conflict. By trying to understand the origins of the various social conflicts Sun thought it would be possible to draw up policies to ensure economic development for all social groups, and hence to preserve the environment and to restore social harmony. *Minsheng* was synonymous with subsistence and the driving force of social change in Sun's ideology (Myers 1989: 240).

In Beijing of the 1920s Sun's term *minsheng* was commonly used to refer to that part of the established social order which supported the material well-being of townspeople. There was a general sentiment running through public opinion at the time that philanthropic projects were necessary correctives to unregulated growth. But politically conscious Chinese also recognized the value of state intervention both in co-ordinating social peace and economic security, and in legitimizing the existing social order (Strand 1989: 285).

The establishment of the Republic saw a big increase in the number of social organizations including charitable organizations; according to a YMCA survey, in 1923 there were more than 370 charities in Beijing alone (Wang J. 2010: 148). Charity in Republican times had two trajectories: on the one hand the development of modern, popular charities, on the other hand the establishment of a state social welfare system. The popular charities were reasonably effective in their endeavours, greatly aided by the modernization of transport and communication. The birth of a modern Chinese press, closely associated with Protestant activities, kick started the proliferation of the Chinese publishing industry in the early twentieth century. There were well over 300 Christian journals alone in circulation in China of the 1930s, including several that dealt with social problems and sciences (Zhuo X. 2006a: 165). The impact of the modern newspapers on the charitable sector was considerable. The press not only published reports on disasters, but also on the relief efforts by the government and the people, which greatly increased public interest and awareness of these matters; this in turn fed the growth of popular organizations (Wang J. 2010: 62). A similar link between new media, public awareness and involvement can be observed following natural disasters in present-day China.

Christian charity primarily manifested itself in projects run by foreign missionaries in the areas of education and health care. Basic hygiene measures, education against the custom of foot binding, elementary education as well as the provision of basic supplies and soup kitchens were associated with Christian missionary endeavours in Chinese localities of the late nineteenth and early twentieth centuries. But Christian funds also contributed towards the education of China's reformers and intellectuals, creating between 1850 and 1950 pioneers in the field of education, health care, media and diplomacy as well as the women's movement, popular organizations and social work, whose activities had a long- lasting effect on Chinese society (Bieler and Hamrin 2009).

The YMCA was perhaps the one organization which most actively promoted the 'social gospel', that is the belief in the importance of addressing social problems as part of missionary work. The YMCA was originally founded in the United Kingdom in 1844, but its Chinese branch, founded in 1895, was the direct result of the growth of the American mission in Asia during the nineteenth century. The considerable economic resources needed to finance the missionary efforts in Asia came from the growth in America's industrializing economy after the Civil War;

the rise of the social gospel that went hand in hand with these missionary efforts was a reaction to the social and economic displacement brought on by the very same processes of industrialization. The social gospel was conceived as a solution to the problems arising from the transformation of the agricultural economy, including rampant corruption at all levels of government, unemployment, poverty and working-class discontent. Proponents of the social gospel wanted to build a new society based on religious liberalism, humanitarianism and 'social science', marking an adaptation of Christianity to a more modern, scientific world (Keller 1996: 33–5).

According to Jesiah Strong, one of the proponents of the social gospel, Americans were the chosen people of a chosen race with the mission to 'prepare the way for the full coming of God's Kingdom on the earth' (as quoted in Keller 1996: 34). But preparing for the second coming included more than just converting non-believers; the obligation to save man's soul expanded to include the improvement of the social, moral, and physical condition of the whole person. The YMCA in China exemplified this approach.

In the uncertain decades following the establishment of the Republic of China, the YMCA and YWCA projected a beacon of social service and spiritual guidance that many believed illuminated a viable path for the country's future (Keller 1996: 2). For example, Emily Honig argues that it was the YWCA rather than the Communist Party, which first provided political education for female textile workers by teaching them how to read, how to speak in public and how to analyse social structures (as quoted in Wickeri 2007: 47). An important goal of the YMCA's programme was to imbue its members with an 'ethic of community' that resulted in voluntary social service and sense of national identity. It was also the largest institution in China practising 'social reconstruction theology', and responsible for coining the Chinese term for social service, *shehui fuwu*.

Social reconstruction theology held that Chinese modernization depended upon the reformation of society to include progressive Chinese values by rectifying the character of individuals and that a social vanguard with a Christian value system could actualize the 'spirit of Jesus'. Some Chinese adopted this idea as an alternative to revolutionary Marxism. Two of the main leading figures in the establishment of the official Protestant organization after the Communist victory in 1949, T.C. Chao (Zhao Zichen) and Y.T. Wu (Wu Yaozong) were proponents of the social gospel and the importance of a social foundation to evangelism. While Zhao Zichen believed in 'salvation by moral character' as discussed in Chapter 2 of this book, for Wu Yaozong Christian engagement had to go further. He emphasized the importance of charity and social welfare, but also the efforts to improve conditions in society (see Lin M.M. 2010: Chapter 4).

Charity in Communist China

The Communist victory in 1949 radically changed the landscape for religious organizations like the YMCA and for charities in general. All charities and philanthropic organizations run by Christians were disbanded and placed under the control of the central government. Philanthropy was no longer considered necessary under socialism and the common Chinese term, *cishan*, in use since the end of the Qing period, was abandoned as it was associated with the bourgeoisie.

The term *minsheng* is still in use in China today, but it has disappeared from core political vocabulary. Still, the now prevalent 'harmonious society' is a term with similar philosophical roots as *minsheng*. Both articulate the ideal of a socially fairer state. Sun's formulation formed part of reconstruction efforts following revolution and civil war, while the contemporary CCP tries to counterbalance social inequality following three decades of industrialization and reform. In both cases, social organizations play a pivotal role for the state. Care for people's livelihood is considered the foundation for stable rule, but neither the Republican state nor the CCP were/are able to deliver this care without the help of social organizations. Allowing the existence of such organizations however also harbours a potential threat to stable rule, the worst being that they may turn into platforms of social protest and unrest. Therefore, control of the organizations then and now serves as the means to safeguard the foundation of stability.[1]

The value of religion in this new ideological project has been officially recognized, in particular where charity and social welfare are concerned (Wielander 2011). Christianity, perhaps more than any other religion in China today, is associated in the public mind with charity and the qualities of sincerity and compassion, honesty and efficiency, which are of particular importance in the third sector. According to David Schak, China's most prominent non-government philanthropic organizations are all (Protestant) Christian (Schak 2011: 81). But at the same time, religion is also considered to be a potentially destabilizing factor in China, both historically and today. Therefore, from the CCP's point of view, this is difficult terrain to negotiate.

In 2004 China held its first national conference on the Harmonious Society and Philanthropy in Pujiang, Fujian. The conference traced the beginning and development of a charitable culture in China, discussed challenges and examples of good practice and tried to determine the role of the government and NGOs in the delivery of charity. Participants ranged from government officials, researchers in China's main social sciences research institutes to representatives of a variety of social organizations including a number of Christian organizations.

Yang Tuan, researcher at the Social Policies Research Centre at CASS and editor of the conference proceedings, distinguishes between 'charity' and 'philanthropy' (using the English terms). She links the term 'charity' to Christ, whereas she explains the meaning of 'philanthropy' as a 'broader love' (*kuanguang de da'ai*) or, with intriguing similarity to Bishop Ding's theology, as 'cosmic love' (*yuzhou zhi ai*). Yang confines the utility of the term 'charity' to tradition, using it to describe pre-modern, non-organized charitable behaviour. She stresses the point that philanthropy has a broader meaning than charity and is therefore the more modern term, labouring to define it within the terms of industrialization and enterprise, without delving into the motivations that drove the great Western philanthropists, whose models she refers to. Nevertheless Yang does concede that philanthropic work is greatly influenced by Christianity, but that this fact has been difficult to acknowledge because of Christianity's link with the semi-colonization of China (Yang and Ge 2004).[2] (While outside the scope of this chapter, it is interesting to note in this context that the rise and success of charitable activity in Taiwan is much more closely linked with Buddhism and Daoism than with Christianity, which in part has to do with its identification with the West by most Taiwanese people.[3])

Since the early 1990s, academics in religious studies have been working on correcting this 'image' of Christianity as a foreign religion associated with imperialism; its contribution to China's modernization through education and medical projects carried out by missionaries play a key part in this. Zhuo Xinping (2006b) has long been arguing for a re-evaluation of Christianity's contribution in Chinese history. He credits Christians as the catalysts for the process of modernizing the Chinese education system and curriculum, which in turn led to other social reforms. He acknowledges Christians' impact on the creation of a modern press in China and praises Christian involvement in medical work and philanthropy. According to Zhuo, 70 per cent of total Chinese hospitals in the 1930s were church hospitals, and 90 per cent of nurses at the time were Christians.

Gao Shining and He Guanghu (2011) also list a number of positive contributions of Christianity to Chinese culture as a result of missionary activity prior to 1949, including the concept of the weekly calendar, monogamist families, an end to foot binding, hygiene matters and hospitals, but also concepts like democracy, rule of law, and balance of power. After a break of 30 years (by which they mean the three decades after 1949) during which Christianity was not able to contribute anything to society, they concede that China has seen an impressive amount of charity conducted by all religions, including Christianity. However, in their view Christianity could and should do a lot more. They point to the high level of Christian involvement in social work in Taiwan or Hong Kong, despite the low Christian population in both areas.

'Social organizations'

The 1980s saw a gradual reestablishment of philanthropic organizations in China. Initiatives emerged on an official level and two of the most successful and longest-standing social organizations today saw their beginnings in the 1980s as a response to high level initiatives. Others were the result of courageous endeavours by individuals, who found themselves in an entirely new professional landscape. Many of the brightest people with initiative went into business; only very few tried their hand in the new field of social service provision.

The increasing income disparity and the wide publication of news regarding natural disasters led to the re-emergence of grassroots philanthropy in the 1990s, although the devastating earthquake in Wenchuan of 2008 is sometimes seen as the real turning point in China's charity scene. The unprecedented, spontaneous outburst of sympathy and desire to get involved hands on showed the Chinese population's capacity for charity, especially from within the religious sector. According to statistics quoted by Gao Shining and He Guanghu (2011), 50 per cent of volunteers to Wenchuan were Christians, 80 per cent of whom came from 'house churches'. Financial contributions from this sector were also substantial. In a context where churches, let alone unregistered churches, were not allowed to get directly involved in charity work, but where donations were needed and the national and international media spotlight was on the scene, a unique moment was created for churches to show their social concern and Christian love in action – and garnering some publicity from it. Susan McCarthy (2012) reports how the Catholic nuns working for Hebei's Jinde Foundation sported religious headpieces to complement their functional protective clothing while working in the disaster relief zone, thereby side-stepping the ban on proselytizing (which was reinforced in special lectures before their departure to Sichuan) yet displaying their religious identity to a much wider audience than ever before.

The 'love' promoted in the official discourse as discussed in the previous chapter is expected to find its most natural outlet in charitable behaviour and in the support for social service provision. However, various scandals surrounding charities which involved the embezzling of funds (as mentioned in Chapter 2) have made the general public wary of parting with their money. Those positively predisposed to charity work criticize that charitable work is used as political capital by individuals and often serves as a stop-over for officials on the way up in the ranks. This means that leading positions in social organizations are often held by people who lack the necessary qualities and dedication to ensure the transparency of funds and success of the endeavours.[4] Appeals to people's charitable nature are often conducted in the style of political movements. People take part in it because they are forced to, often required to make certain donations to fulfil quotas set by superiors (Wu J. 2004: 113).

In this environment, Christian belief has come to be associated with honesty and sincerity in the context of charity and social outreach and is a positive emblem that now also holds meaning for a domestic audience, not least with Chinese urban middle class donors, many of whom have adopted a value system derivative of Christian values. Having said that, Christian organizations, and in particular the official organizations governing Protestantism and Catholicism are by no means free from scandal or corruption. The lifestyle of their leaders and their easy mingling with government officials is one reason why these organizations are increasingly discredited in the public's eye.

All charitable organizations, including religious organizations, fall under the umbrella term 'social organizations', the common way to refer to 'NGOs' in China. Defining an NGO in the Chinese context is not a straightforward matter and the task itself has produced a fair amount of scholarship.[5] Kang Xiaoguang (2010: 4) considers the benchmark as to whether an organization is an NGO as functional rather than conceptual, i.e. as long as an organization, regardless of its background (be it entrepreneurial, social, official, private or religious) engages in the type of work an NGOs would engage in, using the methods of an NGO, then it is considered an NGO. Mapping out the history of NGOs in China, Nick Young (2004) is convinced that China will 'develop its own model, drawing on its specific history'.

In the following, two very different charitable organizations, both inspired by Christian values and linked to Christian initiatives, will be analysed to illustrate the diverging experiences of grassroots initiatives and government approved organizations today and to illustrate the environment in which all charitable work is conducted.

The Amity Foundation

Turning into Nanjing's Hankou Road, just north of the city's bustling Xinjiekou district, one is still reminded of the city's quieter atmosphere in the 1980s. The few cars that make it down the narrow two lanes struggle against cyclists, street vendors and pedestrians, who traverse this thoroughfare to get from one part of Nanjing University campus to the other. Having walked past the old university's South Gate, bearing its name in the calligraphy of its former president Kuang Yaming, one ends up in front of a handsome detached house standing behind a low wall displaying five Chinese characters in the same hand. This is the headquarters of Amity Foundation, one of China's oldest and most successful charitable organizations.

Amity was founded in 1985 on the initiative of Bishop Ding Guangxun.[6] According to Amity, there were two catalysts for its establishment. One was the establishment of the Chinese Welfare Fund for the Handicapped in 1984, the other the active encouragement by Hu Qiaomu, of religious groups to undertake activities for social welfare. As the churches themselves had few resources to engage in this kind of initiative in 1985, overseas churches were approached for their support which yielded a favourable response.

Interestingly, a slightly different version is presented in Ma Jia's biography (2006) of Ding Guangxun's. According to Ma, Amity was established, because the official Protestant church could not very well be seen to accept the funds offered by foreign churches at the time. There was therefore a need to establish an organization outside the church to become active in Chinese welfare. In order to mitigate criticism that this would still go against the 'three-self' policy, individuals from outside the church, including many intellectuals like Kuang Yaming, were invited onto the council of the new organization. Kuang himself was known to have a long-standing interest in religious and philosophical questions and had developed an appreciation of Christian ideas and the work of the YMCA in the 1940s. That he was known in Christian circles for his view that a 'true' Christian and a 'true' Communist both sought to 'serve the people' in their own ways made him an ideal candidate for this role (Wickeri 2007: 216). The calligraphy used in Amity's logo is written in his hand, marking Amity's continued strong connections with Nanjing University and officialdom. Kuang Yaming was directly involved in the '2 June Incident' which formed the starting point of the Cultural Revolution at Nanjing University; he was restored to his former post as Nanjing University's party leader and president in 1978 and was a good friend of Ding Guangxun's (Dong 2010).

Over the last 27 years Amity has grown from a relatively unknown organization with three members of staff into a well-known national social organization with a staff of over a hundred. Amity is enjoying a good reputation both inside and outside

China as an efficient organization able to deliver high quality projects (see Qiu 2004 and Amity Foundation 2010). The organization was heavily involved in the relief efforts after both major earthquakes in Wenchuan and Yushu in recent years, but their projects extend well beyond the scope of disaster relief. They are also engaged in scholarships and fostering orphans, public health and HIV/AIDS prevention and treatment, social welfare (including foster care projects and projects for the hearing impaired, the disabled and the elderly), community development and environmental protection, etc. The majority of these projects take place in remote regions of China, often inhabited by ethnic minorities. But there are also several projects in Nanjing including the Social Service Centre, which is comprised of various projects with disabled people, including the Amity Bakery, where a retired chef from Hong Kong works with a number of mentally disabled adults to produce a variety of breads, cakes and chocolate items.

Amity also has a very strong arm of publicity and resource development; it publishes a sophisticated newsletter, has a very well maintained website in Chinese and English, organizes conferences and public debates, runs a volunteer centre, and has recently opened a 'charity gallery' in Guangzhou. It also organizes education and international exchange programmes. Amity also has an office in Hong Kong, which helps with overseas links, fundraising and volunteers.[7]

Apparently Bishop Ding personally came up with the Chinese name *Aide*, consisting of the two characters for love and virtue and which could also translate as 'the power of love'; the English translation 'Amity' was suggested by Janice Wickeri and was adopted as the official English name (Wickeri 2007: 271–9). The name partly reflects the centrality of 'love' in Chinese Christian theology as formulated by Ding Guangxun, but, if perhaps not considered at the time, has also proven to be a genius decision as far as marketing and the creation of a brand is concerned. Love, probably more than any other philosophical concept, is able to cross cultural boundaries and appeals to people's innate goodness and morality. Visually this is expressed in the internationally recognizable heart symbol, also used in Taiwanese charitable organizations (Madsen 2007: 142). One of the most successful ventures of Amity's bakery is the production of little chocolate hearts, which are sold at fairs and special events to high demand.

Amity's Christian roots were an important aspect of its early identity, and no doubt have contributed to its success. Reliant on foreign partners in its early days, overseas churches chose Amity over other organizations for their outreach work in China. This enabled Amity to establish a reputation of reliability and professionalism and made Amity a link between the Chinese church and partners overseas. Today Amity's Christian roots are not immediately apparent – a fact that is heavily criticized from within church circles. In response to such criticism, Amity are quick to point to one focus of their development, which is cooperation with churches to develop their capacity for social services and has led to the establishment of the Jiangsu Christian Fund for Social Service. Its purpose is to strengthen the cooperation and contact between Amity and all churches in Jiangsu. This organization featured strongly in the recent religious charity week mentioned earlier.

Qiu Zhonghui, Amity's General Secretary, who took over this position from Han Wenzao in 2003, refers to Amity as a 'faith based organization'. According to Qiu, about one third of all staff at Amity are Christians; many have converted during their employment with Amity, including himself. Others are more sceptical about this claim. Kan Renping, the pastor of St Paul's Church in Nanjing, doubts this figure. Asked whether he considered Amity a Christian organization, he was quite clear that he did not. In his view there was no longer enough cooperation with churches and not enough Christian staff at Amity for it to be called a Christian organization. He thought that at the most, a quarter of Amity staff were Christians, but he did not count Qiu Zhonghui among them (author interview, November 2010). Melissa Manhong Lin of the Nanjing Jinling Seminary, too, was quite adamant when saying that Amity was not a Christian organization (author interview, May 2010). Song Tianyong of Gospel Times, an NGO founded in 2006,[8] also hesitated in his answer when asked whether he considered Amity a Christian organization. In the end, he referred to a conversation he had had with a pastor, who works with Amity on one of the church projects and who seems to have contented himself with the notion that 'God works through Amity' (author interview, November 2010). None of the dozen or so Amity staff I met at various occasions, with the exception of Qiu Zhonghui, who said he had converted since working for Amity, were Christian believers. Asked where Christianity came into Amity's work, Anthony Tong, Amity's director in Hong Kong, was hesitant in his answer. His first answer was that Christianity was important at an individual level, and that working with Amity changed people's belief. Ultimately, though, he reverted to the official phrase that Amity was built on Christian love and the ecumenical sharing of resources (author interview, November 2010).

Twenty years after its foundation Amity's (then newly appointed) General Secretary Qiu Zhonghui did not once mention the word religion in his speech given at China's first national conference on charity and philanthropy held in Pujiang. Instead Qiu, who, like his Deputy, studied American and English literature at Nanjing University, presented an organization based on the two equally important pillars of Western management practice and Christian values (but not faith). One of the five key principles he cited as lying at the heart of Amity's success was 'sincerity' which he considers crucial to gaining the trust of the donors. In his view 'honesty and sincerity' needed to embed themselves in society in order to be able to develop a modern non-profit culture and a genuine spirit of public welfare in China, which attracts talented young people willing to get involved (Qiu Z. 2004).

Part of the attraction to get involved with Amity may lie in what Philip Wickeri, long-term coordinator of the Amity overseas liaison office in Hong Kong (from 1985–97), refers to as the 'Amity Spirit'. According to Wickeri (2010), the Amity Spirit draws on Chinese traditional culture, Chinese socialism, and Christian internationalism. It is not 'Christian' and not 'religious', but many Christians and religious believers would see in it a reflection of their values. This constitutes a reflection of Bishop Ding's theology which aimed to integrate socialist values and Christian values, and which now appears to be of far greater attraction to foreign donors than to Chinese Christians.

Chinese Christians more widely are put off by the same factor that makes Amity such a successful organization: its very close cooperation with the government. Qiu Zhonghui is a member of the standing committee of the Jiangsu People's Political Consultative Conference, a role which enables him to raise his organization's profile on an important political stage. In February 2012 China's government newspaper, the People's Daily (1 February 2012), featured an article based on an interview with Qiu, in which his efforts at 'promoting philanthropic culture, improving social harmony, raising the amount of social services purchased by the government and the enhancing the healthy development of social organizations' are extolled. The article does not make any mention of religion and while it does mention Ding Guangxun, it only refers to him as the former vice-president of the National Chinese People's Political Consultative Conference.

Huiling

The founder of Huiling, a charity for mentally disabled adults, also takes a dim view of Qiu Zhonghui's connections, although she does approve of Amity's projects. Huiling came into existence in the same year as Amity. Back in the 1980s, when the trend was to 'jump into the sea' (*xiahai*, the Chinese expression for going into business at that time), especially in China's south, Meng Weina was in Guangzhou contemplating alternative ways to 'make a difference'. In her own words, she did not have the courage to become an entrepreneur, yet had a strong ambition to achieve something (author interview, November 2012). She was deeply impressed by Mother Teresa's work, and her award of a Nobel Prize (in 1979) inspired her to start a small charity, which became China's earliest organization for mentally disabled adults.

Today, Huiling is China's biggest organization of this kind and can be found in 12 Chinese cities, with 250 staff involved in training and caring for over a thousand adults with learning disabilities. Considering the size of China's population and the 1:4 staff to trainee ratio required to implement Huiling's integrated approach, this is still a very small organization. Its vision is to achieve equal opportunities and improved quality of life for people with learning disabilities through integration with society by relying on a community based service model (Huiling 2011). Huiling's approach is pioneering in a society where the approach to caring for the disabled, in particular the mentally disabled, has been one of segregation into specialized 'schools' rather than community based care with a view to integration.

Huiling has relied on different partners and sponsors over the two and a half decades of its existence. To come into existence it relied wholly on funds from a Catholic organization in Hong Kong, which was looking for a project to support in China. They parted ways after ten years of a sometimes stormy relationship in the process of which Meng Weina and her then charges in Guangzhou were also baptized, in her own words without much elaborate preparation. Despite her admiration for Mother Teresa and her continuing support from Catholic organizations (in terms of funds and in terms of staff), Meng Weina's own faith in Catholicism is by no means firm, yet not entirely dismissed by her. While grateful for (and reliant on) the funds and expertise provided, she has also gained insights into the workings of Catholic organizations and the Catholic Church (both in China and in Rome), which have left her very critical. The first-hand experience of a young female embezzler – a case not dissimilar to the Guo Meimei story, which made the headlines in the summer of 2011 – have further dented her belief in the purity of the Catholic church, in particular its Chinese incarnation (author interview, November 2012).

Today Huiling has annual funds of 10 million yuan, which are generated through different channels, including charges for various services they provide, government subsidy, domestic and overseas donations. Their longest-serving partner from overseas is the German Misereor foundation, a charity run by the German Catholic Bishops' Organization, two thirds of which is funded by the German government which has supported Huiling for over 20 years. Considering Meng Weina's reluctance to go into business in the 1980s, it is ironic that Huiling has not succeeded in registering as a people-run non-profit organization but is registered as a business (as many social organizations are).

In total, Huiling comprises of 73 'service points', which are made up of day centres and home care units or 'families', where five to six men or women with learning disabilities live together with one house co-ordinator. Each 'family' member has responsibility for certain aspects of daily life; chores are carried out together and meals are decided collectively. In the day centres the focus lies on building vocational skills for their 'trainees' with the hope that they will be able to find employment and live an as integrated life as possible. The day centres also provide workshops in handicraft like stitching and jewellery making, farming, cooking and house cleaning. Trainees, who do go on to find employment receive follow-up counselling through the centre.

Beijing Huiling is located in an old, un-modernized courtyard house in the city centre, a stone's throw from the main shopping area of Wangfujing. While by no means located in one of the most elegant or renovated alleys in Beijing, the rent for their premises constitutes by far their biggest expenditure. Moving further out of the city would ease the financial burden, but the central location is key to Huiling's integrated approach and also provides one source of income. The courtyard is promoted as a tourist attraction where Huiling's trainees put on cultural shows and cook dumplings for foreign visitors paying for the experience. They have been able to generate 200,000 yuan per year over four years through this activity and are hoping to turn these endeavours into a social enterprise. They are currently looking for potential partners and investors.

Meng Weina's plans for the next few years are to consolidate current projects and to improve standards of service. On the day I met her in Beijing she had received news of one of their trainees in Guangzhou falling (or jumping) to his death from their premises on the fifth floor of a building, which made her question their own policies and precautions. Certainly she is already aware of a variety of inadequacies which impact on their development. Apart from the unstable funding and staffing environment, the ever-changing external landscape including ever-changing concepts regarding social service provision provide a serious challenge.

But there are also disagreements among senior staff at Huiling as to how to deal with the government. The organization wants to keep a distance from the government, but this means they are losing out on vital income as the government in return does not purchase services from them. On the other hand, remaining distant from the government also means that they can refuse to comply with demands like the handing over of funds (as happens during major disaster relief efforts). They are also wary that their unique approach of community based, integrated care would not withstand the integration into the government's realm, where care models are less progressive than the one practised by Huiling.

NGO incubators

One of the most recent new concepts regarding social service provision is the idea of an 'incubator'. While constituting a mild digression from the core theme of this chapter, this deserves a closer inspection as it helps to understand the complex environment in which all charitable organizations operate. The concept has particular implications for organizations, which fall outside the approved realm of activity, which are not registered, or which are simply too 'difficult' to benefit from government cooperation.

The idea of an 'incubator' was first launched by NPI, a major aggregation of several NGO supporting organizations in Shanghai, which places high value on integrated branding, sharing of resources and complementary advantages. The establishment of minimum standards and the sharing of good practice are a key feature for the development of social organizations in China, in particular where the government has become a major funder of social organizations through its purchase of services from them. In this context, older, more established and 'trusted' organizations play a key role in fostering, or 'incubating' grassroots organizations.

Amity started its own 'training centre for social organizations' in 2009. With an expenditure of just over 98.000 yuan in 2010, it constitutes the smallest of Amity's projects in financial terms, but it is nonetheless controversial, as local funds (which could go towards other projects) are raised for it (author interview with Kan Renping, May 2010). Qiu Zhonghui justifies this new venture with the necessity to share Amity's expertise, but it may also have to do with the fact that the Nanjing government now wants all informal groups registered as a result of a change in the registration system (He J. 2010).

The Centre was founded in collaboration with the two local government organizations. Budding social organizations can submit proposals to the Centre, which then get evaluated. If an application is considered viable, the Centre will agree to 'incubate' this budding social organization for one year to prepare it for official registration. During this year the Centre provides office space and computers. They also lend support by providing help with the writing of applications for registration, checking if projects are sustainable (in terms of staffing for instance), if the project is strategically coherent and do-able and if it is financially viable. The Centre will also provide its expertise when it comes to writing funding applications (author interview, November 2010).⁹ One key element which determines whether a budding organization can be incubated is the area of social welfare provision they wish to engage in. This is firmly determined by the government's agenda. Of the seven organizations Amity currently incubates, three are environmental organizations, one works with disabled people, one with elderly people, and one provides educational material for disabled children and one is a travel agency.

Whether an organization will actually register largely depends on its development target. The fact, that according to Amity, 90 per cent of the 14.000 NGOs in Nanjing alone are not registered seems to suggest that the majority of individuals must be content to be involved in very small-scale work at the grassroots level. It may be that the urban elites, who tend to get involved in such projects, consciously resist the embrace of the local state, or that their initiative may simply be stifled or rendered unaffordable by all the processes involved in obtaining official registration. But one must also seriously consider the possibility that many small-scale initiatives take place in areas which are not declared urgent social needs by the government and hence do not stand a chance of either being registered or even incubated by umbrella organizations like Amity.

But this trend for all activity to be captured within the reaches of the state or a proxy (like Amity) can also impact on the way an already registered organization is able to carry out its projects. Beijing Huiling is a registered, legal body, but its community based integrative approach poses real difficulties, as its various 'service points' in different areas of Beijing are not also registered as community organizations in each district. These 'service points' do not amount to more than a small flat which serves as a day centre where trainees take part in arts and crafts activity. But the unregistered status of these 'service points' means that they are not allowed to use the facilities of the community centre in the same district, meaning they do not have access to government resources that would greatly help their daily work. The paperwork and fees involved in registering, however, make it impossible for all the service points to apply for registration.

Nationally, the tendency appears to go in the direction of more red tape rather than less. Wenzhou city introduced a permit requirement in 2012 to standardize the food charity sector dominated by a myriad of small-scale initiatives. An application costs 30,000 yuan and takes three months to be completed. By November only one group had applied. The majority of stall holders quite understandably question the need for this process when all they provide is a free cup of tea for passers-by (Yu R. 2012).

The 'incubator' appears to be one of the many new concepts and initiatives that established social organizations are faced with and feel the need to respond to, if they wish to remain competitive. Even Huiling has created its own type of incubator with the help of Hong Kong's Kadoorie Foundation. Unlike Amity's incubator, which is designed to shepherd small organizations towards registration and integration into the system, Huiling's 'incubator' brings together existing like-minded organizations to share experience and best practice in implementing community based services (Huiling 2011: 37 and 73).

Christian love in action?

Both Amity and Huiling, while different in scope, status and ambition, were inspired by Christian values and role models, have relied on Christian funding and are run by self-declared Christians, and could therefore be called Christian organizations, if 'Christian' is understood as synonymous with 'charitable', which it often is in the European context. In the Chinese context both organizations conform to societal expectations of what it means to be 'Christian' as shown in Chapter 2, but neither organization is a Christian charitable organization in the sense that neither was established by a religious group or organization or guided by religious doctrines or moral codes. Instead both are examples which showcase the meeting of socialist values and Christian caritas, where the former is provided by the Chinese side and the latter by the foreign partner and is primarily expressed in funding, but also through the work of dedicated individuals.

'Real' Chinese Christian charity, understood as the direct involvement of Christians through their churches in charitable work for the community, exists all over China, but is hindered by a variety of factors. Unregistered churches are not legal bodies, a key factor that impacts negatively on their existence in a number of ways, but which also further restricts what they can do in terms of charitable work. But even official churches are not allowed to get involved directly in social projects, but have to find a secular organization (or the local authorities) to whom they hand over their funds and for whom individual church members can volunteer. Churches in Jiangsu, for example, tend to work with Amity.

Crucially, however, the social gospel, propagated by American missionaries in the 1920s, 1930s and 1940s which was popular with early Chinese Christian thinkers, is not a doctrine all churches in China subscribe to. In fact, it is one of the theological fault lines along which the different churches in China segregate. Melissa Manhong Lin, the first woman from Nanjing Theological Seminary to have received a doctoral degree in a theological discipline, is hugely critical of this. Her doctoral dissertation *Ethical Reorientation for Christianity in China*, presented at Graduate Theological Union, Berkeley, in 2007 makes an urgent call for a reorientation of Christian ethics in China today. Lin's starting point is the lack of *chengxin* (honesty and credibility) in Chinese society today. While Christian belief holds the potential to contribute to the moral reconstruction of Chinese society, in her view, Chinese Christians are not doing enough in this regard. In her understanding, which reflects the theological approach of Wu Yaozong and Ding Guangxun, what it means to be a Christian and how to live a Christian life depend on social and historical circumstance. Christian responses to God's commandments will therefore be shaped by the context in which Christians reside (Lin M.M. 2010: 15).

For Lin, China's present social and political environment has engendered more opportunities for the church to make itself understood and to follow Jesus's example to serve the people. However, the fundamentalist character of most congregations together with the political environment of the twentieth century has kept Christians from engaging with wider society and from developing a fuller sense of Christian identity, adopting instead an individually-focused and otherworldly ethic. The political context has now changed, she argues, but Chinese

Christian thinking and identity still lags behind. Theological thinking has not caught up with this change, meaning that the majority of Chinese Christians do not yet live up to what theologian Richard Niebuhr sees as Christian identity, namely to 'follow Jesus Christ, and to identify with the person, the cause, and the community of Jesus Christ' (Lin M.M. 2010: 155).

Lin still sees great value in the social gospel and its application to Chinese social needs as formulated by early Chinese Christian thinkers in the 1920s and 1930s; in today's China this means for Christians to first inform themselves of the needs of society, whether they have related these needs of society to the needs of the church and whether they have considered making contributions to the needs of the people as part of the church's mission. Evangelizing and conversions need not come into this.

For Lin, the most obvious area in which churches can live Jesus's example and 'serve the people' is through work with migrants. This should start with a welcoming attitude towards migrants in the churches rather than considering them a burden on the congregation. They should provide for their spiritual needs through Bible study groups and counselling sessions; material help could come in the form of financial aid, but should also include training sessions for further professional development and legal training to make them less vulnerable in their daily existence. She particularly emphasizes the role of lawyers and legal scholars in this regard. While she concedes that the church will not be able to eradicate the issues migrants face in their working lives, they can help to raise their legal awareness and to join them in protest against the injustice done to them. Furthermore, churches should get involved in providing regular food donations, in setting up private schools for migrant children and in setting up clinics and hospitals. The Christian identity would not be revealed in the names of these projects, nor should the service be restricted to fellow Christians, but these would be ways for the church to show that it shares the burden of society and helps with its needs out of unselfish love as taught in Christian virtue ethics (Lin M.M. 2010: 190–2).

These suggestions warrant further analysis and comment as they need to be understood in the wider context. One of the main problems 'three self' churches are facing is the size of their congregations; there are simply not enough of them to cope with the demand. In this context, the additional influx of a growing migrant population becomes a concern and is viewed as an additional strain on resources rather than a welcome phenomenon. Their large size also means that even where migrants are welcome, they will not receive the same attention and spiritual care as they can within smaller churches outside the official realm. The intimate approach of Bible study groups and fellowships, which are a key feature of religious activity and outreach in 'house churches', may suit the spiritual and psychological need of a migrant population much better. On the other hand, due to their small size, fellowships, Bible study groups and many churches that emerge from this activity tend to be relatively homogenous in their make-up, which means they provide little interaction between the permanent residents of the cities and migrants.

Lin's emphasis on professional training, rights education, schooling and health care is reminiscent of the approach of early missionaries or indeed the Chinese YMCA in the Republican period. These activities potentially have a long-lasting and far-reaching effect on the improvement of lives and prospects of the beneficiaries of this type of charity. They do, however, not necessarily lead to a lot of new converts. Indeed, Lin clearly emphasizes that evangelization, beyond the offer of spiritual support and Bible study groups for those already interested in Christianity, should not be linked to charitable activity and will hence not find an open ear in churches with a different theological emphasis.

Crucially, as Liu Peng (2011) unequivocally points out, under the current regulatory framework and in the absence of a Law on Religion and a Law on Charitable Organizations, religious institutions are not allowed to conduct non-religious activities outside religious venues by providing social services. They are also not permitted to establish charitable organizations and organize and execute charitable projects. To Liu, 'religious charitable organizations' need to have two prominent features: the organization needs to be established by a religious group or organization and be guided by religious doctrines or moral codes; second, the organization does not conduct religious activities, but carries out charitable activities, as suggested by Lin. But in reality a lot of misunderstandings exist about what constitutes a religious charitable organization and therefore religious organizations are, for example, prohibited from using their symbols, or are generally treated with suspicion. They also don't have access to public resources in the same way as other social organizations do, for example in the form of media coverage. Liu sees no chance that projects like those proposed by Lin would be able to obtain permission from the relevant authorities to establish schools or hospitals. This would require not just approval by religious organizations, but also by the Ministry of Civil Affairs and other relevant ministries, a nigh impossible feat.

Religious charitable organizations are also not allowed to engage in fundraising activities, although these may be quite successful as they are considered more trustworthy by general society (as discussed in Chapter 2). They also do not enjoy any tax breaks, cannot use their own property to raise funds and are only allowed to accept a very limited amount of foreign funds. All this means that the range of their possible activities is extremely limited.

Despite all these factors, certainly most urban churches have a charitable aspect, although usually small in scope and dedicated to projects close to home, geographically and spiritually. They may concern the support of members of the congregation who are in difficulty or food donations to migrants or petitioners (who often spend weeks in places away from their home before they are heard). Urban churches may also support rural churches close to their hometown. In Wenzhou, one of China's richest cities with a high percentage of Christian population and a high percentage of migrants, 1,600 small independent street stalls provide passers-by with simple dishes or tea free of charge (Yu R. 2012). The regulatory framework also does not prevent individual Christians from taking part in charitable work or relief efforts as part of projects organized by established non-religious organizations or indeed spontaneous efforts that have not been formally planned. Chang, whom I met in Chengdu, told me of her experiences of engaging in charitable work organized by her church in a small village in Sichuan. She related these actions to illustrate her change of personality since her conversion; she emphasized how she had surprised herself for being able to sleep in the basic conditions and to hug the 'dirty' village children, all as a result of God's love. In this account – as in others referred to by (Kleinman *et al.* (2011b) – the emphasis seems to be on how charitable work makes the individual engaged in the act feel and what it means to their individual identity, rather than its actual effects on those at the receiving end. (From the government's point of view and those, who coordinate large-scale relief projects, the spontaneous, disorganized efforts of individuals, however well meant, are seen as counterproductive, constituting an inefficient use of resources at best and a disruption and further drain on limited infrastructure at worst.)

In rare cases such charitable activity close to home can take on a distinctly political nature. Some churches have started to provide support for members of their congregation who are negatively affected by the enforcement of the one-child policy, for example. The degree to which they do so varies. Wang Yi's Early Rain Reformed Church has gone so far as holding campaigns against the one-child policy in front of schools, but the majority prefer a more low-key approach. Early Rain have also been providing financial support for the families of individuals detained on political grounds. They have supported nine affected families so far, most recently the wife and son of Sichuan poet, who was handed a prison sentence in November 2012.[10] A third charitable aspect they are involved in is support, primarily spiritual, for rural petitioners in Chengdu. All these areas are acutely sensitive and, not surprisingly, not all members of Early Rain are prepared to get involved in them.

Conclusion

The recent encouragement of religious organizations to become involved in charitable work as seen during the religious charity week in September 2012 needs to be understood in the wider context in which social organizations (which includes all charitable organizations) operate. The emphasis on 'long-term, institutionalized and standardized' work during the events of the religious charity week indicates this very clearly. Most churches, due to the nature of their congregations, their legal status or their theological orientation, will neither be able nor willing to engage in this type of charitable work, which inevitably must involve some degree of cooperation with the government, either directly or through an organization like Amity.

In the 27 years of its existence Amity has become an important player in the domestic NGO scene. Its Christian beginnings are important, as it was this particular characteristic that drew in powerful and financially liquid donors from overseas. But from the outset the link to and support of the government was a vital ingredient in Amity's ability to attract foreign donors, as the churches overseas were keen to ensure the viability of their projects and to reach as wide an audience as possible. Once the money was received, Amity has worked with the Chinese government at different levels, in order to be able to successfully carry out the projects. Its ability to deliver very effectively in turn further built its reputation with foreign donors, but also built its name inside China at the various levels of government.

In this process of reorientation away from foreign donors and towards the domestic field and competition of charitable social organizations, it is not only less reliant on its foreign funds, but has also put off some of its international donors as well as domestic churches. Kan Renping was quite explicit in his criticism of this development, which to him was clearly manifested in the greatly reduced number of foreign visitors to Amity's twenty-fifth anniversary celebrations in November 2010 (author interview November 2010). Not only is Amity not regarded as a Christian organization by the wider Christian population in China, but it also appears to have lost the connection to the TSPM churches.

Today Amity's Christian roots are primarily invoked in dialogue with foreign partners and churches inside China, but in reality are probably of negligible importance. When I first visited Amity in 2010, a big photograph of Qiu Zhonghui and Ding Guangxun was propped up against the window and dominated the scene, exuding big symbolic significance. At my next visit the picture had disappeared, but, as I was assured, was now hung properly in a different (but less public) part of the office. Following Bishop Ding's death, no written obituary was posted on the Chinese website of Amity, only a slideshow displaying various images of Ding's, while the (much more rudimentary) English website carried a very short text. Two weeks later, a short article was posted reporting on a memorial service for Ding held at Amity's headquarters (Amity Foundation 2012).

Part of Amity's mission statement is to 'encourage Chinese Christians to get involved in social development work' and to provide a 'new form' in which Chinese Christians can get involved in social welfare. Read in the wider context of China's regulatory landscape for social organizations, this means that Chinese Christians should go through Amity (either by donating or by volunteering as individuals), if they want to engage in charitable projects. The churches do not like this development, but they do grudgingly have to admit, that it is better to work with Amity than without it, if they want to get things done – echoing bigger organizations' views about working with the government. While many overseas Christian donors as well as Chinese churches go along with this despite what they consider a compromise of their religious principle, other organizations like Huiling are loath to be embraced by the government, not for religious reasons, but because it may eventually compromise their own values in terms of what type of service they provide.

While her gratitude for the various Catholic organizations and individuals who have enabled Huiling's work is sincere, and although there are a number of religious images displayed in the small flat Meng Weina shares with her son and four disabled adults, it seemed to me that what really drove her initiative in the 1980s and what continues to motivate her work today, is a belief in socialism, and more precisely Marxist ideals of equality and fair distribution. She is full of criticism for the current trends in Chinese 'socialism', ranging from the failure of the education system to the pitfalls of money and status and the lack of transparency. She is scathing in her criticism of anyone, who appears to detect a 'Chinese model', be it for social organizations or the wider polity. In her view, the so called 'Chinese model' is characterized by double standards, lack of transparency and accountability, and the one-party system. But she is equally scathing in her criticism of Catholic Church organizations.

The current environment puts organizations like Huiling – which is well known and established, but nonetheless comparatively small – in a really difficult situation. It is possible to be uncompromising in one's principles when it comes to working with the government, as far as handing over of donated funds or changing their particular way of working (in Huiling's case using a fully integrative model of care) is concerned. This ensures integrity and a degree of independence, but it also means that the government will not purchase services from this organization, which means that it loses out on vital funds and makes it less competitive; this in turn endangers its existence. Huiling faces this problem on a daily basis, even though it provides social services in a field firmly on the government's agenda.

Despite – or perhaps because of – efforts on the part of individuals within the 'three self' church, philanthropy as social gospel is not emphasized by churches in general. In the eyes of the majority of Christian believers in China, the focus on the social gospel at the expense of an emphasis on faith and salvation is characteristic of the official church's efforts to dilute the doctrine and to enlist Christians for worldly matters in the interest of the state. The lack of adequate laws and the current regulatory framework further complicate, and even disable, organized religious charitable activity.

The urban, educated reform congregations, which subscribe to the ethical aspect of Christianity together with strong notions of salvation, are potentially able to agree with Manhong Lin's proposed charitable work of churches. The most progressive thinkers within the TSPM and other churches share a similar understanding of the importance of social works; so do those with a more left-wing and instinctively atheist orientation like Meng Weina. Theologically and politically they currently stand miles apart, but this may change, if and when 'following Jesus's example' in the sense of the social gospel leads to differences or conflict between 'three self' churches and the government. Considering the type of activity Manhong Lin is proposing, this can happen very easily, provided they are ever allowed to get off the ground.

It is difficult to see how under the current regulations governing charitable activity, including the acceptance of funds by churches, Lin's suggestions of larger projects like the founding of schools and hospitals by churches can be realized. Furthermore, the emphasis on training and basic legal education are potentially sensitive areas that may lead to conflict between the churches and the government as such activities do not currently fall within the government agenda on social welfare. This will be an interesting area to watch as far as the relations between 'three self' churches and TSPM leadership are concerned, which have already become more strained in recent years.

The most likely scenario over the next years is that religious charity will be fostered and 'incubated' to become part of the approved and standardized social welfare provision in areas on the government's agenda. In this sense the Chinese government is signalling its recognition of the importance of the social gospel and acknowledging the positive contributions it can make to Chinese society today, but at the same time it is also continuing its control over charitable activity as introduced in 1950. Today the control is not phrased in ideological terms, but in terms of logistics ('co-ordination') and quality control ('standard of provision'). However, recent signs that the party wants to establish branches and groups within social organizations may also be a hint that ideology is becoming more rather than less important (Shieh 2012a). Currently the government will only buy services from charities (thus providing important funding), which conform to its standards, where standards also refer to the area of social service an organization is involved in and the way in which it delivers these services. This control is not as all-encompassing as the more overtly political control of earlier decades. It is possible to remain outside the system and to resist the embrace of the government, but the social groups or organizations which choose to do so or are forced to do so, will have to be content to operate on the margins, regardless of their religious, theological or political orientation.

Notes

1. This observation, made by Alfred Lin in reference to Chen Jitang's rule can be equally applied to contemporary China (see Lin A.H.Y. 2009).
2. Interestingly no such moral dilemmas are associated with capitalist entrepreneurial structures and practices.
3. Two of the most interesting recent books on religious charities in Taiwan are C. Julia Huang, *Charisma and Compassion. Cheng Yen and the Buddhist Tzu Chi Movement* (Cambridge, MA, Harvard University Press 2009) and Richard Madsen, *Democracy's Dharma. Religious Renaissance and Political Development in Taiwan* (Berkeley, University of California Press 2007).
4. This is confirmed by Lu Yiyi (2008) who also states that NGOs are often staffed by government officials who can be hugely ineffective.
5. For the clearest explanation of the various organizations and regulations see Lu Yiyi 2009: 2ff.
6. Ding Guangxun has been the central figure in the development of the (official) Chinese Protestant church in China since the reform era. He has developed a Chinese Christian theology influenced by socialism and whose central tenet is the notion that God is love. See Wickeri 2007 and preceding chapters of this book.
7. For detailed information see Amity's website at www.amity.org.cn, also *Love Never Ends*, 1985–2010, on the twentieth anniversary of the Amity Foundation.
8. Gospel Times is a web-based organization with the aim to provide information and a communication channel for Chinese Christians www.gospeltimes.cn/ For a detailed analysis see Chapter 5.
9. For a detailed chart of the incubation process see www.amityfoundation.org.cn/project/app/0032/webproject-02lv.aspx (last accessed 9 May 2011).
10. Dissident Writer Li Bifeng sentenced to 12 years www.dw.de/异议作家李必丰被判刑12年/a-16389523 (last accessed 30 November 2012).

5 Protestant and online

The growth of China's Christian population has garnered considerable attention from academia and media outside China, but this pales in comparison to the interest that the growth of the internet has received in the same circles. Chinese 'netizens' have become a special section of the Chinese population whose opinions are closely watched and have at times be able to elicit concessions and unexpected reactions from the government. China's internet users are often referred to as though they were a homogenous group, when ultimately what unites them is no more than the use of a very effective public medium for information, entertainment and comment. In the vast majority of cases, this activity is non-political, but it is undeniable that the internet has been an invaluable publishing and communication tool for interest groups with a more sensitive agenda.

Since the beginning of the reform era, different groups have challenged the existing limits of rights and liberties in the People's Republic of China. Until the crackdown in 1989 it was the members of the 'democracy movement' who used the opportunities afforded by economic liberalization to create and explore niches of public debate in which they demanded political change. After 1989, marking both the crackdown of the democracy movement and the fall of the Iron Curtain in Europe, these activities were documented and researched in the light of an 'emerging civil society' in China (Howell *et al.* 1996; also Madsen 1998). In the 1990s, different social groups, many of them Qigong associations and most notably the Falungong movement, emerged and challenged the government's restrictions on rights and freedoms guaranteed in the Chinese constitution. Since the crackdown on Falungong and the China Democratic Justice Party in the late 1990s, some believe that the most important groups continuing this challenge have come from within the Chinese 'house church' movement (Yan X. 2004). Operating in the first decade of the twenty-first century this group continues the tradition of Chinese opposition movements and of Christian churches, historically and worldwide, of employing the most up-to-date technology to disseminate information and avoid government control. The samizdat magazines of 1978 have now been replaced by online journals, some of which are produced as clandestinely as the former but with the potential to reach a far wider audience.

A variety of religious and quasi-religious groups in China today rely on extensive web-based strategies of text distribution, recruitment and information sharing, often funded at least in part by overseas Chinese groups. The technological resources at the disposal of these groups facilitate the linking up of relatively dispersed smaller groups. Collectively, members and practitioners of such groups construct virtual communities of faith. While these organizational elements are not unique to religious and quasi-religious groups in China, the degree of reliance on the web to maintain their existence in the face of severe government repressions makes the Chinese use of web technology unique (Thornton 2003: 248, 265). From a Christian point of view, the internet explosion in China is seen as part of 'God's work in China', facilitating an unprecedented reach of the gospel far beyond existing church communities. It is seen as a tool created by God, whose full use is the task of Christian intellectuals in order to bring the gospel 'not just to every individual, but also to the collective soul' (Wang Y. 2012a). In this chapter, some of the most professionally produced publications will be introduced. Following a brief outline of their main characteristics and features, this chapter will present an analysis of these publications in the wider context of the church agenda, church-state relations, and the Chinese mission.

Online communities and the online gospel

Originally the term 'community' was based on birth and physical location, but with the increase of technology in particular in transport and telecommunication, a different understanding of 'community' has emerged. In recent years, the strength and nature of relationships between individuals is considered a more useful basis for defining community. Howard Rheingold and Roxanne Hiltz used the term 'online community' to communicate the intense feeling of camaraderie, empathy and support that they observed among people in the online spaces that they studied. De Souza, Preece and Maloney focus on people who come together for a particular 'purpose' and who are guided by 'policies' (including norms and rules) and supported by 'software'. Other ways of approaching online communities have included the identification of key parameters of community life and a search for their presence online. Online communities rarely exist only online. Most of the time there are also offline components and communication is rarely restricted to a single medium. Particularly non-profit groups and voluntary associations use internet tools to keep their members informed and to maintain group interaction (Maloney-Krichmar and Preece 2005).

The latest survey conducted by China's Internet Network Information Center (CNNIC) available at the time or writing gives a figure of 538 million internet users in China by the end of June 2012, with mobile internet access for the first time surpassing desktop access. The growth of mobile access is particularly pronounced among new rural netizens. Overall, internet penetration has reached 39.9 per cent with a slightly unequal gender balance (55 per cent male, 45 per cent female netizens). Perhaps not surprisingly, students form the single biggest group of netizens with 28.6 per cent, followed by independent professionals and other self-employed people (17.2 per cent) and the unemployed (11 per cent). The latter perhaps slightly surprising figure is further supported by the fact that netizens are as likely to be from the lowest income stratum as from the middle-income stratum.[1] The tactical use of the internet for protest purposes is certainly not a reserve of the urban educated elite. Take the example of a farmer's fight against illegal mines and quarries in Hebei, who started to be successful in his endeavours once he bought a laptop and a digital camera and started posting to websites and microblogs (The Economist 2012).

The growth of the 'online gospel' on the Chinese internet is a phenomenon particularly prevalent in mainland China and North America with very close links between the two. But the internet has also become a useful tool for established churches within China, providing one way of easing the strain on capacity experienced by TSPM churches. Churches have their own websites on which sermons are published; in some cases the entire Sunday worship is recorded and can be viewed or listened to online. (See for example the website of Haidian Church in Beijing www.hdchurch.org.) Individual Christians are also using microblogs to express their religious belief (World Watch Monitor 2012). Most recently the 'online gospel' has also drawn the attention of religious regulators, who speak of an 'electronically linked missionary era' and a 'large internet religious world' which has made the 'establishment of a monitoring system for religious websites an urgent task'. In this context the danger of 'outside forces making use of electronic churches' is being evoked (Mi 2013).

Christianity was a 'hot' topic on the Chinese internet right from its beginnings in the early 1990s. Jidian[2] reports on a regular war of words between Christian and non-Christian intellectuals in the early news groups, which were the dominant forum of internet debates at the time. Christians were certainly in the minority then, but the debates intensified as more and more Chinese scholars abroad converted to Christianity and joined in. From 1996/97, BBS (Bulletin Board System) took over from newsgroups in terms of importance. They were hosted by Chinese universities, but the debates on Christianity were often dominated by individuals residing outside China and were joined by Christians from Hong Kong and Taiwan. From the start, BBS had sections on Christianity or the Bible (Ji D. 2006).

From 1997 onwards, with China's connection to the World Wide Web, Chinese online Christians started their own websites, where they compiled Christian writings online; more and more online Christians also wrote for non-Christian or non-religious sites, which resulted in the establishment of good contacts and relations between the two groups. While the early debates in the 1990s were characterized by debates between Christian intellectuals and their humanistic, scientific counterparts, who were sceptical of or hostile to religion, following the explosion of the internet at the turn of the millennium, these debates were largely replaced by discussions among different Christian denominations on theology. According to Jidian, the anti-religious voices of the 1990s had more or less disappeared by then. Christian websites proliferated, some with more popular orientation; others specifically aimed at the cultural field, where so-called 'Christianizing scholars' (*jiduhua xuezhe*) started to exert their influence among young intellectuals, forming a 'new vanguard' after the cultural Christians of the 1990s (Ji 2006).

Apart from the creation of websites, the new century also saw the influx of evangelizing material in the form of books, CDs and films via the internet. One of the first people to engage in this type of media work was Yuan Zhiming, a former Communist Party member, Marxist theorist and co-writer of the 1987 television series 'River Elegy', who converted to Christianity at Princeton in 1992 and has been in the United States ever since (see for example Johnson 2012a). Increasingly, the internet also became a source of comfort, a place of support and a way to get in contact with other Christians, either via email or through online publications, so it started to bear the hallmarks of an online community. Websites based in the United States were specifically designed to help and reach out to mainland Chinese intellectuals and to foster this community. One prime example is www.ccim.org, founded in 1994. This web resource was previously called Chinese Christian Resource Centre (CCRS), but I have not been able to confirm the English name for which CCIM is now the acronym. Based on its Chinese name (*wangluo jidu shituan*) I imagine it stands for Chinese Christian Internet Mission. The site has built up an enormous archive of resource materials, ranging from the early online debates to teaching and preaching materials, helping people to answer questions of their congregations, distance study, etc. They helped *Overseas Campus* (www.oc.org/web/) and *Life Quarterly* (www.smyxy.org/) to come into existence, enabling contact and discussion between Christians in mainland China and the United States. Both magazines are part of the wider 'internet project' in the Chinese Christian mission and are still heavily involved in setting up, authoring and supporting similar magazines in mainland China.

The editors behind CCIM see the site's main function as the provision of news and resources, technological support (to other websites) and online evangelizing. They are associated with a whole host of related sites, each with their particular focus, be it news reporting (www.ccim.org/news), pastor training (www.chinapeixun.org), prayers (www.prayforchina.org) or Bible readings (www.bible.ccim.org). According to the site's editors the use of the internet as a tool to reach out to Chinese mainland Christians is directly linked to China's urbanization and the growth of urban churches. The internet is regarded as a technology and as a medium, and they are using both to the full. The online publications analysed in the following epitomize this characteristic of the 'online Christian' movement.

The main purpose of online church publication is to inform and to educate and to provide a platform for church members to stay in touch. Much of the former is concentrated on the Bible, but the different backgrounds and aims of each publication determine the relative emphasis of their content. Clearly the Chinese 'house church' movement is not just a 'virtual community' but also a real community existing in different geographical locales within China. However, the existence of an online component potentially enables members of these smaller communities to see and identify themselves as part of a bigger community, spanning provinces and if not the globe, so at least the Pacific all the way to North America.

Of the publications analysed in this chapter, all exist(ed) as hard copies as well as electronic journals apart from *Gospel Times*. In some cases, the website consists primarily of an electronic version of the publication; in other cases the website provides additional material for the perusal of the reader, which complements the themes addressed in the actual publication. *Aiyan* (The Banquet, also translated as Love Feast[3]) was founded in 2002 and ran 15 issues until it ceased publication in 2008. It is the focal point of this chapter and presented here as a resistance community using up-to-date technology whose religious message had strong political overtones. *Maizhong* (Wheat Seeds, www.maizhong.org), which aims to 'fill the cultural void' among Wenzhou churches, was founded in 2006 and appears to have run into difficulty in 2012. *Jiaohui* (Church China, www.churchchina.org) also saw its first issue in 2006, had produced 38 issues by January 2013 and it is still thriving. Its main concern is the construction of the church in China and is therefore primarily directed at church leaders, fellow missionaries, preachers and 'all ordinary Christians involved in building the church' in China. *Fuyin shibao* (Gospel Times, www.fuyinshibao.cn) is a new addition and reflects the most recent developments in Chinese Christianity. A non-profit organization registered under Beijing Gospel Times Information Technology Ltd, *Gospel Times* was founded in 2006 in Beijing by young Christians, who converted while at university. It is now a comprehensive website with subpages for several provinces in China and presents a very different Christian identity from the other three publications. These publications are introduced here as a means to contextualize *Aiyan*, the earliest publication among them. They also serve to illustrate the different models of churches and their different agendas and directions.

It is quite customary for churches to produce some kind of reading material or CDs and DVDs for their members. Congregations have their own libraries that are shared among members which will contain different types of materials, including books and films on Chinese Christians or Christianity that may not be available in general book stores; these materials are multiplied for the perusal of the congregation. All the journals and websites analysed in the following go far beyond these small-scale operations. They are well established and professionally produced journals reaching an audience that goes far beyond the members of just one congregation.

Aiyan (The Banquet, www.aiyan.org)

Aiyan was founded by Cai Zhuohua, pastor of a Beijing 'house church'. It was conceived of as a quarterly publication, but both the printed and the online edition had difficulty maintaining this regularity. By January 2008 there were 15 issues of *Aiyan* online, but the website has not been updated since. Cai Zhuohua was arrested in 2003 (his arrest was partly related to his association with *Aiyan*[4]) which marked a crisis point for the publication, from which it subsequently recovered before its eventual demise.

A number of leading intellectuals were associated with and wrote in *Aiyan*. The majority of these intellectuals were leading figures in the field of law working for the main think tanks and universities. A number of them have since lost their positions and have encountered further harassment including imprisonment and house arrest or have gone into exile. According to one well-connected church contact, *Aiyan* was a widely known, nationwide publication received with great enthusiasm, however due to its underground nature it was not possible to establish circulation figures for it. It was written by Christians for Christians, reaching into the general population of 'house church' Christians; quite a few of its articles were rather highbrow.

Aiyan's domain name was registered in California; caution was also exercised when it came to the identity of contributors and editors. Most articles did not give an author's name but only referred to a 'Brother' or 'Sister' sometimes stating a certain province. Where names were given, they were usually Christian names and thus render identification quite difficult. Both content and context of the articles published make it clear that *Aiyan*'s main target audience as well as authorship lay within the People's Republic of China; *Aiyan* appeared to be easily accessible in China.[5] Both the nature of the magazine with its relatively highbrow articles on a variety of subjects and scholarly contributions on China's legal system and its online existence stood in stark contrast to the general depiction of the Chinese 'house church movement' as predominantly rural congregations consisting mainly of old people, women, the sick and the illiterate, as was still the main assumption at the start of the millennium (for example Dunch 2000).

Due to the considerable strain under which *Aiyan*'s paper edition was produced (writing, printing and distribution of the printed copy all took place in different provinces), editors were very keen to get people online in order to access the online edition rather than the printed version. Step-by-step guides on how to get online were a regular feature in the magazine. There was clearly an intention to encourage members to read the online edition in order to increase the readership and to ease the pressure on the production of the printed version. According to the editors, all contributions to *Aiyan* were written by members of the 'house church' community themselves; they were voluntary and unpaid. The online edition of *Aiyan* went through various visual incarnations during its existence while the printed version of was a very simple black-and-white publication which did not change significantly. The simplicity of the printed edition most likely was a reflection of the difficulties under which it was produced; the paper copies of *Jiaohui* and *Maizhong* follow a similarly simple style.

Each issue of *Aiyan* formed a substantial publication with between 20 to 30 different articles, many of which were lengthy. There were regular categories under which articles were published. Quite a big part of these were concerned with personal testimonies and reports from the mission (evangelical outreach work), a crucial component of all churches in China today. Apart from these rather emotional accounts there were also a number of categories under which relatively highbrow and scholarly articles were published. These included articles on theology, law, biographical accounts of famous foreign Christians, science and religion as well as politics and religion. While none of these articles were overtly political, they did have strong political implications in so far as they intended to inform Christians of the legal framework and how to use it. News items, both domestic and international, were linked with prayers and the selection of news reported in *Aiyan* offered very interesting insights into the concerns, direction and intentions of the Chinese 'house church' movement.⁶ So did the sections that directly address specific questions coming from the community.⁷

Reading through the publication, it was possible to discern a number of functions that *Aiyan* was trying to fulfil. Some of these were in keeping with evangelical movements worldwide; others reflected the specific situation Chinese Christians find themselves in. Education was of great importance. *Aiyan's* pages reflected an acute awareness of the need to 'raise the quality' among the Christian population, a task which some people deeply involved in the 'house church' movement consider more important at present than further evangelizing. The aim to raise the educational level within the churches is also reflected in recurring prayers for the timely return of theology students abroad,⁸ for more people within China to engage in Bible studies, and for the aid of foreign churches in this endeavour. In addition to its more specific educational role there was a wealth of more general information available to the readers of *Aiyan*.

News items, which according to the editors were taken from news published in the official Chinese news media, were organized according to domestic and foreign news. These news items were concluded with short prayers for the parties/countries/individuals involved or a more general prayer in connection with the item. Domestic news tended to focus on social problems and ills in China, like unemployment, domestic violence, drug addiction and alcoholism, gambling, smoking, corruption (of teachers, journalists, the government), hepatitis and AIDS, environmental degradation, superstition, China's mafia, and the dangers of the internet. Social groups addressed in these news items cum prayers included, apart from the sufferers of above societal ills, old people, migrants , atheists, poor people, China's middle class, miners, homeless children, etc.⁹

While Christianity is seen as an answer to all of the social ills mentioned above, it was also clear if sometimes only implicit that the social groups listed here also form the main target for evangelizing efforts. An increasing number of domestic news items and prayers (and dominating the news by the last issue of *Aiyan*) referred to detained church leaders, Christians who were mistreated in custody, together with calls for the abolition of re-education through labour and the establishment of a proper and fair legal system in China. This last item appears in every single issue of *Aiyan* without fail.¹⁰

Aiyan clearly attempted to assume a guiding role within the 'house church' community, both in smaller and faith related matters in matters impacting on the whole of society. *Aiyan* contained a feature called 'Question and Answers' which addressed questions ostensibly emerging from individuals within the community. These questions were very interesting reflections of the dilemmas and tribulations faced by the 'house church' community and ranged from the more spiritual to the very practical. All questions were answered in utmost sincerity and at times in very great detail. As these questions were chosen by the editors they presumably were representative to a certain degree. What we learn from them is that members of the community look to the church not just for spiritual and matters related to faith, but also to receive guidance in a rapidly changing society on how to make one's choices and how to take part in wider social activity including political activity.¹¹

Maizhong (Wheat Seeds, www.maizhong.org/wheatseeds)

The first issue of *Maizhong* was published in July 2006. The welcome letter of the editors (no name provided) states that while *Maizhong* aimed to fill the 'literary void' among Wenzhou churches, it was directed at all churches in China. Its aspirations were to publish original pieces of writing, specifically commissioned for the publication, including fiction, drama and music. In its first anniversary issue of September 2007 it goes further and draws parallels between *Maizhong* and *Xin Qingnian*, the seminal publication of the May Fourth Period, which gave a forum to Lu Xun and many other key writers of the period. In this issue *Maizhong* is referred to as a 'luxury good' of the Wenzhou churches who wish to produce their own Lu Xun.

Maizhong's aim is to publish proper literature, not just evangelizing material. In a further reference to the spirit of May Fourth and Liang Qichao, literature is quoted as the most powerful tool to effect change in people's thinking (Xiao Y. 2007) According to China Aid (September 2011), *Maizhong* was founded by Ezra Pan (Chinese name She He) 'together with two other brothers'. Involved in preaching from an early age, Pan graduated from the Christian Witness Theology Seminary in California in 2009 and now edits Gospel Operation International for Chinese Christians (www.gointl.org), a site providing comprehensive teaching and training material for the mission. It also hosts the online edition of a related journal, *Go&i* (The Quarterly Mission Journal of Gospel Operation International). Issue five of *Maizhong* saw a change in editorship and four permanent consultants put in place. They are Ezra Pan, Liu Tongsu, Fan Xuede and Ye Jiacheng. Liu Tongsu also serves as permanent columnist.

Clearly the editors of *Maizhong* felt they had a lot to share with their readers in the first year of their existence. Nine issues were published in the first 14 months, all of them substantial with about 20 articles each. There were special issues for Christmas and for Easter. Finding regular contributors – a challenge for most publications regardless of their background – does not appear to have been a problem for *Maizhong*, which claims in its first anniversary issue that all articles were now exclusively written for publication in *Maizhong*. (This does not continue in later issues, where many articles are reprinted from other sources.) The majority of authors are university students. *Maizhong* is a cultural magazine and its content reflects this. In addition to the poems, songs and stories, essays deal with Chinese Christian traditions, problems within the churches, the best organizational structure for churches and how to ensure growth. The twenty-ninth issue, dated January 2012, is the most recent issue of *Maizhong* available online. According to a China Aid post dated 27 March 2012, the offices and storage of *Maizhong* were searched the day before and four people were taken into custody. A qq (the Chinese equivalent of Twitter) feed of 11 April 2012 by one apparent reader states that *Maizhong* has stopped publication.[12]

From issue 12 onwards, each issue of *Maizhong* focuses on a particular topic. The first one is migrant workers followed by topics covering a wide range, from theological education in China today, Christians on campus, to a Korean missionary captured by the Taliban in Afghanistan, church structures, etc. In October 2008 it announced that the website is up and running, which initially only featured an online edition of the magazine. In January 2010 an unnamed church in Wenzhou held the first conference on the 'Internet Project' (i.e. the use of the internet in the mission), which brought together a range of editors and webmasters to discuss missionary work online including the chances, opportunities and hidden risks involved (Maizhong 21 January 2010). The October 2011 issue reports that the website has now been updated and developed to complement the hard copy of the magazine. The website wants to provide more detailed information and/or further reading to the topics covered in the journal and to facilitate a better exchange between editors and readers through discussion forums. Readers' letters – which only rarely feature – are mostly expressions of admiration and gratitude for the existence of *Maizhong*.

Maizhong established a sister publication called *Taxiang* (Sojourn) aimed at and partly written by migrant workers. It does not appear to have an online edition, but part of its content can be accessed from within the BBS on *Maizhong's* website. It claims to be the first publication on migrant workers' belief and life edited with the involvement of migrant workers. It was launched in June 2009 and came about as the result of a conference organized by an unnamed church and with the help of unnamed scholars and specialists on Chinese migrants. Its aim is to reflect migrant life and to be testimony to the religious journey of migrants, to help migrants develop a 'correct outlook on life' (*zhengque de renshengguan*) and to become their 'intimate friend'. *Taxiang* was planned as a quarterly publication in colour with a circulation of 15,000 copies per issue (which rises to 20,000 at Christmas and Easter; *Maizhong* 20 October 2010).

Maizhong's main concern lies with the best strategy to ensure the continuing growth of the churches. In this context, a considerable amount of words are spent on discussing the utility as well as the challenges and risks for student fellowships (*daxue tuanqi*), which form the main evangelizing units at university. Issue 18 is written with a particular focus on this area. It highlights the difficult transition for young Christians from the familiar intimacy of student fellowships to the regular local churches once they have graduated. At the same time, the model of fellowships and small groups is also proposed as a remedy to the increasingly unregulated nature of churches, which no longer follow proper processes, are too focused on the here and now instead of the ultimate Christian concerns and whose priests resemble CEOs more than religious leaders, as an article in issue 9 claims.

Jiaohui (ChurchChina, www.churchchina.org)

Jiaohui is a journal associated with the previously mentioned CCIM. It is concerned with the construction of churches in China (their organization and growth rather than the actual buildings), internal relations between different churches and the relationship between the churches and society. Its declared target readership are church leaders in China, preachers, fellow missionaries and 'everybody involved in the building of the church in China'. While the site of the publication may be hosted externally, it is clearly written from within China.

Readers can subscribe online and will be sent a pdf copy of the latest issue by email. *Jiaohui* started in September 2006 and as of January 2013 there were 38 issues online with an additional special issue on the gospel; the journal is clearly still thriving. Again, there exists a hard copy, which can also be downloaded as pdf, as well as a website. Unlike in *Maizhong's* case, though, the website's content is identical to the magazine's with some additional useful features, for example one page which provides an index of all articles published in all 38 issues so far.

Author names appear to be either foreign or relatively generic Christian names, which make identification difficult, but also include familiar names of individuals as well as some high profile people like Zhao Xiao, who writes in 2009 about the social mission of Christians following the Wenchuan earthquake. Recurring names belong to men who have been involved in the 'online mission' since the early days; others are well known Chinese evangelists abroad. The two most recent issues of the magazine feature contributions by Stephen Tong (Tang Chongrong), an Indonesian evangelist and founder of the 'reformed evangelical movement' informed by Calvinist theology, which he established with the intention to demarcate his movement from charismatic churches on the one hand and liberal theology on the other. He is greatly admired among intellectuals like Wang Yi and Yu Jie, who shared an excited tweet about finally being able to meet Stephen Tong during the first months of his exile. One may speculate about the connections that were established at that time that led to Tong's subsequent contributions in *Jiaohui*.

Jiaohui mostly focuses on church work and issues pertaining to the growth of churches in China. It will however adopt a more critical and edgier tone on occasion and does not shy away from making wider comments on the role of Christians in contemporary society. A special issue is dedicated to Martin Luther, who is also referred to in an article on the importance of a political theology, published in issue 21 (June 2010). (Somebody on the editorial team must be a Germanist as the occasional German term will make an appearance in the article titles.) In its inaugural issue, Liu Tongsu writes about church and state relations and the issue of registration; a different section of the same magazine features a reprinted article by Wang Mingdao.

Many of the articles are very scholarly and informative, presumably a reflection of the fact that its target readership includes church leaders and pastors. The majority of articles, which focus on the situation within the Chinese churches, provide fascinating insights into the social make up of congregations and the challenges church workers encounter in their daily endeavours. One article in issue 26 (November 2010) for example highlights the problem of gender imbalance in the churches. While rural churches used to be predominantly female, the feminization of urban churches, which used to be much more balanced in terms of gender or even predominantly male, appears to be a recent but prevalent phenomenon, which poses a number of problems for pastoral work and church leadership. Although the gender balance in the general population is skewed towards the male, and although graduates from higher education institutions as well as urban migrant workers are predominantly male, as claimed by this article, in the churches there are often two times as many women as men, sometimes the ratio is as high as 3:1; the gender imbalance appears to be particularly pronounced in the 18–45 age bracket. This appears to be a particularly Chinese phenomenon, as the comparison with Korean and churches overseas seems to prove, according to this article. Apart from outlining interesting explanations for this phenomenon, the article also states that this raises the question of female church leadership and the problem of finding a theological explanation for this phenomenon (Lu K. 2010).

Jiaohui is closely associated with the 'New-Calvinists', the dominant strand of theology in the international Chinese mission and represented by individuals and institutions like Jonathan Chao's China Ministries International and Samuel Ling's China Horizon in addition to Stephen Tong mentioned above. All of them are influential organizations heavily involved in the Chinese mission, both in China and in the United States.

Fuyin shibao (Gospel Times, www.fuyinshibao.cn)

Fuyin shibao is a very different kettle of fish. Like *Maizhong*, it is written and maintained by young Chinese university graduates. *Fuyin shibao's* five point mission statement is printed on the backs of their editors' business cards and includes the following points: to provide a Christian news and gospel information service; to use the platform of the internet to bear witness to the pure gospel and to spread Christian culture; to provide motivational energy for the spiritual growth and life changes of believers; to provide a communication platform that facilitates understanding among pastors, among believers and between pastors and believers; to improve well-meaning communication among the churches and to build a unified body of Christ. It is a formally registered non-profit organization; its website registered with China's CNNIC. It was founded in 2006 and differs from the other examples above as it is not the online identity of an essentially traditional journal, but a rich and vibrant news site. Apart from ten categories under which items are featured, there also exist several regional sub-sites for Chinese provinces and major cities.

During an interview in November 2011, the editor said that since June 2011 each province had its own sub-site, but there appear to be difficulties accessing all of them. *Fuyin shibao* is registered as non-profit organization under Beijing Gospel Times Information Technology Ltd, which provides a certain amount of financial support. Otherwise the organization is sustained through donations and some income through advertising. Their plan to have editors in each province has not been realized and as of November 2012, *Fuyin shibao* only had permanent offices in Beijing and Shanghai. Occasionally they will send their own journalists from the two main offices into the regions, but mostly they rely on regional freelance contributors. Recruiting these is easier in some provinces than in others; often churches will propose individuals. They are usually university graduates, who, following an application, are interviewed and sometimes given some training in journalistic writing. Staff in the head office in Beijing receive regular salaries, but others are volunteers (author interview with editors, November 2011).

Fuyin shibao's content can be roughly summarized as current affairs and general interest stories with a particular Christian focus. In October 2012 these included articles about a company designing Christian clothes (i.e. with Christian motifs); a report on the first media evangelizing conference in Malaysia; a report on the second international conference of Christian entrepreneurs in Texas (including a number of related articles on how to build a Christian entrepreneurial culture). Other items deal with the question of Christian values and the importance of safeguarding the respect for life, including the right of the unborn child, which is considered to fall within the duties of the pastor. The response to the question 'Are you happy?' in an eponymous article lies with faith in God.

Fuyin shibao has very good relations with the 'three-self' church and the *lianghui*. Asked what the difference between them and *Tianfeng*, the official organ of the *lianghui*, was, the editors in Beijing considered *Tianfeng* mostly a propaganda organ for the 'three-self' churches whereas *Fuyin shibao* provided information about Christian life and experience in China today. Their audience are mainly pastors and young Christians with a relatively high level of education, but older academics I spoke to were also very familiar with it (although they were unaware of the other publications presented above).

Fuyin shibao is mostly directed at a 'three-self' church audience, facilitating communication within them and between them. But the same parent company also maintains two separate websites with a slightly different orientation. They employ different staff and hire separate office space for these. *Jiduwang* (Christian Net www.jidunet.cn), judging from its homepage, has a very different feel from *Fuyin shibao*. Items on the home page include articles by Yuan Zhiming, Wang Yi and Wang Mingdao as well as articles on the evangelizing of Muslim and Arab countries together with the usual topics like pastoral work, church building, theological training and family life, etc., that also form the core of sites like *Maizhong* or *Jiaohui* mentioned before.

A second site maintained under the same umbrella organization as *Fuyin shibao* is *Jidu shibao* (Christian Times, www.christiantimes.cn). In terms of articles there is some degree of overlap between this site and *Jiduwang*, although Christian Times has the appearance of a more scholarly endeavour with a more international outlook and more immediately apparent links with networks outside China. Within its 'special topics' pages it features a special series on the work of '*haigui*' pastors (Chinese pastors returned from overseas). The series of articles features many voices from within this group (not necessarily all high profile) who all agree on the particular importance of '*haigui*' pastors in the construction of churches in China, but who also address some of the issues faced in the daily practice of 'returning' which range from the hassles of the required paperwork to the difficulty of readapting to life in China after a prolonged period abroad (Christian Times 2012).

Without having conducted a detailed quantitative content analysis, it is my impression that the content on both *Jiduwang* and *Christian Times* is richer (i.e. there are more and longer articles in more different categories) and more spiritual than the content published on the *Fuyin shibao* site, which with its bright red banner has a drier and more official feel to it.

A complex landscape

Lukas Zhang (2010) distinguishes three different models of 'house churches' in China. The 'Beijing model' is characterized by connectivity, meaning that there is either one pastor for several churches, or that the pastors of different churches meet up on a regular basis to remain informed about developments. They are highly trained, the majority of them graduates of China's elite universities, who gave up significant professional prospects in order to be pastors. They often draw on underground theological seminaries or online training materials; some of them are '*haigui*', meaning that they have returned from studies abroad to take up this work. According to Zhang, the 'Beijing model' produces a strong social force whose members spend a lot of time thinking about the future of Chinese churches, including questions like church-state relations, environmental protection, civil society, and post-modernism. *Aiyan*, which was widely read among Beijing churches, seemed to capture the most political manifestation of this model.

The 'Wenzhou model' of churches, from within which *Maizhong* is produced, is particularly effective in missionary work, both inside China (through people who work in all provinces with their businesses) and abroad, according to Zhang. Within the pages of *Maizhong*, missionary efforts, especially among young Chinese students, with the help of overseas networks, are of far more importance than any political agenda. While the question of registration and church state relations is also touched upon, from the many articles dealing with missionary work on campus and beyond, one almost gets the impression that the aspiration and increasing trend to move above ground and into the mainstream with full participation in social and theological work is seen as counterproductive to the future growth of churches. Instead the return to intimate and private 'small groups' similar to student fellowships is considered the best way forward for the mission.

Zhang's third model, the 'Pearl River Delta model' is described as the result of migration and a particular regional culture which has led to the emergence of 'migrant churches', 'nanny churches', 'boss churches', and even 'public security churches'. This last model does not appear to have spawned its own publications, at least not online, but the migrant journal *Taxiang* (Sojourn) mentioned above, although not from within the Pearl River Delta, may come close to this model.

Readership and finances

Aiyan was quite unique in its more inclusive approach to its target audience. While some articles on the law were relatively highbrow, their aim was ultimately to educate and benefit those who needed to understand the law. All the other publications discussed in this chapter are much more exclusively focused on an educated, urban readership. *Maizhong*, in particular, has a very exclusive feel to it, being primarily focused on and written by young Chinese intellectuals. It is difficult to detect any apparent educational function within its pages, nor does it reach out to a readership beyond the circle of university students and the well-educated middle class.

Instead of trying to create a publication with inclusive appeal for a wider readership the strategy now seems to be to maintain separate publications or websites and indeed organizational units to address different audiences as in the case of *Taxiang* and *Maizhong*, but also evident in the case of *Fuyin shibao* and its sister websites. This is one non-profit organization that wishes to provide a service for 'all Christians in China', and yet it does so through three different platforms. This may be a pre-emptive strategy to the very real possibility of difficulties or crackdown, in which case only one part of the overall operation would be affected. (It is reminiscent of Amity's strategy in Nanjing, where various projects are ostensibly independent of one another, but all linked and co-ordinated by Amity.) But it may also be a recognition and response to the different demands and orientations of the 'proto-denominational' characters of Chinese Christian readership.

All the publications and websites discussed above rely to a large degree on donations and free article contributions. In *Aiyan's* case, only very coy references were made to 'God having already provided a sound basis' without stating any specific sources. There was no advertising, but from issue four onwards there were more and more references and mentions of like-minded organizations and their products. *Fuyin shibao* and its related sites do feature some commercial advertising from companies selling Christian products. The extent of products adorned with Christian symbols and motifs is endless, ranging from mobile phone covers to radios adorned with crosses, from casual t-shirts and hoodies to church paraphernalia including pastor's robes. These products are aimed at a Christian population, which, far from keeping its faith secret, is proud to display this (brand) identity on its other staple consumer items.

Protestant politics online

Aiyan clearly was a vehicle within which attempts to position the Chinese 'house churches' took place, both in the context of state regulation and persecution and in the context of the enormous diversity of unregistered church groups in China. Within the pages of *Aiyan* in particular, attempts were made to draw demarcation lines to other Christian groups as well as to the official church, with the aim of establishing some form of 'house church' identity within China. This tendency is less prevalent in the other publications analysed above, which either have a more inward orientation, or which simply do not have, or avoid, a political agenda altogether.

Within *Aiyan* one of the main aims and in turn one of the central pillars of identity construction was to establish clear boundaries to the 'three-self' church by rejecting their theology as well as their leadership. The official Protestant publication *Tianfeng* (Heavenly Wind) was a further frequent target. Readers often asked for guidance regarding 'three-self' church publications, the 'three-self' church's interpretation of the Bible, how to treat fellow Christians who worship in 'three-self' churches etc. Another clear boundary *Aiyan* was trying to draw was that against so called heretical sects. The state, the 'three-self' church, and other churches all define Protestantism differently. Maybe not surprisingly, heresy as defined by the state and the 'three-self' church is defined more along political rather than along religious lines, that is, if a religious group rejects the 'three-self' church or holds meetings in secret they may be called heretical, which potentially puts all activity outside the 'three-self' churches into the category of heresy. Among other churches, according to Dunch (2000), the disputes are huge; almost all reject the 'three-self' church as non-Christian or unorthodox, but among the different groups huge disputes remain regarding baptism, communion, the marks of true conversion, Holy Spirit, how to hold the Bible, how to pray, etc.

The most important sect against which *Aiyan* was trying to define its constituent readership was Eastern Lightning,[13] often referred to as 'the greatest enemy of the Chinese churches'. A variety of articles relate to the allegedly evil nature of this cult and provide a number of testimonies of individuals who have allegedly been abducted by the cult or lured into joining by devious tactics. (One account tells of how Eastern Lightning deployed attractive young men and women to lure others into their own circle.[14]) Most interestingly, a theory seemed to exist among the churches that Eastern Lightning was a plot by state security and that it was related to the government's attempts to weaken the churches (an idea refuted by *Aiyan*). Other sects are also mentioned, and it is clear that the editors were trying to find a middle ground between the too liberal and worldly orientation of the 'three-self' church and the more controversial or even notorious Christian sects in the country. Interestingly, even though a clear line was drawn to the 'three-self churches', when it comes to denouncing other so called heretical sects, both language and terminology adopted by the 'house church' publications echo the official party language, referring to them as *xiejiao* (literally: evil cult; a term also applied to Falungong).

Maizhong does not have an apparent political agenda. There is no palpable link between this journal and the wider world outside the churches. It has the feel of an inward looking cultural salon rather than the organ of a community engaged with contemporary social issues. Where articles ostensibly tackle such issues, they do this on a merely intellectual, historical or philosophical level. The editorial of issue 16 provides a good example of this attitude. It starts with a reference to the end of the Olympic games and the poisoned baby milk scandal and a comment that China's economic development is not matched by appropriate legal and structural developments, but only uses these as an opportunity to talk about problems within the churches, namely their slow growth and how to adjust church structure to the new circumstances.[15] Scholarly articles, often authored by Ezra Pan or Liu Tongsu, draw lessons from history for the churches today, but in historical comparison again no links are drawn that could be interpreted as remotely political. While the editorial of issue 20 (October 2009) states the historical significance of many anniversaries (a common and comparatively safe way to make comments about the present), the examples cited remain firmly within the confines of church history.[16]

Jiaohui (Church China) does not shy away from more political questions, but these are very carefully framed as religious or theological difference with the 'three-self' church, as representative of the religious system in China, rather than as differences with the political system or the government per se. An article in the January issue of 2009 states that religious faith makes believers good, law-abiding citizens, but where a religious system harms the core of a believer's doctrine and practice, the sanctity of their belief and their freedom of conscience will make it very difficult for them to support the system. The pursuit of a pure belief and doctrine makes people reject the 'three-self' churches for religious reasons rather than political reasons, a position represented so famously by Wang Mingdao. The article rejects the notion that China's 'house churches' were the tool of any political movement over the last 50 years. Indeed it claims that the 'house churches' transcended all political movements, be they national or international (Jiang D. 2009).

The importance of Christian values is of course common to all publications, but on the sites registered in China, one can perhaps detect a more immediate social consideration, especially when it comes to the importance of Christian values in entrepreneurial culture and environmental protection. The latter also finds expression in the visual presentation of journal covers and images used on the websites. Unless they are used to illustrate particular news items, dominating images display green pastures, unspoilt idyllic landscapes, blue skies and crystal clear waters. The contrast to China's actual landscape in the twenty-first century could not be more striking. Quite apart from the visual representation of the pure spirit these images hope to convey, a clean (or cleaned-up) China becomes a metaphorical heaven on earth towards whose realization Christians seem to be called to work. (From the very little data there is, it appears that those who believe in 'one God' versus an 'afterlife' and 'fate' are more inclined to consider pollution a serious issue than those who 'worship ancestors'. Lang and Lu 2011: 256.)

Freedom of religious belief and legalization of status

Religious rights defence was at the heart of *Aiyan's* political agenda. The core issue in this context was the legal status of churches in China and the government's requirement for any social group to register with the authorities.[17] Resistance to the requirement to register was one of the core issues in *Aiyan's* approach to religious rights defence. The freedom of religious belief was considered a God-given right which is guaranteed in the Chinese constitution and which no lower administrative body has the right to limit; a position still held by many churches in China, but not a consensus view. Contributions to *Aiyan* frequently expressed the hope that one day 'house churches' would be officially accepted and legal; they hoped for a transition similar to the one private businesses underwent from the 1980s to the present, meaning a gradual change of status from outside the law or 'underground' to within the law and 'above ground'. In just a few years, this view has become fairly accepted among Chinese churches, although the majority would probably concede that this process involves a process of registration.

The sites registered in China tackle the issue of registration and church-state relations in a different way from sites and publications registered outside China. They go about it in a less politicized way, quoting and reprinting articles from other public sources like the Pushi Institute for Social Science (www.pacilution.com, an independent, non-profit, non-governmental think tank established in 1999 dedicated to the protection of religious freedom in China), or by resorting to the well-tried method of reporting about events or speeches made outside China to raise a particular issue in their readers' minds, who can then come to their own conclusions.

Aiyan's early years coincided with the emergence of *weiquan* lawyers in China's legal scene. (See Chapter 7 for a closer analysis.) Among them were Christian lawyers taking on cases of Christians whose religious rights had been violated and during *Aiyan's* existence these activities were formalized in the Association of Human Rights Attorneys for Chinese Christians (*Zhongguo jidutu weiquan lüshi tuan*). The formation of this group was advertised in *Aiyan* and the names and contact numbers of its members were published.[18] They were all leading scholars in the field of constitutional law with the country's leading research tanks or universities; they were also regular (and in some cases key) contributors to *Aiyan*.

Rights awareness and rights education

Formation of rights awareness and rights education was an essential task and function of *Aiyan* and it went about it in an increasingly organized way as the issues developed. Initially this was done primarily through individual items in the news section, where readers of *Aiyan* were asked to pray for imprisoned fellow Christians or individual court cases. From issue 3 onwards there were regular calls for the establishment of the rule of law in China which according to *Aiyan* should be the concern of every citizen and every Christian. Issue 3 also saw an extensive explanation of the legal framework and clauses relating to religion which was clearly published as a result of a huge reader response to an article in issue 2 on the legal viewpoint of a Christian.[19] This subsequently developed into a special category on law. Under this category articles on the Chinese constitution, a series of articles on the relations between religion and politics, the right to remain silent (justified by Jesus remaining silent when interrogated by Pilate), and a Chinese and English version of the Universal Declaration of Human Rights were published. Issue 13 first mentioned a book called *Yue yu Fa* (The Covenant and the Law, published 2005). The book's author (who remains unnamed) was initially detained by the police in Hainandao, but later released and encouraged to circulate his book. (The authorities allegedly realized it was not just harmless but actually useful.) According to *Aiyan*, the book outlines how to be a good Bible-following Christian as well as a good law-abiding Chinese citizen.[20] By 2008 the book was available to download in its entirety on *Aiyan's* website with explanations and commentaries. It seemed to have replaced the category on Law and had become a special feature or sub-site of *Aiyan*.

In this context there existed clear links between *Aiyan* (or the individuals behind it) and the China Aid Association (CAA) in Texas. Christian rights education is also one of the declared aims of CAA, an organization founded by Bob Fu. According to its own website, China Aid had invited 25 Christian legal scholars, lawyers and 'house church' leaders to the United States for training in the law, Christian worldview and biblical stewardship. CAA is also associated with the Institute of Chinese Law and Religion which hosted a 'Freedom in China' Conference in May

2006 at the Hudson Institute to which all the founding members of the Association of Christian Rights Defence Lawyers were invited. Bob Fu and CAA are also behind *China Monitor*, another organization promoting religious freedom in China. This organization publishes the *Chinese Law and Religion Monitor* journal which can be downloaded from their website (www.monitorchina.org). It is a bi-lingual journal, which was started in 2005. Early issues are dominated by reports on persecution and betray a slightly paranoid character (by going through great lengths to conceal an author's identity), but this changes and some issues, and in particular the most recent ones, feature very serious and scholarly articles often by leading scholars in the field like Liu Peng and Yang Fenggang (often reproduced without seeking prior permission[21]). The dominant topic for the journal is rights defence and the members of the Association of Chinese Christian Lawyers are regular contributors to the journal, in particular Fan Yafeng. One issue in 2006 focuses on the trial of Pastor Cai Zhuohua with contributions from a wide range of intellectuals including Yu Jie, Bei Cun and Liu Xiaobo. With the demise of *Aiyan*, The *Chinese Law and Religion Monitor* seems to have taken over as the main organ for the Christian elements of the *weiquan* movement.

Defiance of the regime

Chinese Christians emphasize that their faith makes them law and authority abiding citizens. In the pages of *Aiyan*, Chapter 13 of the Book of Romans ('Everyone must submit himself to the governing authorities, for there is no authority except that which God has established') tends to be quoted in support of this attitude. At the same time article 36 of the Chinese Constitution is invoked in order to deny any lower authorities (like the Religious Affairs Bureau) the right to infringe upon the constitutional right to religious freedom.[22] Not registering with the authorities is one act of defiance in the face of state control of religion. Some individuals do this more consciously as an act of defiance, others do not register for less overtly political reasons, but when pressed will concede that they consider their belief and worship none of the government's business. In the event of crackdowns and arrests, Christians embrace these hardships in the spirit of Christ; especially in rural congregations these repressive measures are often approached as a test from God and the suffering they entail are seen as experiencing but a fraction of Christ's suffering for mankind. Repressive measures lose their grip where arrests are seen as an opportunity to get a free ride in a car or where stints in prison are seen as a good opportunity to (often successfully) evangelize the fellow inmates.[23] Within the pages of Aiyan, defiance of the regime was not encouraged, but at the same time, the focus on rights awareness and rights education was clearly intended to make individuals and congregations better equipped to deal with repressive measures and to invoke the relevant Chinese laws and sections of the Constitution in the event of trouble. Information of unlawful arrests and trials of fellow Christians was a staple in *Aiyan*; so were letters or poems written by imprisoned Christians. None of the other publications reviewed here adopts quite such a controversial attitude.

Prolific male networks

Several things strike this particular reader of the self-declared 'house church' publications, which can broadly be summarized under the terms authorship, networks and gender. Obtaining enough contributions to fill its pages is one of the greatest ongoing challenges for every publication and extends to online publications and communities (Ling K. 2005). In the publications analysed above, this is reflected in repeated calls by the editors to readers and community members to do their bit and submit manuscripts. These calls are particularly prevalent within the pages of *Aiyan*, which was unique among the publications in the way it combined scholarly and political material with relatively simple testimony by ordinary (albeit mostly educated) Christians.

Although this general invitation of contributions should lead to a very diverse authorship of the publications, there is an obvious recurrence of certain names, who often also act as regular columnists, consultants or editors. These names belong mostly to individuals, who are now residing in the United States, some of whom cannot travel back to China, and some who are probably more aptly described as '*hai ou*' (seagulls) rather than '*hai gui*'. They are part of a wider phenomenon of intellectuals, who despite residing abroad frequently migrate between their new place of residence and China. They appear to be at the heart of several overlapping Christian networks in China, who are involved in the big project of the 'online mission'. These networks (like the publications discussed here) share a baseline of common concerns, but their approaches and their public, often secular personae differ widely. Some networks are focused on the mission inside China; others focus more generally on mission work including countries outside China, often with particular interest in Africa and the Middle East. There are networks, which are primarily concerned with domestic church-state relations, but their ways to problematize these are different; very few can be described as political in the sense that they are overtly critical of the government and involved in hands-on dissident activity.

Some individuals – mostly residing outside China – appear to have connections to all these different networks. Depending on most recent developments, the boundaries of principle that divide the various networks can become blurred or fade. For example, leading academics (often social scientists) can be involved in the most public networks, but may also have a presence in more spiritual networks hosted outside China. The list of contributors to *Xinyang zhi men* (lit. A Door to Faith, www.godoor.net), which includes eminent intellectuals and writers from mainland China, Taiwan, Hong Kong, the United States and Canada provides illuminating insights into the way people, who belong to rather different fields of expertise and professions, come together (or are brought together) in a different context on the basis of their shared faith.

They are almost exclusively male. The male dominance in Chinese Christian intellectual circles is striking, especially as it stands in contrast to the make-up of congregations, which are still predominantly female in the countryside and increasingly so in urban churches also. Women clearly do play an important part in the Chinese Christian experience. But while there are many female pastors, journalists and editors (the main editor of *Fuyin shibao* is a woman, for instance), there are far fewer who make public pronouncements or who are 'leaders' in what I would call an ideological sense. This phenomenon is particularly prevalent outside the 'three-self' church, where churches are dominated by a conservative theology, which rejects contextual hermeneutics in favour of a literal understanding of the Bible as infallible source of guidance and wisdom. As a consequence, very few women are involved in theological work; those who are interested will find a more welcome environment within the 'three-self' churches than in the urban reformed churches, which are more closely linked to the publications analysed here.

In his anthropological analysis of Wenzhou churches, Nanlai Cao presents a vivid picture of gender segregation and gender hierarchy. In Wenzhou churches, to which many of the overseas pastors and intellectuals involved in the publications analysed here are linked, the low quality (*suzhi*) of the traditional female, rural church congregation poses a considerable 'image' problem, which is being rectified by holding events like lectures and banquets for an almost exclusively male audience. Church publications play an important role in this endeavour; indeed in Cao's view, the growing publication efforts can be viewed as an important sign of the rise of rational masculinity in the post-Mao Wenzhou church (Cao N. 2011: 106). Based on the authorship of publications produced outside Wenzhou I am inclined to see this as a wider phenomenon of the Chinese churches, where a conservative interpretation of gender roles coupled with traditional Chinese notions of male intellectual prowess conspire to result in a reality where current agenda and future direction of the churches is determined by highly educated, middle-aged men engaged in debates over contested theological or political issues, reminiscent of similar debates that have dominated the last one hundred years of Chinese intellectual history.

Not only are these 'leaders' predominantly male, but they are also impressively prolific, a trait which they share with all Chinese elite intellectuals in the modern period. Their writings in the publications discussed above make up the bulk of substantive articles in them. They constitute a constant, unedited verbalization of thought, a running commentary on the core issues debated within the various networks, as well as reflections on the problems faced 'on the ground', as seen through their own particular bias. In addition to their contributions to these journals, these individuals also tend to maintain blogs, are active on China's equivalents of Twitter and – where they lead their own churches – spend a lot of time and energy writing sermons and letters to their congregations. The value of these sources when it comes to understanding the current face of Christianity in China today has not yet been explored. Far too often, conclusions are extrapolated from information gained only in interviews that do not necessarily reflect the competitive, occasionally consensual, and decidedly conservative thinking that goes into the question of how to position and develop Christianity in China today.

Conclusion

The selection of publications and websites above should in no way be seen as comprehensive or inclusive. *Christian Times* alone provides direct links to as many as 35 related websites, which have not received any mention in this chapter. All of them provide rich material for further study. While they all differ slightly in their organization and in the way they present their information, they clearly share certain common concerns, which focus on the growth of churches in China, the training of pastors and how to deal with the many challenges of the contemporary world as a Christian.

The start of the chapter presented the Chinese churches as currently carrying the baton handed down by the democracy movement and Falungong in the race towards a democratizing China, their publications following in the footsteps of the earlier *minkan* by providing a forum for debates on the key issue of religious freedom, which links to freedom of assembly, freedom of speech and freedom of association. The ensuing analysis has shown that only the minority of church networks and associated publications will become overtly political. The majority are more concerned with the development and growth of the churches than with social and political change overall. They may join in the protest voices, when their own immediate interests are at stake or when they encounter direct violations of their rights, but are otherwise not overtly political.

The publications introduced in this chapter reflect the diversity of the Chinese Christian population today; *Fuyin shibao's* sub-sites reflect recognition of the different foci and priorities that exist among it. Due to their online nature, it is very difficult to ascertain, how influential or far reaching these publications actually are. They are certainly well known within certain church circles, but many people, who I would consider well informed about Christian matters in China, have never heard of some of them. Arguably, within the relatively small circle of individuals, who are behind these publications, to be engaged in the activity of writing and publishing in and of itself may be the most important aspect in which they testify their own calling. Their writings receive even more exposure through the liberal borrowing and reprinting of articles among the different publications. These journals are published for an audience that is already Christian or interested in Christianity. They are an additional tool in the larger mission that is characterized by work in small groups, sometimes one-to-one efforts. They are in their orientation inward looking in the sense that their main concern is the spiritual nourishment of fellow believers. The newer addition of *Fuyin shibao* suggests that there is also demand for a more worldly, information based Christian publication, although judging from the relative spiritual richness of its sister publications *Jiduwang* and *Jidu shibao*, this kind of Christian audience may well be in the minority in China.

It is tempting to interpret this as a reaction to the harsh repression individuals associated with *Aiyan* and *Fangzhou* (a publication emanating from Beijing's Fangzhou congregation, founded by Yu Jie and with close ties to Liu Xiaobo, but with no online presence) have met with since 2008. There is probably some truth in this; certainly it has led to a change of tactics on the part of the minority of individuals within the churches, who are politically active and vocal. Those, who are still in China and not imprisoned or under house arrest, have changed the urgency of their political message, instead concentrating on more immediate theological and religious matters. The overtly political agenda, albeit often still written by individuals in China, is now mostly published abroad in publications like *Guancha* (The Observer) or the above mentioned *Chinese Law and Religion Monitor.*

But one must also acknowledge that most church leaders simply do not agree with what they consider the political hijacking of churches. Yin Xing, in discussion with Yu Jianrong, is quite adamant that Christians are not less free or worse off than other parts of the population. The type of rights violations that Christians encounter commonly happen to all Chinese and the churches' agenda should not be reduced to this (Yu Jianrong 2008). Their main concern should be evangelizing, the future (growth) of the Chinese churches, and catering for the theological and spiritual education of the Chinese Christian population; the 'online gospel' is one method to work towards this goal.

Notes

1. A full version of the report can be found at www.ccnic.net.cn/hlwfzyj/hlwfzbg/hlwtjbg/2012 (last accessed 3 October 2012).
2. Jidian is the Chinese version of Gideon and the pen name of Cheng Song, a Fudan graduate from Chengdu, who has been in the United States since 1992 and was one of the first people involved in online work for the Chinese mission.
3. 'The Banquet' is the English translation used by the editors. 'Love Feast' probably refers to the Christian Eucharistic practice of the 'love-feast' or agape, although the choice of title is not explained by the editors.
4. Cai Zhuohua was imprisoned for three years and has since been released. For a report on his case see China Human Rights Forum 3.2006.
5. The author checked a number of times in 2006 and 2007. All the author's interviewees in China were familiar with the publication, both the hard copy and the online edition and it continues to enjoy a good reputation among Beijing Christians.
6. Compare www.aiyan.org/2005/05-5/17.html (last accessed 22 February 2008).
7. Compare www.aiyan.org/2005/05-5/16.html (last accessed 22 February 2008).
8. Students abroad will always be enrolled on other courses but may take advantage of opportunities to study theology as an extra subject.
9. For example see www.aiyan.org/2005/05-7/18.html (last accessed 7 March 2008).
10. For example see www.aiyan.org/2005/05-2-13/24.html (last accessed 7 March 2008).
11. For example see www.aiyan.org/2005/05-3/26.html (last accessed 7 March 2008).
12. http://t.qq.com/zhaoyunfneg) (last accessed 24 September 2012).
13. *Dongfang Shandian*. For an evaluation of the sect by China's 'three-self' church see www.chineseprotestantchurch.org/church%20Ministry/shi_dongfang.htm (last accessed 10 October 2007).
14. See www.aiyan.org/2005/05-3/12.html and www.aiyan.org/2005/05-3/13.html; see also Madsen (2003: 277).
15. www.maizhong.org/wheatseeds/2008-10.16/wz/01.html (last accessed 5 October 2012).
16. www.maizhong.org/wheatseeds/2009-10.20/wz/01.html (last accessed 5 October 2012).
17. This registration process is governed by the Regulations Regarding the Formation of Social Groups of 1998. A full English version of the Regulations can be found at www.chinadevelopment brief.com/node/298 (last accessed 11 September 2007).
18. www.aiyan.org/2005/06-15/20.html (last accessed 8 March 2008).
19. www.aiyan.org/2005/05-2/12.html (last accessed 8 March 2008). The Readers' Letters

section of issue 3 as part of which the explanation of the legal framework was published has since been removed. A copy of the document is now held at http://leiden.dachs-archive.org/citrep/wielander2008

20 See news section of *Aiyan* issue 13 www.aiyan.org/2005/05-2-13/24.html (last accessed 2 February 2007).
21 Interview with Liu Peng in Beijing, 10 November 2012.
22 Article 36 of the Chinese Constitution reads: Citizens of the People's Republic of China enjoy freedom of religious belief. No state organ, public organization or individual may compel citizens to believe in, or not to believe in, any religion; nor may they discriminate against citizens who believe in, or do not believe in, any religion. The state protects normal religious activities. No one may make use of religion to engage in activities that disrupt public order, impair the health of citizens or interfere with the educational system of the state. Religious bodies and religious affairs are not subject to any foreign domination http://english.peopledaily.com.cn/consitution/consitution.html
23 Both these examples are taken from Yuan Zhiming's film *The Cross. Jesus in China* (2003).

6 Christian intellectuals

Bridging the gap?

On 11 May 2006, three Chinese men – two lawyers and a writer – met with the then American President George Bush for a prayer meeting at the White House. The meeting was facilitated by a Chinese American pastor based in Texas, who enjoys close connections in Washington. The meeting drew considerable attention from Western media, and it turned the spotlight onto an until then relatively little-known fact: that some of the most outspoken critics of the Chinese government today approach their political activities with deep religious conviction. The political activities of this group of Christian individuals have gone far beyond theoretical or polemical writings; some were close to Liu Xiaobo and are among the first signatories of Charter 08, others are lawyers, who have been involved in the most high-profile and controversial legal cases in recent years. Their activities will be dealt with in more detail in the next chapter of this book.

This chapter adopts a more theoretical approach by investigating the link between Christian belief and the fight for political change in today's China. Links have been drawn between the China's future democratization and the potential role Chinese Christians may play in it and news items on Christians in China are often framed in this context. This chapter proposes the hypothesis that Chinese Christian intellectuals may be able to fulfil a special 'bridge-function' or act as unifying force in Chinese society in a period of political change. After a critical examination of the term 'intellectual' and the theoretical link between Christian belief and political action with particular attention to the Chinese context, the hypothesis of the bridge function will provide the framework for the analysis of developments over the last decade based on academic studies, Christian writings and events on the ground in order to determine, what evidence there is that Christian intellectuals may be a key driving force in China's democratization.

The potential bridge-function of Christian intellectuals

Chen Cunfu (2005) identified two main new types of Christians emerging in China, one the so-called 'boss Christians', the other 'intellectual elite' Christians. Chen considered the latter to be the most important new emerging group, whose development would need to be closely watched. While they may not be likely to become the economic pillars of their churches (like the 'boss Christians'), the intellectual elite's conversion to Christianity was a significant factor in promoting the cultural and theological status of the churches and the communication between the Chinese church and the international (Chinese) Christian communities, Chen argued. While commonly accepted, I would argue that it is difficult to delineate so clearly between Christian sub-cultures. Many 'boss-Christians' are well educated and have forged close links with intellectual Christians at home and overseas. Nor do all churches in the Wenzhou area, commonly associated with the 'boss Christians', fall in this category, but share characteristics with urban churches in other cities. These urban residents, many of whom are Christians, occupy all types of positions in the new economic order. They may run their own businesses, be skilled workers, professionals, business executives, managers or intellectuals. They usually have some kind of political experience and organizational competence. They are young, educated, open-minded, and energetic church goers, some of whom accumulated vast fortunes and new social networks in the reform era (Chen C. 2005: 179). What are then the implications when part of a communist country's intellectual elite has turned to Christianity? Based on the links between Christian belief and liberal democracy as discussed in more detail below, it is possible to hypothesize about a special function of Christian intellectuals which allows them to bridge three important gaps when it comes to China's democratization process.

Christian belief is a great equalizer; in the contemporary churches everybody can pray to God regardless of their intellectual background. In a culture where intellectuals traditionally assume a superior standing to the 'small people', the most important 'bridge' Christian intellectuals can offer is a bridge between the intellectual elite and the common people. The focus in the contemporary Protestant churches is on personal testimony and experience of Christ; in theory, an illiterate peasant's testimony is as valid as a university professor's. When all the qualifications one needs to be embraced by God's community is 'to be hungry for the Holy Spirit' (in the words of a minister in one of the Chinese Pentecostal churches in London), all social barriers are removed. It can be argued that Christian intellectuals are not afraid to leave their desks and mix with the wider population. It would follow that Christian intellectuals may be more successful in bringing political ideas of democracy into the wider population, either through direct contact with people or through writings in publications with a much wider appeal than the prestigious and highbrow intellectual journals the majority of intellectuals prefer to publish in.

Second, Christian intellectuals may offer is a bridge between intellectual theory and political action. The departure from the public sphere of public intellectuals and their disinclination to take a political stance has been a recurrent subject of criticism by dissident intellectuals abroad and within China (for example Idao 2005). Wang Yi illustrates this point of view by likening the importance of New-Left intellectuals in China today to that of giant pandas.

> Our society needs neo-leftism as much as China needs pandas. The neo-leftists have been reduced to being 'animals under first-class state

protection', celebrities without ever lifting a finger. Every once in a while a few of them are sent abroad to show off.

(Wang Y. 2012b: 96)

(The fact that Chengdu, Wang Yi's hometown, has China's biggest panda conservation base may have made this an obvious metaphor.) We can argue that Christian intellectuals, on the basis of their belief, almost inevitably have to enter into the sphere of politics when it comes to issues such as injustice and individual rights. Their belief does not give them the choice to sit back and retreat to theories. Religious protest campaigners would almost always have been able to enjoy greater social approval and worldly success had they not committed themselves to a cause that risked them being ostracized or worse (Bruce 2003: 127). Franklin I. Gamwell argues that Christians are called to democratic activity because they are called to pursue the community of love and to act for justice as general emancipation. He argues further that politics today is a common Christian vocation because the moral principle implied by faith prescribes democracy as a form of political rule and thus democratic citizenship as a general form of Christian witness. It would therefore follow that Christian intellectuals will be engaged in much more hands- on political activities than their secular counterparts in China (Gamwell 2005: 4).

Finally, Christian intellectuals may also be able to bridge the gap between China and the world. Whereas a great number of Chinese intellectuals are still caught up in the polarized view of 'China and the West' and/or in finding a distinctly Chinese way of doing things, one could argue that Christian intellectuals see a global world and promote global values. For them, the realization of democratic values as universal values becomes the ultimate aim which will not only save China but the world.

Reaching out to 'the masses' and putting theory into action were of course central tenets of an equally global communist movement. However, as we have seen in Chapter 2, for many of those most in search for meaning and purpose, disillusioned by the loss of a credible ideology – a feeling exacerbated by the events of 1989 – Christianity has become an alternative belief system offering answers for China's future.

Intellectuals

The in-depth study of Western culture was an important element of the first decade of the reform era. Intellectuals, trying to get to the bottom of the West's success, identified crucial cultural differences between China and the West, which they considered the reason for China's 'backwardness' and the advances of the West. These were visualized in the famous television series 'River Elegy' which was aired in China in 1987 and through vivid symbolic imagery conveyed the message that China needed democracy and human rights in order to throw off the shackles of its own stagnant culture. In the aftermath of Tiananmen Square 1989, the repercussions for those closely involved in the scripting of the series were serious and far-reaching. Within China, however, the study of Western culture including the study of Christianity continued and gathered momentum. Rather than studying Christianity as a religion it was viewed as a culture to which many academics were drawn without initially converting to the Christian faith. The main representative of this group was Liu Xiaofeng, who started a number of publication initiatives, including the journal *Christian Culture and Review*. His most famous publication remains *Zhenjiu yu xiaoyao* (Salvation and Freedom) and *Zouxiang shizijia de zhen* (Towards the Truth on the Cross), which has recently been republished after its first publication in 1992 (see Yang F. 2005; Zhuo X. 2000; Fällman 2004).

But for many Chinese intellectuals, the academic debates on Christianity which characterized the 1980s and 1990s have now been replaced by active Christian commitment. While former 'Cultural Christians' tended to treat their faith as a private matter, there is now a younger generation of Christians, who openly live their faith and who claim that it is God rather than democracy that will save China. Within China, the most prominent examples of this development are public intellectuals like the writers Yu Jie, Bei Cun and Jia Guobiao; the legal scholars Wang Yi, Fan Yafeng, Li Baiguang, Chen Yongmiao, Teng Biao, and Xu Zhiyong as well as lawyers like Gao Zhisheng, Zhang Xinshui and Li Heping. These individuals started to appear on the Chinese intellectual and political scene in the middle of the first decade of this century and have brought a new and for many (not least the Chinese government) a controversial angle to the intellectual debates on China's political future. They have also not confined their activities to intellectual debates alone. Liu Xiaobo had very close affinities to this group of individuals, many of whom are signatories of Charter 08, and since his arrest many of them, too, have suffered harassment and imprisonment. The disappearance of Gao Zhisheng made headlines in Western media, though others have received less attention. Fan Yafeng has been under house arrest for the best part of the last two years, and Yu Jie famously went into exile to the United States in the spring of 2012 after having suffered arrest and torture in China.

The term intellectual needs some clarification. Before the reform era and through the 1980s, the term intellectual set all those who had received higher education apart from the rest of the population. Receiving a university degree almost certainly meant subsequent employment by the state in positions that guaranteed status, but only a very modest living. As the reform era developed and opened up other sectors of the economy, new opportunities emerged for the educated, who now follow career paths very similar to their counterparts in other countries of the world. Some go into business working for Chinese or multinational companies, others open their own businesses. Many will have spent time abroad. Those who want to become socially active can do so by working in one of China's myriads of social organizations; for those, who wish to become politically active and rise into leadership positions the CCP still offers the only accepted option.[1]

The term 'intellectual' is now mostly reserved for individuals, who hold academic positions with one of China's leading universities or research institutions. They become 'public intellectuals' when they comment on social or political issues in a wider forum, set an agenda or coin new terms to feed into the national intellectual debates. Many of them travel frequently abroad and have forged close links with research institutions in the West. The term intellectual tends to be reserved for those who work within the humanities and social sciences, although the astrophysicist Fang Lizhi was a notable exception. Many individuals start their career as academics within the Chinese 'Ivy League', but for various reasons and often not out of choice, move into the private sector by making a living through their writing and professional expertise. However, they continue to be public intellectuals as they continue to address matters that 'concern the nation', although not necessarily those on the official agenda. What these and more mainstream intellectuals have to say is in turn followed by academics, professionals, journalists and a more widely educated middle class. 'Public intellectuals' have been criticized by the government for having their own benefits in mind when claiming to speak for a wider public; the concept of a 'citizen intellectual' was proposed as an alternative (Fällman 2013: 165).

For Jia Guobiao (1998: 48–50) the marker of being deserving of the title 'intellectual' lies not in the individual's association with academia, but with the moral quality of the individual. An intellectual deserving this title must not know self-interest but work solely towards a more just and more democratic society. In an essay dating back to 1989, Liu Xiaobo laments the 'faithless, utilitarian character' of Chinese intellectuals, who will not 'uphold the truth', because they are caught up in the binary positions of either 'serving politics' or 'cultivating their moral selves' in direct protest to politics. As a result of this focus on their own role in the political theatre, they are unable to develop 'pure' academic thinking or theories. Their thinking is unable to transcend utilitarian limitations, hence they have, for example, not been able to develop a religious spirit of ultimate transcendental values, or a metaphysical tradition of hypotheses transcending human experience, nor have they been able to nurture a positivist spirit that enables them to rationally testify to the truth transcending politics (Liu Xiaobo 2010 [1990]: 107–31). Wang Xiaoming (2011) is more sympathetic. He says that as an intellectual, it is only possible to hold on to one's conscience, if one gives up any expectations of society. If one wants to advance within the system, it is almost impossible to do so and have a conscience. Since Mo Yan's award of the Nobel Prize for literature, the debate over the role and responsibility of intellectuals in China's political landscape has surfaced with renewed vigour. Most recently, his fellow writer Yan Lianke has criticized the intelligentsia, including himself and Mo, for failing to speak out on important issues (Branigan 2013).

The Chinese intellectual scene of the reform era is often divided into three broad categories of intellectuals: the new-left, new-Confucians, and liberals. In He Guanghu's view they are about equally represented among Chinese academics, partly because the new-left and new-Confucians receive a fair degree of government support. In his view, liberals have the widest influence in educated circles outside academia, including the media, professionals and educated middle classes. Among them, many who contemplate China's social phenomena and are 'desperate for a solution', are attracted to Christianity, because it is intellectually sophisticated and seems to offer answers to fundamental questions like human nature and the meaning of life as well as core concepts like justice and democracy, which underpin Western liberal political thought (author interview, November 2012).

While some parts of the analysis in this chapter will focus on public and elite intellectuals, the definition of intellectuals applied here is not restricted to this narrow meaning, but includes a wider sector of society, which has received a higher education and works as a white-collar professionals in the fields of culture and technology.[2]

Christianity and democracy

In his study on politics and religion, Steve Bruce (2003) cites many examples from different historical time periods and different parts of the world to show how Christianity and the development of democracy are connected. These links vary tremendously and Bruce puts the emphasis on the relative importance of religious culture and material circumstance. Throughout his study he questions whether it is really religion that matters, or whether religious culture is only a secondary factor to material circumstances which are the real reasons why people act politically at any given time or space. Despite these qualifications, Bruce comes to the conclusion that Protestantism, through a variety of factors, and in many cases inadvertently, led to the development of liberal democracy. According to Bruce, Protestantism encouraged democracy in three ways: first, it played an important part in the rise of capitalism and the growth of prosperity; second, it encouraged individualism and egalitarianism; and third, it created a context of religious diversity.

John Keane (2000: 9) argues that in every known case, religious discourse was a basic pre-condition of the rise of early-modern public spheres, which correspondingly displayed strong traces of Christianity in such matters as constitutional protection of free speech, blasphemy laws, religious holidays and public prayers. In the contemporary context John Keane identifies two particular manifestations of religious protest: a call to the imitation of the life of Christ through extension of ethical concerns to the needy, and the emphasis on the importance of spiritual outreach where believers are called to witness before others in public through forums such as 'house-churches' (Keane 2000: 12). Both elements are strongly represented in Chinese Christianity. As shown in Chapter 4, Chinese Christian theology as developed by early Christian thinkers and the TSPM emphasizes the importance of Christian ethics and social work. The 'New-Calvinists', to whom some of the leading Christian intellectuals belong, also see an important role for the church in society. And witness before others in public is an important feature of all churches in China.

Micklethwait and Woolridge (2009), too, argue that there is a link between Christianity, or rather more specifically, Pentecostalism, and liberal democracy, although in their analysis of contemporary religion, they see the causal chain in the reverse. For them, it is democracy, choice and the market, which produce the highly individualized Christianity at home in the United States and which is being successfully exported all over the world, including, they argue, to China.

Although for many secularism is a pre-condition for democracy, one of the apparent features of secularism is its theoretical and practical affinity with political despotism, says John Keane. He points to various philosophical and political warnings that secularism succours anthropocentrism, which seduces humanity into thinking it can play God (Keane 2000: 13–14). Christianity starts from the premise of the fallibility of man. Contrary to the argument that it is the humanistic tradition of Confucianism that provides the right conditions for democracy in China, Chinese Christians argue that dictatorship and tyranny emerge where people entrust their lives entirely to humans instead of having a faith which, as the foundation of their culture and their psyche, transcends all individuals. The fear of the Lord is the beginning of wisdom, writes Wang Yi. While rules can be discovered by reason, it requires a higher constraint than reason – the recognition of a transcendental force – to obey them, he argues further (Wang Y. 2012b).

According to Yuan Zhiming (1997), Chinese culture's denial of man's sin and limitations is the spiritual root of tyranny, whereas Christian awareness of precisely these human shortcomings is the beginning of democracy.

> The precious source of democracy is not the wisdom of man; if we should think so, we fall into the trap of human wisdom, which will result in various forms of tyranny [...] If we think that the ideas of a democratic system and human rights are founded on man's rational and moral consensus, it follows that with the same consensus we can also override them.
>
> (Yuan Z. 1997: 58–9)

He Baogang (He 1996, 2000) also calls for a complete overhaul of the Chinese approach to rights and a negation of the goal-based morality inherent in Chinese culture in order to build new moral foundations for Chinese democratic institutional design. This new moral foundation should be seen as the result of a long process of moral evolution or an ideological transformation in China: from the supposition of good to evil in human nature (as in Christianity), from duty-centred theory to rights-centred theory, and from a collective approach to an individualistic approach. Among these, he considers the rise of individualism and its notions of individual interests and rights most fundamental. Individuals, according to He, have the inviolable right to dignity and security and any restriction by the state on the individuals' pursuit of happiness should be denied. To Yan Yunxiang this shift has already taken place, ushered in by the realization as early as the 1980s of the huge gap between the lofty ideals of collectivism and the reality in which everybody struggled to achieve their own goals, despite all talk of selflessness. The rush by the political and cultural elite to make money signalled the legitimacy of self-interest, profit-making and materialistic fetish (Yan Y. 2011: 44). But the declining influence of collective values does not mean that collective action has disappeared. Such action now takes place in protest to protect the rights of the individual (to property, clean air, and safe food); in many areas these rights of the individual coalesce into collective rights and interests – environmental protests would be a good example. But the shift from a duty-centred to rights-centred approach is not complete, leading to the conflicted 'divided self' as described by Yan Yunxiang, who, in the absence of individual rights protection by the government may find solace and reassurance in the Christian argument, as put by Yuan Zhiming, that an individual's rights, including life, liberty and the pursuit of happiness, are given by God and not by governments and therefore no government has the right to take them away (Yuan Z. 1997: 58–9).

Ethical concern and an extension of charity to the needy and hopeless is a central tenet of Christianity and China is not lacking those in need of *Nächstenliebe,* or neighbourly love. The dissolution of the socialist system that provided basic social security has left large parts of the population without access to affordable health care or provision for old age, while modernization and urbanization have brought with them not just a range of fears and uncertainties but also a catalogue of social ills including poverty and addiction. Furthermore, the increase of China's middle classes has also seen a rise in anxiety and neuroses among a sector of the population who now has potentially much more to lose than in the past. While Christianity is not the only belief system offering comfort and solace to those in need of it, Christianity has become increasingly popular with the urban middle classes in recent years. Its attraction lies partly in the comforting notion of God's unconditional love, and partly in the perceived link between economic success and Christianity. Links have long been established between the role of the middle classes and the process of democratization (Gilley 2004: 62–6). An increase in Christian belief among this diverse social stratum would add another important factor to the political importance of this group, which is investigated more closely in Chapter 7.

One further important aspect of religion lies in its possible solution to the problem of free-riders in society. The term refers to members of society who are happy to benefit from the outcome of social or political action, but are unwilling to contribute or take part in it.[3] Hu Ping (2003) points to the fact that many people in China believe in democracy, although few are willing to share the risk of active participation preferring instead to sit back and wait until the final outcome has been achieved and they too can enjoy the benefits. In a similar argument, Chen Kuide (Chen K. 2004) bemoans the 'over-cleverness' of the Chinese people, who consider it a clever strategy to sit back while others stick their necks out in the struggle for justice and the respect of constitutional rights in China. Mancur Olsen (1965), who generalized analytically the phenomenon of free-riders, suggested as a solution to find ways to make the participation in collective action a reward in itself. Religion seems to offer this answer.

Steve Bruce (2003) argues that secular reformers may work very hard, but that religious reformers have a special impetus. Evangelical Protestants in particular start with considerable advantage over secular activists, he argues. Highly motivated, used to giving large amounts of time, money and energy to promoting the gospel, religious zealots can deploy vast reservoirs of commitment. History proffers countless examples of people, who engage in protest politics, not because they stand to gain, but because they believe that a wrong should be righted. And while religion is often socially conservative, it is also always potentially disruptive. As Bruce puts it

> Zealots do not deal from the same pack as ordinary people. I do not mean that they are irrational in their reasoning; the point is that they have extra reasons. True believers do not weigh possible courses of action in the same way as people whose political calculations are made with purely secular criteria.
>
> (Bruce 2003: 12)

Both members of Falungong and Chinese Christians consider standing up for their rights and enduring the ensuing oppression as a religious act and experience. For Christians, oppression and hardship are embraced as a chance to experience but a tiny fraction of Christ's suffering on the cross for mankind. Autobiographical literature often refers to a strong belief in God that made it possible to endure the hardship and cruelty of imprisonment and torture, be it during the Cultural Revolution or in labour camps. Nien Cheng, Harry Wu or Han Dongfang are the best-known examples, but Yuan Zhiming's film 'The Cross. Jesus in China' (2003) is full of testimonies from ordinary people relating their experiences in prison or labour camps. These experiences, related through testimonies and Christian witness, in turn feed into the growth of the churches. A lot of rational reasons are cited for the growth of Christianity in China, but according to Tony Lambert the role of suffering has been overlooked (Lambert 2006: 209). Protestantism started to grow during the Cultural Revolution, China's most repressive political period, through small, clandestinely held meetings. Meetings in small, intimate groups continue to be one of the most popular and most widespread forms of Christian congregations; where the enemy can no longer be defined as the state it is reframed as the vice-ridden, consumerist, secular world.

We now return to the hypothesis proposed at the start of the chapter, which speaks of a potential bridge function of Chinese intellectuals in three main aspects: social relations, political theory and action, and the relation between China and the rest of the world. Analysis of the first aspect includes the fields of education, urban-rural cooperation and the demographic make-up of urban congregations as potential indices of the closing of social gaps. The second aspect will be analysed by looking at the involvement in concrete political action by Christian intellectuals, while the third aspect looks at the worldview of Christian intellectuals as expressed in their publications and their personal ties.

Bridging social gaps?

As outlined in the previous chapter, some of the publications written by Christians for Christians (notably *Aiyan*) fulfilled a partly educational role. Within their pages, essays on law and the constitution as well as complex moral issues authored by leading intellectuals in the field sat alongside testimonies from ordinary people and reports from the mission. The publications were a far cry from the usual collection of testimonies in similar magazines worldwide. The publications, which emanated from Beijing 'house churches', reached into the general population of 'house church' Christians. *Aiyan* in particular had a strong educational role which became more and more apparent with each issue and clearly reflected the specific situation within which the 'house churches' operated. It also signified recognition of the make-up of the congregations and a conscious effort to raise the educational standard. In general this reflected a critical awareness of the necessary 'raising of *suzhi*' among 'house church' Christians, an issue that is of great importance and generally exercises the minds of the better educated in China, whether Christian or not. It is also a historical characteristic of Protestant churches. People were trained to interest themselves for their own affairs and to develop the habit of exercising individual judgment. An important factor for the reformed churches was the ability to read and write and to study the Bible. Correct belief is of particular importance where salvation depends on correct belief rather than correct ritual (Bruce 2003: 250).

Consequently, in the Chinese publications educational efforts are focused primarily on the Bible as well as rights awareness. A distance study group had been developed under the mantle of *Aiyan* through which potential missionaries received guidance and training. This was very different in scale from the efforts by web-based organizations abroad which provide extensive material for sermons and theological education for pastors as described in the previous chapter, in the sense that *Aiyan's* study groups were aimed at individuals at the grassroots in different Chinese locales. A further aspect of *Aiyan's* educational function was its focus on the teaching of English. It was intellectuals within the urban churches that had taken on this task and it was one crucial area where intellectual sectors of the churches cooperated with poorer and less educated congregations. These educational efforts also need to be understood in the context of an acute shortage of trained clergy in the rural areas. Publications, and in particular their online editions, provide access to information as well as teaching materials and forge a greater link between urban congregations and the rural congregations.

But the exchange and chances to learn from one another were clearly two-way. On the one hand the members of the urban congregation are better educated and have a lot more valuable professional expertise and connections that can benefit the rural churches in their struggle against oppression, which is harshest in the poorest and most remote areas of the country. The work of the Association of Christian Rights Defence Attorneys[4] (of which more in the next chapter), which offered legal help to individuals who have suffered repression in rural areas, was a significant aspect of rural-urban cooperation. On the other hand, Beijing churches were learning from the rural churches when it came to dealing with continuing oppression and building up resistance. As one of my interviewees close to the Association saw it, the rural congregations looked back to several decades of existence in an oppressive environment and imparted this knowledge to the urban congregations who in general were much younger. The fact that links had been established between more intellectual congregations in Beijing and rural congregations in the context of rights defence was a significant political development;

Aiyan, in which a number of leading intellectuals wrote, was one of the means of communication to facilitate and promote this link.

Fangzhou/Ganlanzhi was a cultural journal emanating from *Fangzhou* church in Beijing and edited by Yu Jie (one of *Fangzhou*'s elders at the time) and Wang Yi. Its first issue was published in 2006 and it existed for at least eight issues. It did not have an online presence. It published a number of items reporting on outreach work by *Fangzhou* congregation members to Shangfang or 'Petitioners Village' near Beijing South Railway Station (Yu Jie 2006). Members of *Fangzhou* congregation visited the village in July 2006 handing out over 300 lbs of food that was bought with money collected in a prayer meeting for the support of blind human rights activist and lawyer Chen Guangcheng. Written accounts of the visit were preceded by quotes from the Bible which not only called for charity but also for release from the yoke of injustice.[5] This is but one example of such outreach work by Beijing congregations which has been going on for some time, although most congregations prefer to do this away from the public eye.[6] This particular aspect of 'outreach' work has increased in scale and significance during the relief efforts for the two major earthquakes which occurred in China in 2008 and 2010 and which before then and since has been carried out by many unknown congregations that did not publish highbrow journals.

Possibly the most significant development in the context of urban-rural cooperation was the establishment of the Chinese House Church Alliance[7] on 20 October 2005 in a Beijing suburb. It brought together urban and rural congregations in 17 provinces and was quoted by the China Aid Association to have over 250,000 members. Its formation marked a new step in collaborative ventures and testified to an organizational virtuosity not seen since the crackdown on the Falungong Movement and the China Democratic Justice Party in the late 1990s. The Alliance was declared illegal by the Ministry of Civil Affairs in 2008, apparently 'because it was determined to be backed by hostile forces in the US' (Wen 2012). Despite continuous harassment, the Alliance remains active and determined to continue to uphold its principle '"to serve the church, be engaged with society, be concerned with public welfare, and act according to the law," and to vigorously advocate for suppressed and persecuted house churches and defending the legal rights of victims' (China Aid 2012).

In conversation with individual educated Christians attending urban churches, one nonetheless detects a palpable gulf between urban and rural Christians which hinges on the key concept of *suzhi*. The growth of urban churches and the influx of theologically trained Chinese from overseas as well as the growth of theological seminaries affiliated with the bigger churches, if anything, has widened the gap between urban and rural congregations in this regard. For example, Nanlai Cao reports that Christian conversion enables migrants in Wenzhou to develop contact and social interaction with the local, urban population. Their Christian identity, even though often doubted by local believers, may even give them limited access to jobs, housing, loans, social networks and even potential partners in the Christian community. But while they may be accepted within the urban church community, these ties do not usually extend beyond society outside the church community where the same migrants may be entirely ignored by their more sophisticated urban 'church brothers'. Wenzhou Christian evangelicals fiercely maintain the boundaries between the urban civilizer and the migrant civilizee and restrict the range of possibilities that can be enjoyed by migrant converts (Cao N. 2011: 144, 149). Hence migrant workers' Christianity exists in parallel to local Christianity, not as part of it. They are not welcome in the local Christian communities as they are considered 'troublemakers' who speak 'poor Mandarin' and have 'no culture'. If they are allowed to serve in a local church, then only in marginalized positions like ushers and cleaners. They have no right to be listened to in the local church, not even as a member of the choir, which stands in stark contrast to the enthusiastic reception of Christian celebrities from Beijing, Shanghai and overseas (Cao N. 2011: 154–6).

While Christian belief has the potential to be a great equalizer, the make-up of congregations, and in particular intellectual congregations, is socially relatively uniform. While 'house churches' exist among all groups of society, the majority of them stay and recruit from within their own social group. The six categories of Beijing 'house churches' identified by Liu Tongsu make this apparent. He lists them as local churches (attended by long-term Beijing citizens), blue-collar migrant churches (*mingong jiaohui*), churches attended by businessmen from outside Beijing, white-collar migrant churches (*beipiao jiaohui*), *haigui* churches (Chinese returned from abroad), and independent student fellowships (Liu and Wang 2012: 273). This can only be partly explained by government restriction. The private nature of the congregations means that they are primarily founded among like-minded people who already know one another and therefore rarely cut across social boundaries within one congregation. Congregations that are too big are also considered less than ideal as they no longer provide an opportune environment to look out for the individual members. Therefore, as the number of urban Christians grows, there seems to be a tendency of greater social fine-tuning rather than opening up across different sectors of society, certainly where 'outsiders' to the local community are concerned.

Interesting exceptions are congregations that are founded around private businesses. In such situations it is quite common for all employees, starting from the manager down to the last worker, to be members of the congregation. As such enterprises often also have employees with a rural background, these congregations do not just cut across social boundaries, but also cut across the urban-rural divide. Christian enterprises exist in all parts of the country, but they have gained particular significance and attention in the Wenzhou area of Zhejiang. Here a new type of urban Christians has emerged, who are not part of the old city population, which consisted mainly of state employees. They are the financial and organizational pillars of their churches, and often male (Chen C. 2005: 179). They are in a unique position to reach a variety of different sectors of society, ranging from their own, often rural background and their workers' to local government officials, intellectuals (by inviting them to give speeches in their churches or to publish in their publications) as well as overseas communities consisting of businesses and students. What forges the link is their Christian faith. But while workers in Christian owned factories in Wenzhou consider themselves to be lucky to work for a Christian boss, there is no trace of a sense of equality, however basic or fundamental, in these relations. For Christian entrepreneurs in Wenzhou, migrants are seen as useful tools to fulfil their ambitions of evangelization. The Christian faith, which often has the effect of changing an individual's temperament or make him or her more inclined to submit to their lot as part of God's plan (or indeed punishment), is also considered to produce a more docile and submissive workforce. Sometimes parallels are drawn between migrant workers and Black American slaves, the latter seen as docile (as opposed to the migrant workers who are often violent) as a result of their Christian faith (Cao N. 2011: 152).

Fangzhou (The Ark) Congregation was one of the best-known church congregations in Beijing in 2006. From the start *Fangzhou* had placed itself as an 'above ground' church, thereby completely denying the existing framework of official and unofficial churches. According to one of its elders, the writer Yu Jie, it was a congregation that was 'above ground' and open to all, regardless of status or profession. It welcomed everybody into its fold, be they foreigners, Chinese intellectuals, migrant workers or peasants. (It has not been possible to verify this claim.) As such, *Fangzhou* congregation was controversial from the outset. As some of its leading members or elders were well-known writers and scholars as well as dissidents, the congregation had been under surveillance with the PSB taking a keen interest in both the congregation as well as individual members. The congregation was subjected to raids in January 2006 with continuing interest from the authorities. This declared open approach also led to severe criticism from within the 'house church' movement at the time. Other Beijing 'house churches', who claimed to be equally inclusive and involved in political activities, felt that *Fangzhou*'s public statements were merely driven by a desire to protect individual members from prosecution. (Individuals in the public eye, especially in the international media, are much less likely to be arrested.) It was the unanimous opinion of all 'house church' elders outside *Fangzhou* whom I spoke to in 2006 that *Fangzhou*'s declared open approach endangered the activities and existence of other congregations by drawing the attention of the Public Security Bureau to them, too.

Since 2006, the distinction between unregistered churches worshipping within the confines of a private home, and official churches, meeting at dedicated places of worship, have become more blurred. Many churches have grown in numbers and as we say in Chapter 1 and mostly no longer meet in somebody's home. They rent public spaces, and where prevented from doing so – as was the case with Beijing's Shouwang Church and Chengdu's Early Rain Reformed Church – have gathered in open, public spaces, displaying a continuation of this open approach pioneered by earlier congregations like *Fangzhou*. They have thus forced the issue of freedom of religious belief as well as the related issues of freedom of association, assembly and speech into the public arena, which has resulted in several public comments by leading non-Christian intellectuals on the question of 'house churches' in China today. (One example is Yu Jianrong's essay based on conversations with people from 'house churches' (Yu Jianrong 2008).)

In the context of the Chinese government's Regulations for Social Groups[8] which in theory still prohibits the unauthorized gathering of more than 25 people and the close watch the government keeps on some intellectual congregations, the splitting of church groups once they reached a certain size was a common and necessary phenomenon. Unfortunately this also seemed to have been the easiest way out when the slightest conflict arose and was clearly common practice. In 2006 many of my interviewees referred to individuals who used to be part of their congregation but had since started their own, and almost all of them felt compelled to make derisory remarks about other intellectuals and their congregations. For example, the decision by the three men, who met with George Bush, to exclude a fourth man from the meeting at the last minute, made huge waves in Chinese intellectual Christian circles and prompted a lot of hostility against the three; the decision was also in itself a sign of the differences and rifts among this group of people.

Judging from more recent developments, the tendency to split seems to have lessened, partly because of a relaxation in the management of 'house churches' on the part of the government, and, paradoxically, partly because of the resulting increased focus of government repression on particular congregations with a more overt political agenda, or who are led by individuals, who are outspoken critics of the government. The experience of targeted house arrest, harassment, 'kidnap', torture, imprisonment and ensuing exile of key campaigners over the last few years, has not only resulted in a fragmentation of the movement, but it also seems to have resulted in a certain 'closing of ranks' by the rest. On the other hand, the less strict enforcement of the regulations also makes the character of Chinese Christianity more clearly visible. Many (urban) churches grow out of student fellowships or small groups (often Bible study groups), both deemed the most effective forms of evangelizing and adopted by the Christian mission in many locales, including the UK, where this format cannot be explained by government repression or the over subscription of existing churches. Articles in publications like *Maizhong* and *Jiaohui* (see previous chapter), indicate that small groups remain the favoured form of Christian communion and indicate that in particularly evangelical and theologically traditional circles, small-scale, private, intimate gatherings are preferred to open worship, quite regardless of what the government thinks of it.

Early Rain Reformed Church in Chengdu has managed to weather the storm over its outdoor worship and has been able to secure fixed premises for its church through the private purchase of a property. It is well known in Chengdu and welcomes everybody into its fold, although in practice the church congregation consists mainly of urban educated middle-class believers. So do other churches in Chengdu, which are led by leading intellectuals. Early Rain's patient negotiation with government officials together with its open, affirmative approach, has won the church many admirers outside its congregation. So have Wang Yi's writings on the internet. At the same time new 'gaps' have emerged. Despite their focus on openness and inclusivity and despite a large proportion of women in the urban churches, church leadership is predominantly male. While many women are content with this situation by accepting male leadership as biblical truth, there are also accounts of people leaving certain churches as a result of this attitude.

Therefore, it would appear that despite the equality of all people before God, in the congregations themselves, this remains an ideal that has yet to be achieved. Intellectual congregations just like others, instead of opening up and breaking through social boundaries, seem to be even more exclusively focused on their own peer group than others. In an interview with the author in 2006, Yu Jie likened intellectual 'house churches' to cultural salons or exclusive clubs rather than Christian congregations, although I personally remain unconvinced that he himself was not guilty of the same charge while an elder at Fangzhou church. (Certainly his publication, while undoubtedly daring in its political overtones, was highly elitist.) Where individual intellectuals gained prominence because of their actions in society they often expected an elevated position and respect among their congregation as a consequence; celebrated lawyer and very recent convert Gao Zhisheng for instance was criticized for 'preaching' from the lectern during meetings rather than take his humble place as part of the congregation and leave the preaching to the minister. In general it would seem that intellectuals find it easier to bridge the gap between the elite and the common people in the written word and through teaching rather than through personal contact.

Bridging theory and action?

A number of intellectuals involved with the 'house church' movement are considered public intellectuals in so far as they no longer confine their writings to their own fields of expertise but will comment on the 'state of the nation'. In recent years many of them also moved their focus away from cultural and spiritual China to political and grassroots China. According to Cheng Yanghong (2006) Liu Xiaobo was one prime example of this type of intellectual. Liberal intellectuals like Liu and Yu Jie looked towards real society and tried to effect real change. In the process they increasingly approached grassroots society and gained a deeper understanding of China's complex realities, relations and conflicts. As a consequence, according to Cheng writing in 2005, they found themselves in conflict with local authorities over very concrete and real issues and used the law, the administrative process and public opinion to achieve actual visible results.

Liu Xiaobo and Yu Jie were introduced by the writer Liao Yiwu and both belonged to the circle of people, who drafted Charter 08 (see following chapter). Liu Xiaobo's fate following the publication of this document is of course well known in the West. The empty chair placed at the Oslo Nobel Prize awarding ceremony has become a powerful and iconic image which symbolizes as much the wrongful imprisonment of a political writer and campaigner as the West's single-minded focus on such matters in its coverage of China. Yu Jie is far less well known in the West, although he was one of the three men, who prayed with George Bush in the White House in 2006 (and at three further occasions, which did not receive much media coverage). Outside China he is best known for his attack on Wen Jiabao, whom he dubbed China's most famous actor in a book published in 2010. In his own words, he was deeply affected by the events of 1989 (when he was 17 years old) and which informed his disillusionment and disdain for the authoritarian regime. He converted to Christianity in 2003, a fact that further fuelled his already prolific writing. Similar to other Christian intellectuals he founded his own church, which attracted a high profile intellectual membership. Drafting and signing Charter 08 was an undeniably public, political act in which his congregation was closely involved; but while a number of signatories are Christians, the document itself as well as its signatories does not necessarily have the support of the Christian population at large.

On the contrary, getting too involved with politics and using the churches as a base for political activity is fiercely criticized from within the 'house churches' on theological grounds. Engagement with worldly matters like politics is associated with liberal theology, from which many 'house church' leaders want to distance themselves (Yu Jianrong 2008). Considering the disdain that Yu Jie and other prominent politically engaged Christian intellectuals have for the liberal theology as represented by Ding Guangxun and the TSPM, this is ironic yet in keeping with disagreements and disputes over doctrine (in the widest sense) by Chinese intellectuals since the May Fourth Era. The disagreements over this particular issue also illustrate the importance of theology, in particular where the definition of the relation between the religious and the secular is concerned.

Liu Tongsu (2007) sees three possible options for religion in a dictatorship: to attach itself to power, to rebel or to escape. In contemporary China, of course, he sees the 'attachment school' represented by the TSPM, which went through three phases. The first phase after 1949 Liu considers as more 'pluralistic' in terms of the reasons why they attached themselves to power. He concedes that at the time there was an illusion that the CCP would be led democratically and that the churches would be able to operate independently of the state apparatus, a hope that was finally eradicated in 1957. In this first phase there was also an element of nationalism, that is the satisfaction of a Chinese church and certain idealism by individuals like Wu Yaozong that communism may bring the realization of the gospel. In the second phase from 1957–78 Liu argues that Ding Guangxun saw his approach as a choice between two evils: either accommodating to the actual situation and strike a compromise in order to ensure the survival of the church to some degree, or to shun compromise and risk complete destruction. According to Liu, Ding chose the former. But this has led to the third phase, where attachment to authority is no longer to do with ideals or strategy and is all about the benefits of the individuals and institutions affiliated to TSPM. Therefore today, the TSPM is just another secular institution, according to Liu.

'House churches' have emerged as active resistance to this development, Liu argues further, but they, too, have to face the question as to how to enter public life and give up their complete retreat into the private as a response to the 'adjustment school'. They have to become part of the world yet transcend the world. They need to realize that while there certainly are still traces of dictatorship, there are also seeds of pluralism in contemporary China and that it is the churches' role to contribute to this pluralism. Churches should be part of public life, but they should not belong to or be attached to any independent social force of public authority. Hence political dissidents, who enter the churches must learn new ways, their radicalism must be toned down and the churches must be careful that their involvement in society does not reflect the radicalism of the political rebels (Liu T. 2007). Following the very serious repercussions after Charter 08 this has already happened. Churches with a politically minded leadership are now restricting their actions to smaller, more easily controllable acts closer to home. The charitable efforts by individual churches as mentioned in Chapter 4 are smaller if still sensitive examples of bridges between political theory and action. They reflect a conscious positioning in society and a belief that Christians are called to act upon their principles and faith in wider society.

Still, there is uniform agreement among Christian intellectuals that it is their duty as Christians to bring their belief into society at large and to do what they can to spread Christian values and the gospel. How political and indeed how public this engagement becomes largely depends on the individual's profession. For lawyers the call to bring their faith into society has particularly political implications. China's constitution safeguards a catalogue of rights and liberties, and China's legal system has improved vastly over the last two decades. However, violations of rights, in particular on the side of local authorities, and the invocation of 'catch-all clauses' where the government is determined to eliminate people from the public realm are standard. So are deviations from or violations of proper legal processes. In this context, legal scholars and lawyers have become the most daring and outspoken hands-on human rights activists in the first decade of the twenty-first century. A great many of them are Christians and members of the Association of Christian Rights Defence Lawyers.

A 2006 issue of *China Rights Forum* focuses on human rights lawyers and the rule of law camp and features a number of Christians who also write in the publications introduced in the previous chapter. Wang Yi is quoted on the back cover, saying 'Rule-of-law discourse has given the rule-of-law camp the resources to promote political dissidents, human rights lawyers, social activists and even members of future political opposition parties with greater courage than most humanist intellectuals' (China Rights Forum, Issue 3, 2006). At the time, the trial of Beijing pastor Cai Zhuohua, who was also the driving force behind the publication of *Aiyan,* for printing Bibles and distributing religious literature, was an important test for rule-of-law camp intellectuals. The formation of an Association of Christians Rights Defence Lawyers was advertised in *Aiyan* and the names and contact numbers of its members were published. They were all leading scholars in the field of constitutional law with the country's leading research tanks or universities. The list consisted of Wang Yi, Fan Yafeng, Li Boguang, Teng Biao, Guo Yan and Gao Zhisheng.

According to a source close to the association, who spoke to me in 2006, they did not only take on high profile cases; primarily they were contacted by Christians across the country and asked to represent their cases. The majority of these cases were in rural areas and funds to finance these lawyers' travel expenses and fees were generated from within the community, either the rural community asking for help or the urban community should the rural community be too impoverished.[9] While united in their Christian belief and fight for justice, there were also disagreements among this rather small group of individuals which were centred on issues like depth of belief, the timing of and duration since an individual's conversion to Christianity and the sincerity of their motives, all of which had a bearing on how they related to one another and which were potentially divisive.[10]

Bridging the gap between China and the world?

In the history of the Christian mission in China, how to manage relations with Chinese tradition has been a central issue. One of the approaches was to speak of a distinct Chinese approach to Christianity. In the secular realm too, searching for a 'Chinese way of doing things', be it 'socialism with Chinese characteristics', or a distinctly Chinese model of democracy has characterized official intellectual endeavours. Christian intellectuals do not speak of special Chinese qualities; they demand that an individual's belief and attitude towards Christ need to be the same all over the world. According to Wang Yi (2006b: 36), Chinese Christians today should display more similarities with English Christians in 1650 or Malaysian Christians in 1990 rather than their atheist fellow countrymen.[11]

Christian publications offer an interesting glimpse of a Chinese Christian view of the world which is informed by the preparation for the second coming of Christ. Thus the world falls into Christian countries and countries yet awaiting Christianization. In this context particular focus is given to Muslim countries that lie between China and Jerusalem. Among some sections of China's Christians it is considered to be God's special task for Chinese Christians to convert these countries to Christianity, hence considerable amount of writing is devoted to this field.[12] Apart from the Middle Eastern countries, Chinese Christians also want to move into the areas around the equator, particularly in Africa. In concrete terms, this vision means the sending of Chinese missionaries into Muslim countries; a task for which these Chinese Christians consider themselves uniquely qualified. On the one hand they would encounter less suspicion than Western missionaries and could rely on the good diplomatic relations the countries in question enjoy with the Chinese government. On the other hand Chinese Christians consider themselves tougher and better able to endure oppression than their Western counterparts. One crucial problem seems to be that it is mostly newly converted Christians as well as rural Christians who are enthusiastic about outreach into different parts of the world, whereas intellectual or older Christians (who would after all be the best placed to fulfil such a missionary role) tend to be unwilling to go into developing countries.[13] It needs to be stressed, that this project of evangelizing China's minorities and the Middle East is not a commonly shared ambition among Chinese churches and in many cases outright opposed. In addition, and according to Lambert (2006: 199), the size of the 'Back to Jerusalem' movement is hugely overstated abroad; he estimates that there are perhaps only a few hundred people involved in it.

For many intellectuals, the gap between the West and China is certainly narrowing on an individual level. Considering the frequent travel between China and the West (mostly the United States), which these individuals undertake, the term 'Chinese' also needs to be problematized. Many individuals (mostly men), who are closely involved in the 'house church' movement, are permanently based in the United States. Those, who can, undertake frequent journeys to China, often spending several months at a time working with different churches. Among the best known men are Yuan Zhiming (introduced in the previous chapter) and Bob Fu of the China Aid Organization. Bob Fu was involved in 1989, applied to be a party member, but subsequently escaped China in 1996 to Philadelphia via Thailand. He settled in Midland, Texas, where he runs the China Aid Organization, an 'international Christian human rights organization' with close connections in Washington and in China. China Aid has played a crucial role in helping both Chen Guangcheng and Yu Jie into exile, to give the two most recent examples. His organization is partly responsible for the tenor of the media discourse on Christianity in China in the United States, which almost exclusively focuses on the aspect of suppression and persecution. Within China, his work evokes very mixed reactions among Christians.

Neither Yuan Zhiming nor Bob Fu are able to travel to China, but not all Christian intellectuals overseas have left China under duress. Liu Tongsu, formerly a legal scholar within CASS, was invited to Yale Law School in the early 1990s, transferred to the theological seminary at Yale and stayed in Boston where he has been involved in several Chinese churches. He is actively involved in the Chinese 'house church' movement including several publications published from within it. Other examples were mentioned in the previous chapter. All of them are leading 'pastor-intellectuals', who, while based in the United States, have strong ties and influence in China. It is perhaps not surprising that some observers are struck by the similarity of Christian churches in the affluent eastern coastal regions of China and the United States (Chen C. 2005: 196). There is little evidence of any interest by this group in cultural areas outside these US based theological communities.

Both Yu Jie and Wang Yi credit the emergence of the concept of a constitution to the Anglo-American Puritanist movement. All the non-Puritan constitutional systems of Europe are considered to have failed; their current success credited with the postwar revisions that took place under Anglo-American guidance (Wang Y. 2006b: 37). Many of them also wrote in support of America's war with Iraq. This orientation towards North America is strengthened further through the Christian networks associated with 'New-Calvinist' or reformed theology as mentioned above and in previous chapters. These networks provide theological (in the shape of textual material and people) and financial support, but are not seen as advantageous by all. After all, the biggest obstacle to the blanket toleration of churches remains the accusation or suspicion that they are critical of the government, and worst, that they are used as tools by dissidents abroad. 'Abroad', in this accusation, is largely defined as the United States.

This focus on the United States is far less evident in the older generation of 'Cultural Christians', some of whom studied in Europe and many of whom draw on European theologians of the twentieth century in their writings, or indeed among the church leaders of Wenzhou, who have close ties to Chinese communities in Europe, especially France and Italy, as well as Africa. (However, prominent 'pastor-intellectuals' are often invited to Wenzhou for talks and seminars.) There are also close links to theological seminaries in Malaysia and Indonesia, both home to large Chinese populations. The role of the Chinese diaspora in the growth and theological development of Christianity in China is an interesting and thus far under-studied phenomenon. It also means that at least in the context of the discussion of Chinese Christianity the terms 'Chinese' and 'foreign' as employed by the Chinese party-state are unreliable labels of culture or nationality but arbitrary labels where 'Chinese' is reserved for all that is considered acceptable and compatible with the general thrust of China's social and political development, and 'foreign' is everything and everybody, whose involvement is seen as disadvantageous or a 'threat'.

There is, however, an interesting global aspect to the Chinese Christianity, outside the lofty circles of intellectuals. Chinese Christians – as individuals or as part of small groups organized by their churches – do increasingly travel to other parts of the world outside the English-speaking West and Europe, notably countries in Africa and Latin America. While those I have met did this on short journeys organized through their churches, it will be interesting to observe whether the increased Chinese presence on these two continents will bring with it increased efforts by the global Chinese mission.

Conclusion

Can the hypothesis of a 'bridge function' of Chinese Christians be upheld? The picture that emerges is relatively complex. There is clear evidence that their belief compels many Christian intellectuals to engage fully in hands-on political activities which can be analysed in the context of the fight for political transition to democracy. The activities in recent years by Chinese human rights lawyers are of particular importance in this regard. The guiding motivation for the political activities of the individuals discussed here seems to be religious rather than secular and appears to be not so much the establishment of a democratic polity, but the preparation of the world for the second coming of Christ (although some fellow Christians doubt how strongly they are really guided by this particular belief). A democratic China seems but one step on the way towards achieving this ultimate goal rather than a goal in itself. But does this matter? After all, the work of Christian intellectuals is important at this stage, and despite their culturally often precarious position and their 'fringe' status (Yue S. 2005) they do share points of principle with other liberal intellectuals as well as well-connected, affluent business communities, and it is possible to envisage a political consensus between the various groups in a period of political transition. One can therefore argue that these Christian intellectuals can play a crucial role in a period of political transition and may well contribute to its success, regardless of a possible second coming of Christ. Han Dongfang is a good example in this context. He may not consider democracy the ultimate aim of his work, nor a tool to save China, but there is no denying that his work with the China Labour Bulletin is an important example of how one man has decided to dedicate his life's work to a cause he passionately believes to be right and which contributes to the plurality of voices.

However, in this context the importance of work done by individuals and congregations away from the spotlight and with less direct political ambition also needs to be stressed. The organization of charity work, the formation of NGOs, or simply the involvement in the organization of church activities imparts valuable lessons in active citizenship and self-governance, which have an indirect but lasting effect on political attitudes and awareness. Historically, Protestant sects and denominations themselves formed an important part of the civil society, but they also provided the organizational templates for other associations; and they provided ordinary people with training in public speaking, committee management and small group leadership (Bruce 2003: 250).

In the absence of any officially tolerated alternative political organization, small Christian congregations – the format favoured in China today – offer an opportunity for people who have ideas and leadership skills to 'gather a flock' around them and discuss topical issues and how they impact on the individual. In the vast majority of cases, these will not stray beyond what is in the mainstream and officially accepted. But in a small number of cases they will become a platform for more 'radical' or uncompromising political ideas. In response to the question, whether she thought that some Christian intellectuals were politically involved as a result of their faith or whether they had found Christianity as a result of their political activism, Gao Shining was quite sure that neither was entirely accurate. In her view, most of these individuals had been searching for something; as we have seen in Chapter 2, a number of them had found the party before they turned to the church, which currently offers one very convincing alternative for people with a 'mission'.

The strong ties which exist between Chinese Christians in exile in the United States and the leading Christian intellectuals in China ensure financial support, legal and theological education as well as political intervention on behalf of individuals where necessary. While these activities are intended to help the Chinese Christian community, they are not necessarily welcome or seen as advantageous by all and it would be a mistake to assume that the voices of Chinese Christians in the United States are representative of 'the Chinese Christian experience'. The vast majority are far more conciliatory and interested in good relations with the Chinese government so that they can go about their lives, including their spiritual lives, with as little struggle as possible.

The smaller Christian intellectual scene that does become politically involved is also a diverse and often divided group. This has implications on the way they choose to work together (or not), on the way in which they are perceived by others, and therefore ultimately, on the extent to which they achieve their potential in the pursuit of a common goal. Recent reactions (or rather lack thereof) to a petition by leading liberals within the party and the events around *Nanfang Zhoukan* in January 2013 from this group are also indicative of their uncompromising stance towards others, who do not belong to their own movement. The inability to see common ground and to compromise is a theme that recurs in Chinese opposition movements from the days of the early revolutionaries through to the post-1989 democracy movement. It yet remains to be seen whether a shared Christian belief enables this particular group of political activists – whether inside or outside China – to bridge the gap between individuals' egos and their claim to the right way and to contribute in a constructive fashion to China's ongoing transformation.

Notes

1 The definition of an intellectual in the Chinese context has led to a sizable body of literature. Lian Xi's article on 'Cultural Christians' (2013) provides an overview of the discussions. Hao Zhidong (2003) provides a detailed note on the concept in the appendix.
2 This is also the definition applied by Liu Tongsu in his survey of urban churches. See Liu and Wang (2012: 271).
3 For an analysis of the problem of freeriders see Stanford Encyclopedia of Philosophy http://plato.stanford.edu/entries/free-rider/#1 (last accessed 11 February 2013).
4 *Zhongguo jidutu weiquan lüshi tuan*. The formation of this group was advertised in *Aiyan* and the names and contact numbers of its members were published. They are all leading scholars in the field of constitutional law with the country's leading research tanks or universities www.aiyan.org/2005/06-15/20.html (last accessed 8 March 2008).
5 One account of this visit published in *Ganlanzhi* was preceded by a quote from the Book of Isaiah, Chapter 58, Verse 7, which reads: 'Is it not to share your food with the hungry , and to provide the poor wanderer with shelter, when you see the naked, to clothe him, and not to turn away from your own flesh and blood?' (Yu Jie 2006: 4). However, the unprinted previous verse, with which the deeply religious readers of the publication would no doubt have been familiar, reads: 'Is not this the kind of fasting I have chosen: to loose the chains of injustice, and untie the cords of the yoke, to set the oppressed free and break every yoke?'
6 One of my interviewees was particularly resentful of *Fangzhou's* approach.
7 *Zhongguo jiating jiaohui lianhe zuzhi*. An announcement can also be found in the Gospel Herald at http://ca.gospelherald.com/template/news_view.htm?code=mis&id =252 (last accessed 24 October 2006).
8 A full English version of the Regulations can be found at www.chinadevelopment brief.com/node/298 (last accessed 11 September 2007).
9 Information obtained in an interview with a source close to the Association in September 2006.
10 Information obtained in interviews with leading intellectuals in Beijing and Hong Kong September 2006.
11 The context in each case is one of a beleaguered Christian population; by drawing these parallels Wang Yi is calling upon his fellow Chinese Christians to think and act politically (Wang Y. 2006b: 36).
12 See for example www.aiyan.org/2005/05-2/4.html or www.aiyan.org/2005/05-2/5.html (last accessed 20 May 2008).
13 Information obtained in interviews in Beijing in September 2006.

7 Politics and the transcendental

On 10 December 2008 a document called Charter 08 was made public in China.[1] Inspired by the Charter 77 of Czechoslovakia and published on the sixtieth anniversary of the Declaration of Human Rights, it was initially signed by over 300 individuals from inside and outside the government and across wide sectors of society. The document consisted of a foreword, in which the authors provided a brief overview of failed political reforms since the Opium Wars, a second part, which constituted an affirmation of principles of the authors, followed by 19 'recommendations on governance, citizens' rights and social development'. Instead of advocating steady reform, the document called for fundamental change to the political system in China and is considered to be the embodiment and synthesis of theoretical and intellectual achievements by Chinese liberal intellectuals over a decade (Feng 2010). One year after the publication of Charter 08 Liu Xiaobo, one of the men responsible for drafting the document, was sentenced to an 11-year prison sentence for subversion. The image of the empty chair placed in his honour at the Nobel Prize award ceremony in Oslo has become a powerful symbol of the entrenched positions as far as the question of human rights and political reform in China are concerned.

During an earlier prison sentence in 1999, Liu Xiaobo, an active participant in the democracy movement of 1989, read and made extensive notes on Christianity and political action. Revised in 2005, the resulting article was published in the second issue of *Ganlanzhi* (originally named *Fangzhou*, published by the eponymous church in Beijing) magazine, edited by Yu Jie and Wang Yi. *Caesar tamed by God, Power Subjugated by Faith* is an exposition on the history of Christianity and an analysis of its main social and political characteristics. Two main issues appear to capture Liu's imagination in particular: that Christianity made the transition from a persecuted religion to the official religion of the Roman Empire, and that the Christian faith became the transcendental basis for the processes of the rule of law. Liu argues that since the Second World War the military colonial aggression which had facilitated the spread of the gospel in non-western countries has been more or less replaced with peaceful methods, and that the twin processes of secularization and rationalization have meant that Christianity has been amalgamated into secularized liberalist values. He sees the propagation of the gospel as part of the globalization process of liberalist values not just in the form of the global liberalization of the economy but also in the form of a global democratization of politics (Liu Xiaobo 2006).

His contemplations of the utility or power of Christian faith in political protest led him to the consideration of peaceful resistance as practised successfully by Gandhi and Martin Luther King Jr. As Liu argues, peaceful resistance was bound to be futile under dictators like Stalin, Hitler or Mao, but under a totalitarian regime, which, in the face of the global tide of liberalization and democratization, cannot help but at least pretend to respond to it through the hypocritical use of terms like 'freedom', 'democracy', 'humanism' and 'human rights', Liu sees its chance greatly improved. For Liu this 'hypocrisy', as he calls it, may be the very first step in a development towards a 'good government'. With admiring references to Solchenitsyn and Vaclav Havel, Liu concludes with the following thoughts:

> Respect for human dignity is the natural source of a sense of justice. If a system or a nation allows its people to live in dignity, then people will identify with the system. To quote Thomas Aquinas, political virtue manifests itself not only in the stability of the system, but also in the establishment of human dignity. If this is not the case, then all kinds of protest movements will ensue, as people's conscience makes it impossible for them to obey. The reason why a liberal system can gradually overcome a dictatorship, why the conclusion of the Cold War is seen as the end of history, lies in the fact that the former recognizes and respects human dignity whereas the latter not only disregards human dignity but wipes the floor with it. God says: Believe me; the criminal will turn into a just person. Man's natural instinct says: guard your conscience and a bad government can turn into a good government.
>
> (Liu Xiaobo 2006: 96)

This chapter continues the theme of the previous by focusing on Chinese Christian liberals and the way faith and politics are linked in their theoretical writings. It investigates the links between Christian liberals and other liberal groups as defined by Feng Chongyi (2010), who distinguishes between (non-Christian) liberal intellectuals, Christian liberal intellectuals, human rights lawyers, liberals within the CCP, grassroots rights activists and democracy movement activists.[2] As will be shown below, the distinctions between these categories are blurred insofar as Christian liberal thinking has had a profound influence on representatives in all these categories of liberals over the last decade. This chapter also introduces the nascent attempts at formulating a political theology in China, which stipulates the importance of the transcendental source of values in the construction of a polity as well as in the emergence of a true civil society in China. Finally it explores the likelihood of the emergence of a wider political consensus based on the notion of 'transcendental values', and 'conscience' in contemporary China.

Liberal intellectuals and Chinese Christian liberals[2]

The concepts of peaceful protest, following one's own and appealing to the moral conscience of others are evident in the wording of Charter 08. Central to its reasoning is the difference between the existence of laws and the rule of law and the difference between the existence of a constitution and a true constitutional government. Both issues are central to the writings of all Chinese liberals. While the reformers of the 1980s still mostly approached China's future through the framework of Marxism, liberalism has become the most important political orientation among reform minded intellectuals in China since the 1990s, although by far not all, who consider themselves liberals, agree with the desirability of a multi-party democracy in China.

Similar to politically liberal groups in China of the 1940s, which represented a 'third way' before they got swept under in the violent polarization of CCP and KMT, Chinese liberals today not only strive for individual freedoms and seek to replace the Leninist party-state with liberal democracy, but also address the issue of social inequality. In their view, the unfair distribution seen in China today is a direct result of the continuing power structures which dominate the allocation and control of resources through political power and privileges established in the decades before the reform era. These structures were criticized in pioneering activity as early as the 1960s by, for example, Yang Xiaokai. Yang was born and grew up as Yang Xiguang in Changsha, Hunan province, where he experienced the Cultural Revolution as a member of the Red Guard generation. In 1967, aged 19, he penned an essay called *Whither China?* which turned into a key document in the factional struggles within the CCP and saw him in prison and labour camps for the following 11 years.[3] The document promoted the virtues of direct democracy as practised in the Paris commune and also referred to the Yugoslav political theorist Milovan Djilas; its content was a direct response to Yang's intimate knowledge of the privileges and power structures within the new communist elite in China.

Chen Kuide (2010) concedes that it is mostly with hindsight and knowing his later intellectual developments that one can understand Yang's writings during the Cultural Revolution as tender shoots of liberalism in forbidding times. Certainly Yang and others, who voiced daring alternative opinions during the Cultural Revolution, can be understood as small islands or stepping stones that bridge the temporal gap between pre-1949 liberals and the liberals of the reform era. In this landscape Yang Xiaokai is of particular significance to today's Christian liberals. After the Cultural Revolution Yang went on to become a celebrated economist, who was twice nominated for the Nobel Prize; he died in Australia in 2004. He first encountered Christianity while at Princeton, but only converted later in life, after his first successful struggle with cancer, much to the astonishment of his atheist friends. Yang is firmly claimed by today's Christian liberals as one of 'theirs', partly because of his Christian faith late in life and partly because of his advocacy of a constitutional democracy, a central political demand of Christian liberals today. Thoughts on Yang's conversion as articulated in a letter to a friend are published in an early issue of *Aiyan*, a publication close to Christian liberals and the Christian *weiquan* lawyers;[4] Yu Jie also dedicated an essay to his memory (Yu Jie 2010: 193–5).

The aim to create a link between China's liberal traditions and contemporary Christian liberalism is also evident in the naming of key publications. In the 1940s the main Chinese liberal publication was a journal called *Guancha* (Observer), published in Shanghai, which stopped publication after 1949. In the 1980s reform minded intellectuals placed themselves in this legitimizing tradition by founding *Xin Guancha,* a forum for their ideas, until its closure in 1989. It was revived by a website called *Guancha,* begun in Washington in 2002, which carried on the liberal tradition of its eponymous predecessors with close involvement by Chen Kuide and Harry Wu (Wu Hongda). It was refashioned in 2012 as an 'independent overseas website focusing on research and criticism', with a very clear political agenda that is directly related to the clauses of Charter 08. Since his exile in Washington, Yu Jie has joined the editorial team which consists of Harry Wu, Zhang Dajun and Yang Lili, which means that the editorial direction of *Guancha* is now firmly in Christian hands.[5]

Debates take place among liberal intellectuals and Christian liberals as to the exact nature and aim of liberalism. There exists a range of different aims and emphases which in a multi-party context would manifest itself in different party affiliations ranging from social-democrats to neo-liberals. Their critiques from the left equate Chinese liberals with American neo-liberals, but Feng Chongyi (2010) argues that they differ fundamentally from this group through their concern for social equality. There is however no denying that Chinese Christian liberals have a close affinity to American Republicans. There was great admiration for George Bush on their part and their allegiance during the 2012 American presidential election lay with Mitt Romney.

While the older generation of liberals was mostly atheist, the importance of transcendental values is increasingly explored by the younger generation. Zhu Xueqin, one of China's leading non-Christian liberals, defined liberalism's characteristics as follows: 'it stands for empiricism in contrast to transcendentalism; it rejects all historical determinism; it requires a representative democracy, a constitutional government and a legal system as proof against dictatorship; ethically it requires the protection of differing values' (cited in Wang C. 2003: 105). Zhu, one of the 50 most influential public intellectuals as published by *Nanfang Renwu Zhoukan* in 2004, suggests that liberals, while advocating empiricism and endorsing the market system, should also pay close attention to the 'increasingly pronounced social divisions and conflicts of interests around us' but believes that only by developing further the weak Chinese market can income disparity and endemic corruption be reduced. He attributed the rise in conservatism, by which he referred to a tendency to remain quiet, to 'an exercise in survival skills' on the part of intellectuals (Wang C. 2003).

Wang Yi is a self-declared conservative, although not in Zhu's sense; he, too, featured on above mentioned list of 50 leading intellectuals. Wang Yi is a liberal intellectual and constitutional theorist, internet essayist, and leading church figure from Chengdu. He co-edited with Yu Jie the Christian cultural magazine *Ganlanzhi* (originally called *Fangzhou*), and is a regular columnist for *Guancha*. He is also the pastor of Early Rain Reformed Church in Chengdu, one of the biggest and best known unregistered churches in China, which operates entirely above ground. They have recently purchased fixed premises for their congregation and run their own theological seminary. Wang Yi regularly writes about constitutionalism from a Christian perspective and is working towards the development of a political theology.

Christian liberals consider the political ideals of democracy and freedom under a transcendent moral ethic, thereby returning to their religious source, forgotten or ignored by atheist liberals, claims Wang Yi. Theirs is, as Wang Yi contends, an understanding of freedom that is between man as God's creature and God, and thus forms a new development in China's wave of liberalism. In a speech given at a conference entitled 'Christianization and Democratization' in December 2005 Wang Yi (2006b) explains the understanding of liberalism from a Christian perspective. According to his explanation, Christian liberals make the belief in Christ the firm basis for the secular value of liberty and equality. The Christian understanding of freedom goes beyond the classic understanding of freedoms and does not just mean the binding existence of rights among people which must be respected by governments. In fact Wang Yi rejects the possibility of contracts among people in the absence of a higher transcendental power. The Christian understanding of contracts and hence the constitution lies in God's willingness to restrain his own power in his covenant with Noah. Christian freedom derives from God's self-restraint, which is also proof of God's love and his willingness to save mankind. Love and redemption lie at the heart of the covenant (Wang Y. 2006a). Freedom then means the willingness to submit oneself to God's word. Wang Yi distinguishes clearly between secular liberalism that talks of freedom on the basis of the relations between society and the individual, and Christian liberalism which talks of freedom as a noumenon, as a thing in itself (Wang Y. 2006b: 36).

The emergence and existence of a constitution is seen from a strictly religious point of view in the understanding of the Christian liberals. Man's guilt and fallibility as well as the rule of God's justice are seen as premises for the constitutional system. Without the Biblical notion of a covenant and the power of judgment, constitutions would not exist, they argue. Wang Yi cites the 'Mayflower Compact'[6] as further historical evidence for God's covenant with man and the religious basis of modern constitutions (Wang Y. 2006a: 100). For Wang Yi a secular constitutional government is one of the results of mankind's falling into sin, but that it is also one of the remedies that God is offering mankind before the second coming of Christ, the certain and ultimate event that guides all Christian activity. A constitutional democratic government is therefore merely considered to be the least bad system of government; one which the gospel does not necessarily wish to aid to establish, but it is the one that least hinders the spreading of the gospel. It is a system that enables the peaceful co-existence with secular rights and freedoms of Christians and non-Christians. It is considered a system used and spread over the world by God in preparation for his return to earth. In the Chinese context, communism is seen as the greatest movement of idol worship in political history and an unprecedented trial of Satan holding power in the history of mankind. According to Wang Yi, wherever the location of this trial will be the location of God's triumph over Satan (Wang Y. 2006b: 38). This equation was first established by a Californian Pentecostal multi-millionaire's foundation, the Full Gospel Business Men's Fellowship International, which preached that capitalism represented God's will from which followed the corresponding corollary to communism and Satan, a message particularly welcome in parts of the world, which had suffered from communism in a variety of settings (MacCulloch 2009: 961). Theologically this is a long way from the Puritanism and 'New Calvinism' otherwise embraced by Christian liberal intellectuals and illustrates the tendency to liberally and uncritically draw on a variety of sources to support their argument (Fällman 2013: 162).

Transcendental values and a political theology

In the fall 2012 issue of the *Chinese Religion and Law Monitor*, Wang Yi writes about *The Possibility of Political Theology: Christianity and Liberalism*, where he develops these thoughts further. Among the liberals Wang increasingly sees the differences between those, who understand the transcendental background of liberalism and constitutionalism and firmly believe in it, and those, who accept values and freedoms as transcendental values, but who see its source as void or solely dependent on human reason. Wang understands constitutionalism as a kind of self-constraint and self-limitation by those in power. To him, the highest domain of constitutional civilization is 'covenant' (*yue*), which includes metaphysical moral constraints, as well as specific, institutional constraints and textual constraints from tradition. 'Covenant' manifests the transcendental source of constraints and refers back to God's covenant with himself and God's covenant with mankind. God is essential to the concept of constraints, which derives directly from the two aspects of (God's) love and justice.

> The essence of constraint is love. Out of love for man, God gave up his unlimited will and imposed restraint on himself. This kind of love, in terms of its source, is without cause or reason. From the absence of cause and reason comes covenant and also love.
>
> (Wang Y. 2012b: 110)

Love here is not understood as a social value that can improve social relations among people, as discussed in Chapter 3, but as the core attribute of God together with forgiveness, which finds worldly representation in the legal framework, and specifically in a criminal law system that allows for pardons. As Wang sees it, the human realm needs to be 'opened up' to let 'God's love and the fountain of justice' come in. In this conception it becomes God and God's love that render a government accountable and not the fact that power was invested in them by the people (through democratic process).

Wang consistently uses the term '*yue*' (covenant) in his writings, but accepts that others may want to use the terms '*dao*' or '*yuanze*' (principle) instead, acknowledging that thinking about the importance of transcendental values need not be confined to a Christian spiritual context. This signals a cautious willingness to work together on the formation of a political theology that draws on a wider basis than Christianity. Wang argues that all, who rely on a transcendental source of values regardless of their source lean towards moral constraint. In fact, behind political philosophy and political commonwealth, there always exists a dimension of political theology in his view. Asked whether he envisaged working with other non-Christian liberals who speak of 'transcendental values' in order to develop further his preliminary thoughts on a political theology, Wang Yi had to concede that there was very little direct contact between them and very few fora or opportunities to meet with each other. There are currently plans for the sixth China Theological Symposium to be held in Oxford in the summer of 2013 at which organizers are hoping to bring together representatives from the new left, the new Confucians and liberals to hold face-to-face discussions on this matter.[7] For now, though, Wang Yi's formulation stays firmly within Christian concepts.

> the pursuit of a constitutional polity and the acceptance of and submission to transcendental values is a simultaneous process. From the Christian perspective, if that is not happening simultaneously, then constitutionalism is simply the Tower of Babel and is doomed to fail.
> (Wang Y. 2012b: 115–6)

On the basis of this political theology Wang Yi and others stress the importance of the existence of a new Christian elite in China, who take their belief into all fields of work and expertise, and who, equally importantly, make their joy and optimism visible to all in daily life; a theological tenet reminiscent of Abraham Kuyper's Neo-Calvinism. Among this social elite, intellectuals are seen to have a particularly important role; for Christian liberal intellectuals it means that China's democratization and Christianization need to be linked together. Wang calls for the spirit of the gospel to enter and pervade not only all academic disciplines, but all areas of public opinion, knowledge and ethics so that it can become a part of mainstream culture. He considers this to be the main task Chinese Christian intellectuals must fulfil today. In political terms, the existing Chinese constitution becomes a core element seen as separate from the Chinese government, in particular as it guarantees a number of rights and freedoms, including religious freedom, which are currently not yet implemented.

Civil society and a 'transcendental spirit'

The conception of a constitutional government, which stipulates the firm belief in a Christian God, will not be easily accessible to others. It nonetheless seems to find an audience among other liberal intellectuals. In the 2010 fall issue of the *Chinese Law and Religion Monitor* Liu Junning – firmly placed in the group of non-Christian liberals by both Feng Chongyi and Wang Yi – writes that the value source of all constitutions is the transcendental value of religion. He calls a constitution without holy support just like a decree from Caesar. Liu considers the freedom of religion the most important freedom of all, from which all others follow, because freedom of religion guarantees freedom of the soul, without which no subject can develop a conscience. But the freedom to follow one's conscience instead of authority is the key to human dignity, Liu Junning writes in words very similar to Liu Xiaobo's quoted earlier (Liu J. 2010: 44). Freedom of religion – a fight mostly fought by the 'house churches' – is starting to be seen as pivotal for all other rights, but in particular for the right to peaceful resistance and political change.

The importance of transcendental values is also invoked in the context of civil society and a true 'citizen spirit'. He Guanghu, an academic at Renmin University and signatory of Charter 08 (as well as one of the earlier generations of 'Cultural Christians') does not speak of a political theology, but makes a clear link between the establishment of '"citizen society" and the "transcendental spirit"'. In his eponymous article (no date) he argues that the key question to resolving China's mounting problems lies with politics, and the root with the will of the people. Plenty of historical examples have shown that economic reform without political reform ultimately destabilizes the economy, and that culture and social life are equally affected by the political system. To He, the only answer to all of China's problems, including its social development, lies with the establishment of democracy and the rule of law. He defines the latter as the control by law of all members of society without exception. Democracy, in turn, is the opportunity for every member in society to be involved in the establishment of the rule of law and in the management of society. Only those, who take part in the process of establishing the rule of law, can truly be called 'citizens'.

While the development of such a 'citizen society' may hinge upon the transformation of the legal system, He Guanghu emphasizes the importance of people's awareness of the links between them and society, and in turn the links between social management and politics. People have to start to think like citizens and consider the benefits of society beyond their own personal gains. In order to be able to do so, their thinking and actions need to be guided by a 'transcendental spirit' that enables them to transcend their own selves. To him, the most developed transcendental spirit is religious faith that transcends this world, because only in the face of a true object of faith can men and women realize their own smallness, temporality and limitations and hence transcend their own selves. He concedes that terms like 'God' or 'spirit' are difficult to accept for some people, but the term 'transcendent' is more widely considered to be in an interesting concept by liberals, as it can help overcome the prevalent 'pragmatism' in society and at a most basic level can just simply mean the ability to step outside oneself to see the bigger picture and to overcome differences, 'like Romney and Obama, who shake hands after the election is over'.[8]

He Guanghu (no date) further argues that on a social level, this transcendental spirit means that the individual is able to recognize the equal character and the equal rights of others, leading to mutual respect, equality and common recognition of the same rules, which in turn leads to a 'society of citizens' (or civil society). Furthermore, imbued with this transcendental spirit, citizens will not only obey the law, but they will keep a critical eye on society as a matter of conscience. Aware of the superior nature of God's law these citizens will be aware of the relative nature of man's law and will therefore constantly apply themselves to the improvement of society and the true establishment of the rule of law. In classic Chinese rhetoric style He concludes

> The basis and the aim of political reform is the establishment of a society of citizens; the prerequisite and the result of a society of citizens is a raised citizen awareness; and the raising of citizen awareness and the rising of people's will in turn require the re-awakening of a transcendental spirit as part of our moral qualities.
>
> (He G. no date)

Gao Shining (2005: 310–5) also emphasizes the importance of a system of ethics or morals to be based on a religion, that is, for its values to be derived from a source outside human rationality in order to be able to transcend ideology, to provide historical continuity and to be as widely accepted as possible. While she did not yet see a profound Christian influence on society, she did think that the reform era had led to an emergence of scholarly research, a mass culture and personal space outside political ideology, all of which meant that the individual now had the opportunity to 'think about the soul'. In this space Christianity as well as other religions had a chance to be effective and to influence a bottom to top change in the formation of civil society in China.

For He, Wang and other Christian liberals, politics is not defined by the political dictator, nor is it confined to the field of political power. It is understood as a public life and in Havel's sense of 'anti-political politics' that advocates the re-introduction of ethical and moral norms as the guiding principles in people's lives (Havel 1989). For Christians in general this means a conspicuous and public upholding of their own standards, including evangelization and testimony in public, but also the right to defend their beliefs and the human rights of others. An open declaration of faith and moderate but determined rights defence action are the first way forward and have characterized the behaviour of churches over the last decade. Christian lawyers and legal scholars have played a key role in this; not just as educators and advisors, but also as leaders of their own churches.

Christian rights defence

Since the beginning of the reform era, lawyers must have been the most rapidly growing legal profession of all. In 1978 there was barely a single lawyer in the country while it can now count about 140,000 registered lawyers, the majority of whom have a law degree and are registered with the Chinese bar (see Lynch 2011). Following the drafting of numerous laws and regulations in recent decades and the promotion of the 'rule of law' by the government, lawyers of all ilk, be it corporate, criminal or private, are in high demand. At the same time, practising law is also one of the most difficult and most frustrating professions in China; possibly as a result lawyers are also one of the most politicized sectors of society today. According to a survey conducted among more than 1,500 Chinese lawyers in all provinces of China, Chinese lawyers value political rights far more than economic rights and they were least happy with the extent to which their aspirations for democracy were realized (Michelson and Liu 2010: 311). More than half of the lawyers surveyed self-identified as being *weiquan* lawyers, or 'rights-protection' lawyers, sometimes also rendered as 'human rights lawyers' in English. This stands in surprising contrast to the estimate by Teng Biao (one well-known *weiquan* lawyer) that 'only a few dozen lawyers focus on citizen's rights' (Teng 2009).

Weiquan lawyers started to appear at the start of the new century. They by and large accept the legitimacy of the political system, but use the existing legal framework to protect the rights of citizens within these constraints. Fu and Cullen identify a spectrum along which *weiquan* lawyers operate ranging from moderate to critical to radical. Different individuals may move along this spectrum and while by far not all *weiquan* lawyers have become radical, most radical lawyers started out as moderate lawyers who became radicalized as a result of their sympathy for, and later identification with, their clients and their frustration with the legal processes (Fu and Cullen 2008 and 2011). Some of the most radical lawyers today, who have since suffered severe harassment and imprisonment, including the still missing Gao Zhisheng, have started out as 'poster boys' for China's officially promoted rule of law. As Elizabeth Lynch (2011: 539) argues, these *weiquan* lawyers seek to vindicate individual rights promised by many of China's laws, and unlike their colleagues in corporate law they are motivated by a sense of justice rather than by the promise of a profit.

Religious rights defence is one area of many in which *weiquan* lawyers have been active; it is also one area where the nexus between *weiquan* lawyers and a more general *weiquan* movement is most apparent. The focus on religious rights awareness emanates from recognition of its importance in the context of the 'house church' movement. The previous culture among churches 'not to talk about politics and not to talk about theology' (*bu tan zhengzhi, bu tan shenxue*) has slowly changed over the course of the first decade of the twenty-first century, and certain publications emanating from the dual context of Christian belief and rights defence were the leading organs promoting this change. Wang Yi contends that the rise of the *weiquan* movement, with which Christian lawyers and legal scholars have been closely associated confirmed that liberals were the primary force actively engaged in the advancement of social and political rights, 'finally putting the boot into the credibility of the new left' (Wang Y. 2012b).

The fact that many of the most radicalized *weiquan* lawyers are Christians, is not really touched upon in the growing academic literature on them, although Fu and Cullen do mention in an earlier version of their China Journal paper that there is a close relationship and a growing synergy between law and religion, and *weiquan* lawyers and church leaders, which has led to a particularly active *weiquan* community surrounding the issue of religion and religious freedom in China. Lian Xi also includes them in his recent article on 'Cultural Christians' (Lian 2013). This community centred around the Association of Human Rights Attorneys for

Chinese Christians mentioned in the previous chapter, which consisted of individuals who were not only eminent figures within their academic fields but also devoted Christians with their own 'house church' groups. Among them were Gao Zhisheng, Wang Yi, Li Baiguang, Teng Biao, Guo Yan and Fan Yafeng.[9]

The *weiquan* movement is now of course much larger and goes beyond Christian circles. Law in particular, and *weiquan* lawyering even more so, is a challenging experience. Many young lawyers leave the bar in the first few years because work is so difficult and frustrating (among other things, clients often do not pay). Michelsen and Liu argue that the importance Chinese lawyers place on political rights and their dissatisfaction with the level of democracy in China is a direct result of their occupational vulnerability. They back this up by the finding that lawyers, who identified themselves as *weiquan* did not display any different political values to the rest. Generally speaking, support for political reform increases when people have had negative direct experience with state actors (Michelson and Liu 2010: 323–8).

The connection between *weiquan* lawyering and Christianity is multi-faceted and complex. Clearly, some of the individuals closely associated with the beginnings of the movement were already Christians when they started to get involved in this work. More have converted to Christianity at a later stage, and certainly in 2006 there were great doubts and misgivings among the group of self-declared 'true' Christians as to whether Gao Zhisheng or Guo Feixiong for example, who are now regularly referred to as Christian *weiquan* lawyers, could really be considered Christians. The professional vulnerability of *weiquan* lawyers may be a result of their willingness to accept cases that expose them to vulnerability as a result of their pre-existing values. At the same time, though, their vulnerability may also make them more open to spiritual and intellectual support offered by Christian colleagues. The majority of *weiquan* lawyers operate out of Beijing (although their cases are all over the country), and many, who took up *weiquan* lawyering moved their offices to Beijing in order to be close to the centre of the *weiquan* movement and to be able to tap into the available support. This support (often financial) increasingly also comes from overseas. Some also claim that they have converted to Christianity, because they realized that rule of law and democracy in China lack the necessary deep foundation of faith and morality (Renminbao 2005), and are thus becoming involved with Christian liberal discussions on constitutional government and the necessity for transcendental values as outlined above. Therefore the lines between *weiquan* lawyers and Christian liberals as drawn in Feng Chongyi's analysis, are becoming blurred in the same way as the lines between Christian liberals and other liberal intellectuals are not as clearly drawn as they used to be.

Within the majority of churches outside the immediate influence of *weiquan* lawyering and Christian liberals, the link that has been created between radical *weiquan* lawyering, political theology and churches is controversial and not necessarily welcome. In discussion with Yu Jianrong, Shen Helin, a leading church figure from Jiangsu, distinguishes between rational and radical rights defence within the churches. He agrees with the former, which fights for legal redress within the existing administrative framework, but he has sharp criticism for radical rights defence carried out by dissidents within churches. In his view, they use the issue of regulation and other religious rights issues as a reason to go into opposition to the state, using the churches as their political platform. As a result, rights defence has become an extremely sensitive matter for churches. While both the rational and the radical rights defenders want to improve justice and citizen's rights, he sees their values and methods as very different. Shen appreciates rational rights defence, which restricts itself to protests against the administrative processes and particular cases where help is required. The radical rights defence, as Shen sees it, uses cases to negate the regulations per se, which swiftly leads to conflict and leads to harm rather than benefit for the individual involved in the case. This usually happens where politically idealistic intellectuals lead the charge and use the churches for their voices and ultimately invoke the question of religious freedom. In the eyes of most churches, these are political Christians, who are associated with a liberal theology, with which Shen's church groups do not wish to be associated (Yu Jianrong 2008). As liberal theology is normally associated with the TSPM churches, which is widely rejected by the 'house church' movement and most violently by the most politicized individuals, this is an interesting charge and indicative of quite how deeply the fault lines run.

Liberals within the party

In his musings on the historical success of peaceful protest, Liu Xiaobo conceded that their success was facilitated by a broadly shared value system between protester and government as far as justice is concerned, which led to a degree of shame and insight on the part of the government in the face of the peaceful protests. Liu's observation mirrors the British sociologist Steve Bruce's, who argues that protest movements are more successful, if the protesters share the same value system as those against whom they protest. Bruce, too, cites the example of Martin Luther King Jr. and the black clergy who were able to call on the common value system to shame those whites who would not concede the need for change. This could lead one to conclude that therefore, a Christian led protest movement, or at least one that is perceived to be imbued with Christian values, is unlikely to succeed in China at the present stage. But it is also one reason, why the uptake of Christian values in the official discourse, as well as the conversion to Christianity in communist circles is of particular interest. As Chapter 1 has already shown, the binary thinking regarding party membership and religious faith is no longer appropriate.

The economist Zhao Xiao, whom we have already encountered in Chapter 2 and 3, not only moves in circles frequented by other Christian academics, but he is also actively involved in missionary outreach work, blogs prolifically and has over 7 million followers on China's equivalent of Twitter. Despite being a leading economist and government advisor, Zhao Xiao has become most famous for a short essay, first published in 2002, in which he exhorts the importance of churches in the market economy. Writing after a few months' sojourn in the United States, Zhao concluded that the secret of America's economic power was its churches.

The physical presence of church buildings was a clear symbol for Zhao that a legal framework and punishment alone were not enough to encourage ethical behaviour in the market. In his view, the collusion between government and business, the amassing of wealth only for personal gain and the dishonesty prevalent in the Chinese market economy were all the result of a lack of belief in any force outside the human realm, which guided human trust and agreements. Like Wang Yi, Zhao quotes the Mayflower Compact to illustrate the importance of a covenant in the name of God as the only reliable way to close a contract (Zhao X. 2002).

Nearly ten years after the essay was published, Zhao considers the possibility of a social crisis that may lead to a political crisis as the most pressing issue in China. Following 30 years of reform, people's economic needs have been largely fulfilled and have moved on to a social and political as well as religious level. In his speech presented at the Fourth Chinese Theological Forum in Seoul Zhao (Zhao X. 2011a) warns that government reform is so far ill prepared for these demands, which comes at a price. Zhao argues that budget expenditure towards maintaining domestic stability now surpasses expenditure for national defence meaning that China is holding on to stability (literally) at all cost. This may not be sustainable if the challenges rise further, as they are likely to. He therefore presents an economic argument for social and political change, which in his words will be a 'change of the cross'. Zhao sees China's industrialization and urbanization as a huge opportunity for China's evangelization and harbours a personal vision of '30-30', which means the hope that by 2030 more than 30 per cent of the Chinese population will be Christian (a vision he shares with David Aikman). The majority of these envisaged converts are likely to come from China's urban middle classes. Although Zhao Xiao faces outright hostility from Chinese Christians abroad, who go so far as comparing him and those who follow him to the Nazi's Volkskirche (for example Shan 2012), Christian intellectuals I met in China did not express many concerns about his continued party membership. He seems readily accepted as a Christian and his (and presumably other party members') paths frequently cross those of other Christian public intellectuals. In this context it is also worth remembering that many of the individuals, who play a leading role in the theological direction, publications and 'ideological leadership' of the Chinese churches, who were mentioned in Chapter 6, were themselves party members before they converted to Christianity. They often still have senior family members inside the party and therefore enjoy high level connections and access at least at a personal level.

The possibility of a social crisis and the worry about China's future has informed the publication of a petition signed by 71 academics and lawyers from 'within the system' on 25 December 2012. In order to prevent a significant Arab-spring style social uprising, the signatories call on the government to implement the country's constitution which guarantees the freedom of speech, assembly, publication and religion as well as the freedom to demonstrate. They plead to lift the controls on the internet, on social organizations and the press. While stopping well short of other demands made in Charter 08, like the establishment of a federal republic and direct elections, this recent petition does demand an independent judiciary and non-party candidates in elections to people's congresses and actual inner party democracy (see The Economist 2013 and Ming Pao 2012). The signatories of the petition include well known liberals like He Weifang and China's 'first human rights lawyer' Zhang Sizhi. The majority of them took part in a public discussion forum on reform held in the week after the eighteenth party congress in November 2012 and are close to the reform minded journal *Yanhuang chunqiu* (Annals of the Yellow Emperor). While there is no suggestion that this latest initiative is informed by Christian faith, its emphasis of the Chinese constitution and its proper implementation as key factor of China's political reform was pioneered by Christian liberals and *weiquan* lawyers and is now shared by all liberals, including those within the party. This latest initiative may be an indication that the 'conservatism' of intellectuals within the system is a thing of the past. There has been no public comment on this petition by the supporters of Charter 08 abroad.

Middle-class grassroots activism

Feng Chongyi (2010) lists individuals like Chen Guangcheng and Guo Feixiong as liberal grassroots activists distinct from other groups of liberals. However, Guo Feixiong is a relatively well known Christian *weiquan* lawyer, albeit at least initially considered as very controversial by Christian liberals like Yu Jie. Following his remarkable escape from house arrest and subsequent exile to the United States, Chen Guangcheng, the blind lawyer and activist against human rights violations in the government's enforcement of the one-child policy, has received considerable support from Chinese Christian groups in the United States (who would like to interpret his actions as representative of a Chinese pro-life movement), although Chen himself is not a Christian. They are two well-known names in the myriad of grassroots protests and activism, in which China's middle class plays an increasingly important role. Therefore rather than focusing on individuals (as Feng Chongyi does) this section on grassroots activism looks at the political 'liberalism' of an increasingly vocal sector of society.

The political importance of an emerging middle class (in such cases often measured in GDP figures) has been recognized in modernization and democratization theories (for example Gilley 2004). Zhao Xiao (2011a) argues that based on the example of the 'four little dragons' (Hong Kong, Singapore, South Korea and Taiwan), freedom of the press usually occurs when a GDP per person of $6,000 has been achieved, and political freedom arrives when a GDP per person of $12.000 has been reached. (China's GDP is projected to be $6.890 in the year 2013,[10] whose start was dominated by unprecedented protests against censorship and political interference in Guangzhou's *Nanfang Zhoukan*. It would be interesting to hear Zhao Xiao's opinion on these.) Studies of the political orientation of China's middle classes seemed to show a tendency towards political conformism and support of the state, apparently disproving the arguments that the drive for political change will come from this sector of society. More recent studies, though, paint a rather different picture.

A team at CASS found that China's middle class is more critical of the current social and political situation and less confident in government performance than other strata of society. The study also suggests that middle-class consciousness or middle-class values sometimes differ from mainstream consciousness. They often express above average doubt about official ideology and the present power structure (Li C. 2010b: 73). In recent years middle-class grievances against government policy have become more evident and there is even concern that the middle class may become 'angry'. Li Lulu argues that in authoritarian regimes the nascent middle class may originally rely on the political system, but as members of the middle class become more autonomous they also become more critical and may even challenge the political order. In this context, values become of particular importance (Li C. 2010b: 76). As outlined above, Chinese liberals see the root cause of China's social inequality in the ongoing dominance of pre-reform power structures that impact negatively on distribution in society. The social representation of the results of these power structures may lie in what is now referred to as a 'black-collar class'; urbanites who dress in black, drive around in black cars, have hidden incomes and links to the mafia and to state owned enterprise CEOs. They are increasingly seen to be the true beneficiaries of reform by the 'white-collar class' and as the real political ally of the Chinese government (Li C. 2010b: 79).

Members of China's middle class already have a higher rate of participation in elections and rights-protection activities than other groups and there is an expectation that middle-class political participation will become an important factor in community governance not least because of the high involvement of this sector of society in China's NGOs (Li C. 2010b: 74–5). China's urban middle class acutely feel the pressures of the costs of health care, housing, old-age pensions and inflation. According to the results of a recent survey published in China Daily, only 1 per cent of the surveyed urban population felt that their lives had improved while over 40 per cent said their quality of life had declined (Zheng X. 2012). For middle class professionals, who can afford it, moving overseas has become one way of escaping the pressures of life in China's cities. The first decade of the millennium saw a 45 per cent increase in the numbers of white-collar middle-class professionals leaving China for other developed countries. Pollution, a disintegrating social and moral fabric and political uncertainty are all quoted as reasons for their exodus (Johnson 2012b). The large majority who stay behind are making their voices heard. While in cases of corruption people may think 'I would have done the same' (Wang X. 2011), the public's reaction to the scandals involving contaminated food, drinking water and hazardous substances has been less understanding. Large-scale environmental protests have been taking place in China's big cities in recent years, fuelled by anxieties and safety concerns of urban residents.

At this point we revisit Ci Jiwei, who called the rise of political liberalism in the 1980s which culminated in the 1989 democracy movement a 'sublimation of hedonism', under circumstances of prolonged frustration (Ci 1994: 8). At the time, liberalism captured the imagination of a society thoroughly disillusioned with utopianism but without enough opportunities for escaping into hedonism. Twenty years later, people have had plenty of opportunities to escape into hedonism, but this has not made them immune to the unfair distribution of the goods of hedonism caused by official corruption and the continuing existence of old power structures. Thirty years of reform have not only created more wealth, but have also led to a harrowing catalogue of environmental problems and other, often man-made disasters as outlined in Chapter 2, whose root cause is increasingly seen to lie with institutional structures and those in power. During the Mao years vague feelings of unhappiness over these power structures were prevented from becoming fully conscious and the potential for widespread social discontent was kept in check largely by a stringent morality in which collectivism demanded the subordination of the individual to society and altruism called for the sacrifice of the self for the sake of others (Ci 1994: 78). These moral parameters no longer bind Chinese individuals in the same way, but the declining influence of collective values does not mean that collective action has disappeared, as the myriads of incidents of collective protest testify. These protests are not just about protecting individual interests (which in the case of environmental protests are often also collective interests), but also about an increasing awareness, especially among the young, of global values and that China must engage these values.

Apart from the participation in protest action during acute crisis points, individuals also start to challenge and resist an ethos they find wanting (something that is 'not right') by taking a calculated risk. This risk may be easier to take when supported by a strong moral conviction like faith. A young, recently converted Catholic music student in Chengdu told me that his faith was primarily expressed on Sundays during mass, but did otherwise not really influence the way he acted during the week. However, he did say that since his conversion he had become even more resentful than before of the indoctrination that takes place on campus. Students have to take political classes in order to be able to graduate, but his personal act of defiance is no longer to attend the collective singing sessions of revolutionary songs, which form part of the 'political education'. (The fact that the school authorities reduced his yearly financial support from 3,000 yuan to 1,000 yuan after learning about his conversion to Catholicism will not have increased his enthusiasm for singing odes to the party.) So it is, to begin with, less a form of political criticism than an experience of moral resistance; while conversion itself may not take place as a conscious political act, the new identity informs a new self-awareness and confidence when dealing with the world around oneself.

Where individuals feel vulnerable, they tend to seek protection from social institutions. However, due to a lack of social trust, an underdeveloped rule of law, a lack of transparency and controlled media, social institutions in China cannot fulfil this function. Indeed they are often the main objects of distrust. In this sense the moral crisis in China is also a political crisis, as political changes are necessary in order to put in place preconditions for social trust and functioning institutions. The big question remains as to what moral system should function as the basis for moral and institutional reconstruction. As was shown above, there exists a correlation between professional vulnerability and heightened political awareness and dissatisfaction among lawyers. We can argue that the more dissatisfaction and frustration, and the more vulnerable China's white-collar middle-class individuals feel in interaction with state actors and in the face of a privileged 'black-collar' class, the more likely it becomes that their already higher than average political participation may become 'radicalized'. It is also likely that they, too, will be receptive (as they already are, seen in the fastest growth of Christianity in this particular demographic in the last decade) to the comprehensive evangelizing endeavours of urban churches, the political gospel of transcendental values, and the appeals to their 'conscience' that promise to restore morality and social justice. More immediately, churches can offer a spiritual haven and comfort from life's injustice and vicissitudes.

Democracy movement activists

Liu Xiaobo is a veteran of the 1989 democracy movement and while he himself is not a Christian he is considered to be the Chinese political dissident with the closest affinity to Christian thinking. Since Liu's arrest and since Yu Jie's move into exile, the latter has written a book about Liu Xiaobo as part of a campaign to disseminate Liu's thinking more widely. This creates a sense that Liu is claimed by Christian liberals in a similar way as Yang Xiaokai has been claimed. Support for Liu is now starting to be voiced more widely (and is certainly not confined to Christian liberals), including most recently by Wang Dan and Wuer Kaixi, both, like Liu, veterans of 1989. As has been shown in previous chapters, several democracy activists, who escaped China after 1989, have converted to Christianity and now play an active and highly influential role in evangelical work in China as well as religious rights advocacy. They are often those, who are most outspoken and most uncompromising in their criticism of the Chinese government. Their contributions are not always constructive and often dismissed as irrelevant by those, who operate within China and who adopt a much more cooperative and conciliatory stance with a view to achieving gradual change.

But 1989 is also an important date for many of the people I interviewed for this study, especially those over 40. They identify the crackdown on the students as a key moment in their lives, when their youthful idealism – at that time often still associated with the party – was shattered and they turned to look for something else. While they have found a new idealism in the form of their faith, they have retained their disillusionment with the party and what it stands for. As such, 1989 still resonates in the minds of ordinary people including Christians and continues to feed a sense of injustice and distrust of the authorities in this generation.

The importance of 'conscience'

Feng Chongyi's analysis of liberalism in China today distinguishes between six different categories: liberal intellectuals, Christian liberals, human rights lawyers, liberals within the CCP, grassroots rights activists and democracy movement activists. As was shown in this chapter, there exists a great overlap between these six categories. Core principles of Christian liberalism, which can be summarized as the emphasis on a transcendental source of democratic and societal values, the notion of 'conscience', and the emphasis on the constitution are starting to have an impact on all of them. At the same time, the disillusionment created by corruption and the effects of distribution of wealth linked to existing power structures mean that a wide sector of society is starting to develop a strong sense of justice and is looking for a belief system (in the widest sense) that can form the basis of an improved moral political order. This usually starts when people feel personally negatively affected by the existing system, regardless of whether or what kind of religious beliefs they hold. A young Christian IT specialist who recently graduated from CASS, was quite understanding of the government's need to control and crack down on religious groups, including Christian groups, who don't have the 'correct belief', as he called it. There was little awareness of rights that may extend to all believers, or the problematic of who decides what constitutes 'correct' belief. However, he held very strong views about the injustice of the housing market in urban China, saying that the combined effect of government control, developers' greed and bank charges mean it has become impossible for people like him to 'get on the property ladder' as one would say in the United Kingdom. He clearly had very strong feelings of injustice in this regard, calling the situation 'not right' (*bu dui*) several times. In this context he referred to the Bible and the notions of economic equality expressed therein. He also expressed hope that 'somebody would sit down and analyse the Bible' in order to derive a set of basic principles from which a more just legal system could be built. Hence the formulation of a political theology by Wang Yi, as spurious as it may seem to the outside observer (where outsider refers to anyone outside the evangelical Christian mindset, whether inside or outside China), may mature over time and develop into something that will find a wider consensus among liberals and other politically engaged elites as well as a ready audience among ostensibly less politically engaged individuals. Already there are voices within the party and in the wider 'middle class' that support and promote Christian values.

Although notions of the 'covenant' are firmly rooted within Christian thinking, the concept resonates with Chinese cultural concepts like '*dao*' or '*tian*' as a code of belief centred on a source of morality outside the human realm. One can also find notions similar to the Christian notion of 'conscience' in Chinese rural moral discourse. Ellen Oxfeld (2010) speaks of the importance of *liangxin* in the village where she conducted field work. She renders *liangxin* (one of the two Chinese words translated as 'conscience' in English; the other is *liangzhi*[11]) as 'virtuous mind/heart', defining it as a quality of those individuals, who remember their moral obligations and act upon them. A person lacks *liangxin*, if he or she violates their moral obligations, even if they are troubled by this later. Therefore, for Oxfeld, *liangxin* is different from the English 'conscience' as it not only implies an inner voice, but also the actions it should prompt (Oxfeld 2010: 53). Oxfeld here makes the error of reducing the English 'conscience' to the meaning of a 'troubled conscience', a rather narrow and restricted understanding of it. Certainly the Judeo-Christian understanding of 'conscience' includes the importance of corresponding acts. The main difference as I can make out based on Oxfeld's study is that whether one's action in the village were considered to be *liangxin* depended on relative moral obligations of one individual towards another based on a shared history whereas the Christian 'conscience' is guided by absolute moral guidelines known to all (who share the faith). As Oxfeld says 'In Moonshadow Pond commonly quoted aphorisms make reference to the connection between memory and morality. For instance "when you drink water, remember the source" refers to the necessity of remembering who is responsible for assistance you may have received' (Oxfeld 2010: 56). For Christians the ultimate source is always God; one's moral obligations are not towards another human being but one's actions need to pass muster in the eyes of a higher force. In the absence of a shared history and closely knit moral community, shared moral frameworks which lay out what is 'right' and what is 'wrong' become of growing importance for China's increasingly urbanized society, where social relations need to be built among strangers; Christianity is a strong contender for providing such a moral framework. In a political sense, the notion of conscience expressed as *liangxin* or *liangzhi* in Chinese, resonates with Chinese cultural sensibilities, but has gained significance in guiding one's actions in the context of resistance against what is seen as 'not right'.

Conclusion

Chinese Christian liberals like Fan Yafeng argue that at the grassroots 'house churches' as the largest group within China's popular organizations, together with liberal theories and the internet, have been the most prominent and most successful political force in China in recent years (Fan Y. 2009: 10). But it is very difficult to argue, that this applies to all churches or that a political consensus has emerged among churches. The fault lines seem to run along historical, organizational and denominational identities. The radical, political model associated with a drive for political change seems to be mostly at home in Beijing. Further south there appears to be more focus on the continued growth of churches and the importance of evangelism, although this will also depend on the individual. At the occasion of the National Prayer Breakfast in Washington in February 2011, Chinese delegates, who included Bob Fu from China Aid Association, blasted the Obama administration for its lack of support for religious freedom in China. Zhang Leguo, a representative of a Zhejiang church, stated that 'house church Christians prayed for the re-election of President Bush' while 'the Chinese government sanctioned church was praying for John Kerry' (Birnbaum 2011). Considering that neither were running in the 2012 election, this would indeed have required a miracle, but the statement shows the polarizing nature of the discourse emanating from certain Christian church circles, which alienate the majority of Chinese Christians, whether they attend 'three-self' churches or other congregations.

There may be a different link between faith and political activism. Churches and *weiquan* lawyering offer an opportunity and outlet for politically engaged and ambitious individuals. A young Chinese Christian accountant in London, who remains in close touch with her church in Beijing, told me that the *weiquan* lawyer, who recently represented an imprisoned pastor in Xinjiang, has now changed over to Shouwang Church, 'because our church was too boring for him'. What she meant by this was that the politicized nature of the Shouwang church better suited his disposition and his interests. Christianity may provide a value system and a transcendental basis for the establishment of civil society and a sound legal system, but one also has to consider that Christianity and its associational manifestation offer an opportunity for ambitious people to act politically. Churches, especially small congregations, offer the opportunity to discuss current social affairs in the context of the Bible, but they also offer a chance for leadership personalities to come to the fore and inspire others to make a difference. Christian churches are certainly easier to join than the party, which remains the only formal political organization open to Chinese citizens; and if the doctrinal direction of one particular church does not suit the individual, they can join another, or even found their own.

Restriction, harassment and continuing crackdowns by the government lead to a radicalization of the rights defence movement, which alienates many within the churches, who prefer a more moderate approach. But it also does not reflect well on the government and lacks a wider popular support basis. Even those, who disagree with the politics of the Charter 08, find it increasingly difficult not to admire the personal integrity, if not the politics, of individuals like Liu Xiaobo, who have paid a very high price for listening to their conscience. In their daily lives, people are acutely aware of things that are 'not right' or which they simply cannot abide on the basis of their own convictions. The spontaneous support by ordinary citizens of the staff at *Nanfang Zhoumo*, who went on strike in protest against interference with its editorial policy, is one of the most recent examples. (Yu Jie, on the other hand, has declared that he had 'no sympathy' for the staff of *Nanzhou*, who he considers to be part of the 'save the party' school.[12]) It is perfectly possible to see this particular aspect of the Charter 08 movement – the emphasis on an individual's conscience – become the baseline for a wider consensus and resistance where people respond to their conscience rather than to state ideology, whether they are Christians or not.

Notes

1   A full translation of Charter 08 by Perry Link can be found at http://en.rsf.org/IMG/pdf/Charter08-2.pdf (last accessed 10 October 2012).
2   By 'Christian liberals' this chapter (and Feng Chongyi's article) means political liberals of a declared Christian faith. They are to be distinguished from 'liberal Christians' or liberal Christianity, which is a term that refers to Christians adhering to a liberal theology, something China's 'Christian liberals' decidedly do not.
3   His 'memoir' of this time is published as Yang Xiguang, *Niugui sheshen lu. Wenge qiujinzhong de jingling* (Hong Kong, Oxford University Press 1994). The English edition is Yang Xiguang and Suzanne McFadden, *Captive Spirits. Prisoners of the Cultural Revolution* (Oxford University Press 1997).
4   Yang Xiaokai de jianzheng (Yang Xiaokai's testimony) www.aiyan.org/2005/05-3/15.html Accessed 15 October 2012 – the article must have been reprinted from an earlier source, as it appeared a year after Yang's death, which was only mentioned in issue 10 of *Aiyan* (page no longer available).
5   Harry Wu was born in Shanghai in 1937 and sentenced to 23 years in labour camps in 1960 as a 'counterrevolutionary rightist'. He was released in 1979 and after having worked in a Chinese university for a few years was able to leave for the United States

150 *Politics and the transcendental*

where he eventually dedicated his life to the study of the Chinese 'reform through labour' (*laogai*) system. He published a number of books on this subject and in 2002 founded the 'Laogai Research Foundation' (www.laogai.org). Zhang Dajun is the director of Transition Institute, a Beijing based think tank devoted to education about democracy and one of the 'people from the house churches' involved in discussion with Yu Jianrong in his 2008 article. Zhang is also a writer for Chinese Independent Pen and has translated John van Til's 1972 book *Liberty of Conscience, The History of a Puritan Idea* into Chinese (Fan T. and Zhang D. 2011).

6 The 'Mayflower Compact' was signed by 42 of the passengers of *The Mayflower* in 1620 and is considered to be the foundation of the US Constitution.
7 Author interviews with Wang Yi in Chengdu and He Guanghu in Beijing, all November 2012.
8 Author interview with He Guanghu, Beijing, November 2012.
9 www.aiyan.org/2005/06-15/20.html (last accessed 19 October 2012).
10 The Economist, The World in 2013, December 2012.
11 Zha Changping, a scholar of Chinese philology, said there was 'no difference' between the two words *liangxin* and *liangzhi*; both denoted 'conscience'. In his view *liangxin* displayed slightly more Chinese cultural sensibilities, whereas *liangzhi* was a more Western term. But the term *liangxin* is also used in translations of Western works, for example John von Tils' *Liberty of Conscience* which has been translated as *Liangxin de ziyou* (Zhang D. 2011).
12 Yu Jie on Twitter https://twitter.com/yujie89/status/289934964940754945 11 January 2013.

8 Christian values in Communist China

A conclusion

Two days before Christmas, in 2010, ten renowned Confucian scholars published an open letter addressed to different levels of government and 'all followers of Jesus's teachings (*yejiaotu*) who love Chinese culture' to protest in no uncertain terms against the construction of a new church in Qufu three kilometres away from the 'holy sites' of Confucianism. The surprisingly aggressive letter claims that a church building so near to the Confucian temple was an affront to Chinese culture, that no other religion in China's history had ever so blatantly disregarded the centrality of Confucianism in Chinese culture, and that its presence would lead to religious strife and conflict. The letter stresses the point that Christianity is a foreign religion, and that the attempt to build a church in Qufu was a manifestation of the conflict between Chinese and Western culture. At the same time, the letter also referred to Confucianism as a religion, comparing Qufu to Mecca, and Jerusalem and Vatican City. Conceding that the construction of the church was entirely legal and had obtained all necessary permits and finance, it nonetheless made the following demands: that the construction of the church be stopped immediately; that if there had to be a church in Qufu, that it be built outside a 50 Chinese mile (*li*) radius of the Confucian 'holy sites'; that it should not allowed to be built to the planned height of 41 metres , nor to the planned capacity of more than 3,000 so as not to create the impression that Christianity was more important than Confucianism. The letter concluded by calling on the central government to afford Confucianism the same status as other officially recognized religions and to stop the exploitation of religious sites like Qufu for commercial and tourist purposes so that the spiritual function of these sites could be reinstated (Rujia zhi xuezhe 2010).

The letter, signed among others by the scholar Kang Xiaoguang[1] (known for his calls to make Confucianism a state religion), was successful; the construction was indeed stopped and moved an (even more) considerable distance away. The letter also prompted a delayed response from a number of Christian intellectuals following the Fifth Chinese Theological Forum held in Massachusetts in September 2012. Their letter – drafted and signed by He Guanghu and Yuan Zhiming among others – aims to clarify two major misunderstandings that underpinned the Confucians' demand to halt the building of the church: namely that Christianity was equal to Western culture, and that Confucianism was a religion.

'A rich and dialectic relationship'

The document systematically explains that Christianity, rather than being synonymous with Western culture was a global religion, which had originated in the East. It had indeed profoundly influenced Western culture, but Greek and Roman non-Christian humanistic traditions and contemporary scientific and humanistic non-religious factors were of equal significance in an extremely pluralistic Western culture, which had left the Christian faith behind in many aspects. The authors of the document stressed the point that Christianity did not belong to one people or one culture, but that it was a global religion that had influenced many cultures. Chinese culture, one of the richest, most complex and most diverse in the world, rather than being static, had been shaped in dialogue, competition and complementary, peaceful co-existence with other religions over many centuries.

For the authors Christianity and Chinese culture are engaged in a 'rich and dialectic relationship' that is a relationship between a global, enlightened faith and a complex and diverse national culture. Chinese Christians adopted different attitudes towards different elements of Chinese culture in this dialogue. Towards the classical philosophers, Christians were rational and respectful so that present generations could draw benefit from them. To traditional religions Christians extended friendship and dialogue in order to enable co-existence. And Christians discriminated carefully among modern social trends to choose those that were conducive to moral elevation. Christians treated Chinese culture in the spirit that all was God's creation and lived God's teaching to 'love the other like yourself'. Christians were dedicated to self-improvement, to living together peacefully and to doing good deeds to benefit all (He, Wang *et al.* 2012).

The Confucians' letter shows, if further proof was needed, quite how significant religion and the spiritual have become in contemporary Chinese society. Rather than negate the importance of religion in Chinese cultural identity, the signatories call for the opposite: for the elevation of Confucianism to the status of a religion equal to Daoism, Buddhism, Islam and 'Jesus's teachings' and for this to be officially recognized. Quite apart from the obvious hostility against Christianity, expressed by refusing to refer to it by the commonly used term and the repeated insistence on its foreign character, the letter also puts a question mark over the generally accepted notion that all Confucians are non-challenging supporters of the state. It puts into perspective the notion that the Chinese party-state can rely on Confucians to provide the necessary secular ideological framework to dress up its continuing Marxist ideology with Chinese characteristics. As referred to in Chapter 2, the fierce intellectual debates among different Confucians soon turned out to be a can of worms the party leadership would rather have left unopened and swiftly withdrew from, only picking key terms to invest with new meaning, much in the same way as has been done with core Christian terms like 'love'.

The open letter also shows that core issues surrounding the place of different cultures and religions, as well as the role of religion in China, continue to be debated as fiercely as they were a hundred years ago. The concept of religion and its importance in national identity formation emerged during the debates on China's national salvation at the start of the twentieth century The proposal to make Confucianism China's state religion was first made by Kang Youwei; to introduce a Confucian calendar (which is used by the signatories of the open letter) was first suggested by Liang Qichao in an essay on New Historiography as one of many remedies to strengthen China and rebuild its national confidence. A hundred years later, China's political and economic strength are unquestioned, but its Confucian identity – and the confidence of those promoting it – is less certain. The signatories see this church construction as a sign of Chinese cultural degradation. The demands of the letter seem to be evidence of an almost comically Freudian inferiority complex, where the significance of Confucianism fears being dwarfed by the sheer height of the new church tower. The solution is to ban it, if not entirely out of sight then into a significant distance, so that at least visually nobody would be able to conclude that Christianity was bigger than Confucianism. The exchange thus neatly symbolizes how important Christianity has become and as how threatening some perceive it; it also shows how carefully and confidently Chinese Christians want to respond to such challenges.

What social and political impact?

The question posed at the outset of this study was whether and, if so, what social and political impact Christianity has had in contemporary China. Are Chinese Christians a new moral vanguard? And if so, does this moral vanguard constitute a challenge or a pillar of support for the Chinese leadership? Will Chinese Christians usher in political change or would they even welcome it? Is there a significant link between political liberalism and Christian values, ideas and faith in China today? The different chapters of this book have approached these questions from different angles.

Chapter 2 analysed contemporary Chinese Christianity through the lens of morality and values, generally considered to be lacking in today's China and manifested in the huge scale of corruption, scandal, malpractice, environmental degradation and all time low levels of social trust. It based its analysis on Ci Jiwei's (1994) philosophical understanding of China's history from the 1950s to the late 1980s as a move from utopianism (under Mao) to hedonism (under Deng). For Ci, calls for political liberalism as voiced in the late 1980s were a sublimation of hedonism by people, who had not had enough opportunities to indulge in hedonism. Chapter 2 argued that in recognition of society's increasing diversity and plurality the party-state has since been developing the 'harmonious society' as a new utopia which hopes to accommodate this new plurality, including religious plurality.

While the party developed this new ideological framework, however, many Chinese, including uncompromising, highly intellectual individuals, who never were placated by hedonism, found a new utopia in Christianity, which provides an all-encompassing new moral code based on a code of belief that in turn determines a code of behaviour. This has created a new Christian elite inside and outside China, who, albeit relatively small in number, is developing into a serious moral voice and able to draw on an impressive network and connections both in evangelical circles abroad and within influential circles inside China, including the party. Their voices – expressed in prolific writings published in a variety of publications, including letters to their own congregations, which are circulated more widely – are also gaining credibility among a wider Christian population, who in their daily lives is caught in the moral dilemma of abiding by the moral principles of their faith and living in interaction with wider society, which does not share the same moral standards. They were presented as examples of what Kleinman *et al.* (2011b) have called the 'divided self'; individuals who are divided between their individual moral standards and society's expectations. How they negotiate this conflict depends on the individual's strength of faith. In this particular conflict, the moral voices of Christian leaders, who are heard beyond the immediate circles of their own congregations, are gaining increasing importance as a source of support. Christian faith has also become an important factor in judging the moral distance and trust extended towards strangers. This is of particular importance among fellow Christians, who instinctively trust each other more than they trust non-Christian strangers. But the societal expectations of Christians' moral goodness has also led to the paradox that non-Christian Chinese are more likely to trust a Christian than a fellow non-Christian.

From an ideological perspective, this sector of society with its strict moral standards also presents a dilemma for the party-state. On the one hand, Christians present a new 'moral vanguard' and are potentially new model citizens, combining a hard work ethic with high social and business ethics and an altruistic concern for others. On the other hand, the source of their values lies with a higher morality than the party-state, and while the majority of Christians are non-confrontational law-abiding citizens happy to contribute to a better Chinese society as idealistically imagined in the 'harmonious society', all Christians will have their own individual 'bottom-line' which determines the point at which no compromise between their own principles and those of their surroundings is possible. Contributing to a better society also does not necessarily demand support of the party-state in the understanding of individuals with strong moral principles, Christian or not. Indeed it often seems to dictate the exact opposite. Herein lies the problem for the party, which has tried to square the circle by signalling that the values of the 'harmonious society' and the values of Christians are compatible and complementary, and that their contributions to society are welcome.

This attitude is expressed most obviously in the context of love, both as key term and core value of the new ideological drive and as harnessed emotion to provide the cohesive lynchpin in romantic relationships between Christians and non-Christians, and, by extension, between Christians and the party. Chapter 3 presented the argument that the emphasis on 'love' in the official socialist discourse was a conscious effort on part of the ideologues to use existing popular concepts and invest them with new meaning. In ideological terms, love is solidarity in an emotional reincarnation. In linguistic terms this is expressed through the new, monosyllabic use of *ai*. While there are several words in Chinese cultural traditions that can be rendered as 'love' in English – most notably *bo'ai* of Confucianism or *jian'ai* of Mohism – the monosyllabic use of *ai* to express love has been an exclusive and key feature of Chinese Christian theology as developed by Bishop Ding Guangxun. Considering the political influence Ding enjoyed as president of the National Chinese People's Political Consultative Conference, the excellent connections of certain Christian individuals within the party and the wide acceptance of the term and value of 'love' in the wider population, it is reasonable to assume that the use of *ai* in the official discourse was at least partly 'inspired' by Chinese Christian values. There are signs that Christians recognize these attempts for what they are, and harbour little enthusiasm for them.

On an individual level where romantic relationships between Christians and non-Christians are concerned, the value of love gains new significance. Gendered expectations regarding emotions and spirituality together with the complementarian view of gender relations prevalent in Chinese churches mean that it is often Christian women who do the loving while their non-Christian husbands continue to conform to generally held expectations of male professionals and business people, with possible minor adjustments. The main purpose that Christian love here, then, fulfils is improved marital relationships, an effect that the party-state is hoping to emulate on a larger scale between an emotional and spiritual Christian population and a rational, business-like party-state.

The area in which Christian ethics and values are potentially most pertinent and most practical is charity work. It is in this context where Christians are called on most explicitly to make contributions to society. The two case studies presented in Chapter 4, Nanjing's Amity Foundation and Beijing Huiling, gave insights into the complex realities in which charitable organizations operate. This operational context together with the legal realities means that Christian social service is expected to be channelled through non-religious organizations like Amity. This meets resistance among Christians for two main reasons, both grounded in theology. The first reason is the association of the 'social gospel', that is the involvement in social work as Christian calling, with official theology, which is widely discredited. Calls upon Christians to act out their faith through involvement in social work are seen as a way to reduce Christian faith to a set of ethics, which can be enlisted for the purposes of the party-state, an accusation often levelled against TSPM leadership and its theology. For many Chinese Christians focus on the spiritual and personal salvation is of greater immediate concern than charitable behaviour that is unlikely to lead to more converts.

Christians like the 'New-Calvinists', on the other hand, who do consider social engagement a key factor of their religious existence, are unlikely to work with non-religious organizations like Amity, preferring to organize their own, small-scale projects instead. For these congregations, charitable behaviour becomes one aspect of the collective identity of the congregation, however small scale the operations. Involvement in them not only helps the recipients of the charity, but also helps to reinforce the Christian identity of those engaged in the act. As Anthony Tong of Amity Hong Kong put it in response to the question where Christianity came in (as far as Amity is concerned), his instinctive answer was that it only mattered on the individual level in as much as it reinforced the faith of the individual Christian. For the time being, Christians can only get involved in charitable work at an individual level or through 'illegal' collective activity of their congregations. In the absence of laws on either religion or charity, religious organizations are in fact unable to set up charitable projects.

The diversity of Christian voices and worldviews find representation in diverse Christian publications online. Chapter 5 introduced some of the most professionally produced and best known publications, which form part of the 'internet mission', a project of particular relevance in the ties that have formed between China and North America. Different publications target different audiences which results in content of a different nature. To a certain degree the publications also reflect the different geographical areas from which they originate. At the same time, the influence of prolific male networks around key 'pastor-intellectuals' from overseas on all the publications is hard to ignore. The various names that recur in the journals suggest that there is a fair degree of communication between them and Christian intellectuals in China, including an earlier generation of 'Cultural Christians' and Christians within or close to the party, although the practice of liberally reprinting other peoples' articles in different media without necessarily asking for the authors' permission may contribute to this impression. Judging from the experience of earlier journals and the general direction of those still operational, there has been a shift away from a more political agenda (which is now primarily published, though not necessarily written, outside China) to a focus on theological and spiritual matters including church building, theological training and intellectual nourishment of a Christian readership. What we learn from these publications is that the Christian readership is diverse, confident, and largely non-political.

The role of 'pastor-intellectuals' and their written output was further examined in Chapter 6, which proposed the hypothesis of a bridge-function Chinese Christian intellectuals can fulfil in a period of political transition. This bridge function referred to social relations, a bridge between political theory and political action, and between China and the world. The chapter went on to test this hypothesis against data gained from interviews, anthropological studies of Chinese Christianity and analysis of Christian publications. While historical evidence and theoretical links between Christian belief and democratic political behaviour suggest that there are sufficient grounds to assume that such a hypothesis is justified, the reality that emerges in the concrete Chinese context is rather more complex. Although Christian belief has the potential to be a great equalizer, it is quite clear that cultural concepts like *suzhi* play an important role in determining social relationships among Christians. Urban, rational, theologically educated Christians claim a higher standing in the hierarchy of *suzhi* and discriminate against Christians who are rural, spiritual and theologically less well trained. Conversely, Christian faith becomes a marker of urban sophistication and superior moral and educational standing and thus something to aspire to. Intellectuals play an important role in education – in 'raising the *suzhi* of the Christian population' – and as such do not really break new ground in Chinese intellectual history. Still, there is uniform agreement among Christian intellectuals that it is their duty as Christians to bring their belief into society at large and to do what they can to spread Christian values and the gospel. How political and indeed how public this engagement becomes largely depends on the individual's profession. It has been shown that the role of Christian lawyers is of particular significance in this regard. And while Christian values are considered to be global values, for the 'pastor-intellectuals' involved in the Chinese mission the world outside China consists primarily of North America.

Chapter 7 looked more closely at the influence Chinese Christian liberal thinking has had on the different categories of Chinese liberals as identified by Feng Chongyi (2010). The importance of a 'transcendental source of values' outside the human realm and the innate knowledge of what is 'right' and 'wrong' on the basis of such transcendental values, commonly referred to as 'conscience' (*liangzhi*), are the main aspects which are core to Christian liberal thinking but are starting to be used outside Christian circles. Both concepts are not alien to Chinese cultural traditions; they resonate with concepts like '*dao*' and '*tian*' and notions of '*liangxin*' as used in contemporary rural China (Oxfeld 2010). They will gain in importance both at the grassroots and at the level of ideology as individuals rely on available and credible moral frameworks to articulate their grievances and bring meaning into their increasingly insecure world.

But the government in the form of the party-state, which on an ideological level continues to be guided by notions of fairness, (more) equal distribution and enabling a basic livelihood (*minsheng*) is equally keen to propose a new moral framework which binds individuals, including its own party members, into ethical behaviour. There is great potential here for the development of something new; the series of open letters and petitions that have emerged in the months since the eighteenth party congress in November 2012 are a sign that core issues championed by Christian lawyers since the start of the millennium and contained in Charter 08, like the proper implementation of China's constitution, have now become widely accepted. Much depends on how the party decides to respond to these voices. The first major policy declaration by the Xi Jinping administration started with the words belief and faith. 'Belief, faith, confidence and real action are the guarantee for the success of our undertakings' (*Xinyang, xinnian, xinxin yu shigan shi women shiye chenggong de baozheng;* 'Eight Musts' 2013). The 'Eight Honours and Eight Shames' (*barong baru*) of the Hu-Wen administration have been replaced by the 'Eight Musts' (*bage bixu*) as guidelines for the party and its cadres, which put more emphasis on social fairness, justice and common prosperity than the more abstract tenets of the 'harmonious society'. This may reflect a realization on the part of the new administration that in the growing plurality of public voices the party will need to re-establish its own political platform, which lays out what it stands for rather than what it is against (corruption, chaos, wholesale westernization). In addition to a credible political programme, the party will also need to find a more confident way of dealing with voices of protest and dissent. The sacrifices individuals like Liu Xiaobo or Gao Zhisheng have been forced to make are respected by many, who do not necessarily agree with their politics or share their faith (in the case of Gao), and contribute to the mistrust of the party-state and its organs.

An additional strong voice

The main role Chinese Christians play in China's social and political transformation is that of an additional significant voice to what is already a much more diverse and pluralistic society. While comparatively small in number, Chinese Christians have gained a reputation as a result of their principled behaviour and what are considered to be superior moral standards. The stronger an individual's faith, the more difficult it is to compartmentalize and display one set of behaviour in daily life and another during Sunday worship. Even when keeping a low profile, Chinese Christians are recognizable for their behaviour, often through what they no longer take part in as a result of their faith and resulting code of ethics. Strength of conviction is an important factor in bringing about change. For each and every individual this change may be small: the refusal to join the compulsory singing sessions; the refusal to take financial hand-outs when the source of the funds is dubious; the refusal to engage in business practices and banquets involving sexual encounters.

Belonging to a church community provides the moral support necessary to act upon one's convictions during the week. It also offers opportunities to organize and carry out collective activities, which require negotiation, compromise and democratic decision making processes. For highly able, idealistic and ambitious individuals, churches also provide a chance to lead and to promote new ideas and ideals and to potentially influence current thinking beyond the immediate circle of their own congregations. This last function is of particular significance for a generation of church leaders and 'pastor-intellectuals', in whom the events of 1989 led to a profound disillusionment with the formerly held belief in socialist ideals and the party and to a reorientation towards Christianity. It is this generation that is best connected and most influential and most determined to contribute to China's change.

It is always important to bear in mind that Chinese Christianity is diverse and that much of what cosmopolitan intellectuals are saying will be irrelevant to local Christian experience in Chinese rural areas. However, considering China's increasing urbanization, which now stands at 52 per cent and is predicted to reach 70 per cent by 2035, together with the fact that growth of Christianity is now biggest in China's cities, the current trends and developments in urban Christianity are important predictors. More and more Christians will join the ranks of Yan Yunxiang's 'unbound individuals', who as part of their newly urban existence, will find themselves interacting with strangers rather than being part of a village community that may have shared a broad understanding of moral duties and obligations. The relative psychological security of belonging to a new type of community (through church) together with the aspirational level of *suzhi* associated with urban Christianity may prove to be a potent combination.

But within urban Christians, too, there are differences in theological orientation, which put varying emphasis on the individual's engagement with society as a Christian. They also have different ways of expressing faith and spirituality. Practices usually associated with rural Christianity which focus on the healing quality of the gospel and bodily experience of Christ can also be found in urban churches where these experiences may be articulated in more 'scientific' or intellectual terms without changing their basic nature. It will be interesting to see whether the increasing urbanization of Chinese Christianity will result in a general 'rationalization' and 'intellectualization' of the faith led by 'New-Calvinist' theology. It may be more likely that it will lead to an increasing diversification of urban Christianity, which will display the full spectrum from 'spiritual' to 'rational' that we currently associate with rural and urban Christianity respectively.

When speaking of the impact Christians may have on China's social and political transformation it is important to point out that those voices, who are most articulate, who have the best connections and the strongest public voice, are very conservative voices indeed. Their actions are guided by a worldview that promotes complementarian gender roles and considers homosexuality a sin. They display little tolerance for those they consider to hold an 'incorrect' Christian belief, only modest interest or tolerance for believers of different faiths and remarkably little sympathy (certainly not one that is expressed publicly) for the plight of Tibetan Buddhists even in publications overseas.

In the following I will lay out a number of issues that have emerged from the previous pages, which in my view warrant further study.

Male rationality vs. female spirituality

As a woman, it strikes me that patriarchy and traditional gender roles and expectations are replicated and reinforced in the contemporary churches to a considerable degree. This is most obvious where church leadership, theological direction and the mission are concerned. One rarely finds female leadership figures in the contemporary Chinese churches, and one is more likely to find them within the TSPM churches. The most prominent voices in the debates on Christianity, whether it was Cultural Christians or the younger generation of Protestant intellectuals and church leaders, whether in China or abroad, are predominantly male. As pointed out in Chapter 5, it appears that traditional gender roles and notions of male intellectual prowess conspire to result in a reality where current agenda and future direction of the churches are determined by highly educated, middle-aged men whose leadership many educated women unquestioningly accept.

Male Christian entrepreneurs may shun the Chinese business practices of banquets and karaoke that involve hostesses and girlfriends, but they seem to have replaced it with a different practice that shows their rationality and cultural superiority by organizing exclusive lectures on business and theology that are difficult to get into and are mostly attended by men. At such events women, while not sexualized in the same way as in the business banquets, still play the role of 'hostess' in the more literal sense of being receptionists, who need to be 'tall and pretty with a sweet voice' (Cao N. 2011, Chapter 5). The 'obvious' answer to the gender imbalance in churches (which as congregations are predominantly female) is to focus evangelizing efforts on educated men (the demographic with the lowest representation in churches) in order to even out the gender spread rather than concentrate on the leadership training of women so as to reflect the gender makeup of the churches in their leadership (Lu K. 2010).

Generally speaking people find the Christian faith because they are looking for something; this may be an answer to a big philosophical question (what is the meaning of life?) or problem (how can China's problems be solved?). But in the majority of cases, it is the small, daily physical and psychological aches and pains to which faith may be able to provide an answer. The predominance of women in China's churches is a sign that often it is women, who look for something to help them deal with the daily pressures and troubles of marriage and home life. Even though both partners may be equally well educated, it is the men, who have better careers, are often party members, and who practise a life style that creates tension and friction at home. In their professional and business dealings they will often encounter men, who have second or third 'wives' in different cities, an environment their wives find difficult to accept, yet if they are too assertive in their condemnation of these practices, their marriages will suffer. It is such psychological dilemmas and conflicts which bring people (but mostly women) to churches, where they find solace in the preaching that you should love those who are not lovable, that all humans are sinners and that therefore everybody needed theirs and God's love.

In post-Mao love stories (Louie 1989) we find idealized men of superior moral quality who are loved by women. In these stories it is the men's role to be impressive and the women's role to love and look up to them. In the non-fictional relationships today, men are no longer the idealized lover and may have lost their superior moral standing, but it seems that women are still called to do the loving and understanding, which, in the complementarian view of gender relations prevalent in most Chinese churches, including TSPM churches, often means a quiet deferral to the men's leadership and wishes and the helping role of the woman. Therefore one could argue that the churches actually perpetuate patriarchy, although they undeniably contribute to the women's individual well-being and happiness, where this view of gender roles is willingly embraced. In many cases (as the predominantly female congregations would imply) it is only one spouse, the wife, who is part of the church, or at least first finds the church, often encouraged by their husbands. Of course faith also gives rise to the hope that husbands may change their ways, ideally through conversion to the Christian faith themselves.

The fact that more women attend church than men may also be to do with gender expectations regarding the expression of emotions. In Chinese culture, spirituality is often expressed through crying (Lee 2007); consequently, the more emotional an individual's expression in church, the more receptive they are seen to God's spirituality. Women are seen to have the ability to build remarkably intimate relationships with God, using language and bodily experiences, important features of the more 'Pentecostal' congregations in rural areas where female leadership is more common, including those groups, which are most fiercely opposed and branded as sects. But tears as an expression of spirituality are also a common feature in urban Christians. For many men, however, expressive self-disclosure and emotions in public ritual is a sign of immaturity and lack of self-control, and therefore damaging to masculine identity (Cao N. 2011: 113). Deep devotion in men, especially educated men, is therefore more likely to find an expression in advanced theological study resulting in theology being a male dominated Christian space and a 'rational' church leadership that is based more on words than on feelings.

Small gatherings

The Chinese term for 'small group' is *xiaozu*, which is different from a congregation (*juhui*) or a church (*jiaohui*). *Xiaozu* are usually no more than a dozen people and focus on the study of the Bible or discuss particular social or psychological matters. They serve a particular function in the process of evangelizing and in keeping converts on board and feeling related to the church. They are often the first way a person is introduced to Christianity and are considered to be an important element in the Chinese Christian mission. By small gatherings I do not mean these units, but am referring to all gatherings, including congregations and churches, which do not go beyond a certain number and often (but not always) meet in an individual's home. The ideal size of a congregation should not be more than 50 people to ensure a sufficiently personal experience for members, for example.

While TSPM churches are often quite large in order to meet the increasing demand for places of worship (as the dimensions of the planned new church in Qufu would confirm), the majority of Christians, who meet in unregistered churches, are used to this smaller and more intimate religious experience, which has often started in small fellowships or Bible study groups consisting of only a few individuals. Because the regulations governing social groups restrict all legal gatherings to a limit of 25 people, and because of the focus on restrictive measures in many studies of Christianity (and certainly its media coverage), the generally accepted view is that Christians meet in smaller groups, because it is safer, implying that this form of meeting is a result of government suppression.

Based on the literature emerging from Chinese churches and conversations in China and with Chinese pastors involved in the mission in the United Kingdom, I am inclined to view this as a false assumption. Small gatherings clearly hold an additional appeal, which cannot only be explained by the need to hide – a need that is in any case much less present now – in particular as it is also the preferred pattern of the Christian mission outside China. (For Chinese pastors operating in London, the smaller and more family-like gatherings are the best pattern for church planting.) Some, who meet as Christians, do so in small groups, because they do not feel welcome or represented in the churches. As a well-known, openly gay, Catholic film maker put it, he had already 'graduated from the church', seeing no value in attending conservative and judgemental congregations. Many artists abstained from attending churches preferring to meet privately, creating their own 'atmosphere'.

But Christians are not the only ones whose meetings follow such a pattern. Groups, who meet for the purposes of intellectual, spiritual or psychological elevation, are many and varied. They commonly use texts as the basis for their discussions, which may range from classical Marxist texts to ethical books used in kindergartens and primary schools in the United States and Europe (Yan Y. 2011: 38). It may be that the text or the moral system around which groups meet is almost secondary to the inherent value of the experience of regularly meeting as a small group itself. It seems that great psychological comfort is derived from such gatherings, which provide a fixture in the week when one will spend a couple of hours in the company of trusted and like-minded individuals engaged in 'self-cultivation'. They constitute small moral islands of meaning in an otherwise challenging social environment in which mutual trust is at a record low. More work will need to be undertaken to understand the cultural roots of such gatherings and the psychological needs they meet. Such studies require acceptance that these small gatherings are not exclusive to religious believers and are not dictated by government suppression, but a chosen and preferred form of a 'meeting of minds'.

The role of the Chinese 'diaspora'

There is no question that Chinese outside China, many of whom left China post 1989, whether as a direct result of their involvement or as graduate students in the early 1990s, are an important part of contemporary Chinese Christianity. They are partly responsible for the link that has been created between Christianity and political resistance by framing the religious question in China as a human rights issue and thus putting it on the agenda of human rights organizations abroad. They have also created their own organizations, either advocacy or mission based. Some of the individuals involved in them are fiercely anti-Chinese government and have found an open ear with sections of the US media and lobby groups, who are connected to the American evangelical movement. They can draw on considerable resources and influence and have helped a number of Christian individuals in China and their move into exile, where necessary. The most recent and most prominent example is that of Chen Guangcheng, who, although not himself a Christian, is an important figure for the Christian human rights lobby, which likes to (falsely) interpret his groundbreaking actions in the context of a pro-life agenda. The fact that Chen's case resulted in the US Secretary of State negotiating the conditions of his exile with the Chinese government shows quite how well connected this group is.

It may be the best connected, but it is not necessarily representative. More moderate and nuanced voices belonging to individuals, who frequently travel back to China, who are closely involved with church building in China and have first-hand experience of the situation far better reflect the Chinese Christian 'public voice' as far as one can detect one. These voices, who tie in much more with voices inside China, urge caution and conciliation, cooperation and consensus – as far as it is possible – in the dealings with the Chinese government. As the main theological trend to which these individuals belong is the 'New-Calvinist' school, which expects a degree of social engagement of their believers as individuals and through their churches, staying clear of conflict is not always easy. But there is no great sense of urgency for political change; emphasis is placed on the changes already underway, like the increasing pluralism and diversity in Chinese society, which are expected to lead to eventual political change. How long this will take is less important than the more immediate work of church building, theological training and spiritual elevation.

From the party-state's point of view, the role of the Chinese diaspora in the contemporary Chinese mission in China presents a delicate issue that questions the boundaries between what or who is considered 'Chinese' and 'foreign'. Generally speaking, the Chinese diaspora is considered to be beneficial to China's modernization and globalization. 'Overseas Chinese' are among the biggest investors in China and are encouraged to contribute to the glory of the 'motherland'. But the government differentiates between different categories of overseas Chinese and adopts different policies towards them, depending on how long they have been abroad. And as a result of much easier travel and communication, new categories have been introduced referring to Chinese returned from a prolonged period abroad (*haigui*) and those, who frequently travel between their new country of residence and China (*hai'ou*). The Chinese diaspora actively involved in church building, theological development and shaping church-state relations has representatives in all these categories with different roles and functions assumed by each of them. A great many of them grew up in mainland China and have only lived abroad as adults. In this context the juxtaposition of 'Chinese' and 'foreign' as presented in the Confucians' open letter, acquires new meaning that has nothing to do with ethnicity or nationality.

But difficulties do not only exist on the level of official discourse and policy. In daily practice, the relations between the '*haigui*' pastors and the local Chinese community can be ambivalent. They are welcome for the positive contribution they can make courtesy of their wider theological understanding and their help with the particular challenges churches are facing in a changing China. In general, their influx is seen to have a positive effect on the churches in the field of structure and organization. These pastors form a bridge between Chinese and Western culture and spiritual resources, an essential experience for the Chinese 'house churches' who have to adapt to a changing environment, where they are in increasing contact with other churches and institutions inside and outside China. '*Haigui*' pastors are also expected to play a key role in Chinese missionary work outside China. But their overseas training can lead to them feeling distant or superior to the local churches and critical of spiritual traditions which do not conform to their particular theological training. This may lead to a situation where new churches are established rather than working with existing ones, which are looked down upon as not 'proper' or 'real', especially when their views on how to handle state-church relations differ (Zhang L. 2010). Even more 'alien' are the attempts to politicize the discourse or to use unregistered churches as a platform for a political agenda, a practice widely condemned in Chinese Christian circles.

Overlap between government and Christian agenda

The emphasis on the suppression of religion and persecution of individual Christians obscures the view onto what I consider to be a considerable overlap between the government agenda and the agenda of the Chinese Christian mission. Far from the relationship between Christianity and the government being a one-way relationship of oversight and control, both local and central governments are willing to learn lessons from Christian organizations and individual Christians. But Chinese Christians can also become actors in the interest of the Chinese party-state.

As mentioned in Chapter 2, Christian entrepreneurs are considered pioneers in the post-Mao 'socialist market economy' and an important partner of the state development project. Christian entrepreneurs have earned much recognition and respect for their economic success by the state, which in turn has meant that some Christian entrepreneurs have become actual partners of the state in governing the local community. This way the local government makes pragmatic use of the social standing and proven managerial ability of certain (Christian) individuals, thereby enhancing its legitimacy, while the benefit of such cooperation with the state on the side of the Christian entrepreneurs lies in social stability (achieved through good governance) which is necessary for economic success.

In a similar example, the central government seems to have learnt from Amity Foundation's development project of China's west in formulating its central policy regarding this region. In 1993 Amity's Board of Directors, led by Ding Guangxun, proposed two related strategies. Based on an analysis of poverty distribution in China, Amity decided on a comprehensive development program of villages by 'Going West'. Eight years later, China's central government proposed 'Opening Up the West' as a key policy, which in essence emulated Amity's earlier strategy (Qiu 2004: 219). Considering the high level political involvement of Ding Guanxun through the National Chinese People's Political Consultative Conference, it is difficult to see this as a co-incidence. The government's policy also 'opened up' this area for missionary efforts.

Looking at the work of contemporary Chinese missionaries in minority regions generates interesting questions. As we know, the work of Western missionaries in China has been viewed through the lens of colonialism and imperialism. Seen from the point of view of ethnic minority groups, however, it is the Han – as representing the Chinese state – who occupy the role of colonizer. As Francis K.G. Lim (2013b) points out, a prominent feature among ethnic minorities who had converted to Christianity in Yunnan in Republican times was that many of them had been dispersed throughout the province after protracted struggles against the Han and sinicization. They embraced Christianity as a rejection of sinicization while regarding Christianity and contacts with foreigners as offering alternative pathways towards modernization. This tied in with the efforts by Western Christian missionaries to bring to the minority groups not just the gospel, but also the 'civilization' of modern Christian nations, including health, science and technology (Lim 2013b: 109). The written script (and scripture) was a very important aspect of this endeavour leading to the translation of the gospel into the languages of these ethnic groups, even the invention of a writing system where this was lacking as in the case of the Hua Miao.

In contrast, today's Chinese missionary efforts in China's 'minority regions' all rely on the Chinese Bible and Mandarin as the medium of evangelization. The 'salvation' brought by the contemporary Chinese missionary projects is difficult to distinguish from the salvation from cultural poverty and backwardness which was key to the central state civilizing project of 'sending culture down to the countryside' started in the late 1990s, but which also existed during the more socialist periods of China's recent history. Where Christian migrant workers are involved in rural evangelizing, they consciously act urban and preach in Mandarin, to show their extended urban experience, thus linking Christianity with aspirations, high *suzhi* and Mandarin. I have also heard accounts (but was unable to verify them independently), that the Chinese Bible was used as a text to teach Chinese in Uyghur speaking regions in Xinjiang. Thus, instead of reinforcing an ethnic or local identity, the contemporary Chinese Christian mission colludes with the Chinese state project by bringing not just 'modern civilization' as enabled by the Chinese state but also modern Chinese identity as represented in the speaking of Mandarin and the adoption of new cultural practices to 'backward' areas of China.

The question of language is closely related to the question of terminology. On an ideological level as an example of how another Christian term has found its way into Chinese official discourse, the use of the term *xiejiao* and its application should be mentioned. It was originally used in Ming and Qing times, but has recently made a return in the People's Republic of China in the context of the banning of several groups which had been denounced as heretical by the official Christian associations, but which is also used to denounce Falungong, for example. As David A. Palmer (2008) argues, the contemporary reappearance of term *xiejiao*, which replaced the outdated 'reactionary secret society' label, is associated with Christian and foreign groups. It is used as a translation of the Western term 'cult' and all its associated categories, which in North America is dominated by Christian interests. The Chinese discussions on *xiejiao* combine elements of Christianity, sociology and psychology and often included references to the Bible or the history of Christianity (Palmer 2008: 128).

The persecution of Christians as part of the two campaigns against spiritual pollution and bourgeois liberalism in the 1980s is condemned by voices from within the mission, but the suppression of what are deemed cults by both the government and the evangelical movement is considered a 'success' by the same sources, even though it was carried out as part of the same campaign (see for example Lambert 2006). It is difficult not to conclude that the (often questionable and illegal) methods of the government are condoned when they target 'real' cults, but condemned when they are used against 'true' Christians, thus however involuntarily creating a degree of collusion between the 'true' Christian agenda and the government's.

There was also little doubt about the rightfulness of the government's crackdown on Falungong among the people interviewed for this study. Only Yu Jie agreed that the freedom of religious belief also extended to non-Christian groups and that they were (in 2006) looking into a possible cooperation with Falungong. However he conceded that this potential collaboration was fraught with difficulties, partly because of disagreements between individuals, and partly because of the widespread intolerance of Falungong by Chinese Christians (author interview,

September 2006). The fact that Falungong had been declared illegal of course further complicated any possible collaboration as it put the Christian community at risk.

'Moderate' or 'rational' Christian voices are keen to distance themselves from practices that are too closely associated with superstition, like speaking in tongues, dreams and visions, an attitude which ties in with the rationality of the Chinese party-state's modernizing project as mentioned above. As was shown in Chapter 1, tales of miraculous healing as they emerge from the Chinese rural churches are treated with scepticism, while they are quite readily accepted when they are presented in a more 'scientific' way or when the healing is ostensibly proven by medical tests or expressed in medical terminology. For the outside observer, this is a conflict that is hard to ignore. Apparently some miracles are genuine, but others aren't; but who is qualified to make this judgment? In their efforts to draw the line between what is orthodox (*zheng*) and what is unorthodox (*xie*), the Christian groups concerned with this question come very close to the benchmarks employed by the party-state, when more rural, spiritual, and genuinely indigenous Christian groups as they have emerged in the reform era, where Christian belief meets with traditional folk religion, are branded backward, unenlightened and dangerous. Instead of condemning the ways and methods employed in cracking down on these groups, concern is reserved for the 'true Christians', who find themselves caught up in these campaigns. As Lambert says, 'Local cadres have little detailed knowledge to distinguish bona fide believers from cultists' (Lambert 2006: 139), implying that it is more important to educate those carrying out the campaigns than changing the methods employed in them or indeed question the campaigns per se.

This also leads to the question as to the future role of Mandarin in the global Chinese mission. Already, an interesting correlation can be observed between the nationalist sense that it is the turn of the Chinese to leave their mark on the world and the contemporary Chinese mission. Far from being confined to the rather controversial 'Back to Jerusalem Movement', there is a wider sentiment that the Chinese now play a crucial role in the global Christian mission, and that this in turn is linked to the establishment of a 'harmonious society' on a global scale. While the 'Back to Jerusalem' movement is mainly concerned with evangelizing the 'Muslim block' that stretches from the west of China through South Asia and the Middle East to Jerusalem, a similar ambition is also present in wider Christian circles, which show an interest in Africa and Latin America. The Chinese Christian organizations in the United States also have an interest in these regions. China's involvement in Africa and Latin America has resulted in many detailed studies of its economic effect and has raised questions of a political nature. But so far much less attention has been paid to China's 'soft power' in these regions, which includes educational programs promoting Chinese language as a new lingua franca. The teaching of English has played an important role in the international Christian mission, certainly since the Second World War. Indeed many urban Christians and certainly many of the leading Christian intellectuals have encountered Christianity through the teaching of English on campus or at least through the person, who teaches these classes. It will be very interesting to observe what role Chinese and the Chinese Bible may start to play, or is already playing, in the international Chinese mission, which follows on the coat-tails of China's development and its entrepreneurs in these regions.

The framing of the religious question in China through the lens of political repression, human rights violation and dissent, especially in the context of Christianity, has perhaps resulted in the wrong questions which have misled us in our quest to better understand the role and function of Christianity in China today. We need to question the seemingly most obvious and step around the signposts planted by various interest groups in order to gain a full view and a more direct access to the complex and dynamic realities of contemporary Chinese Christianity.

The Christian declaration in response to the Qufu protest emphasizes the adaptive nature of Chinese culture. But Christianity itself, of course, looks back on its own two thousand years of adaptation and reinterpretation (and not inconsiderable conflict), a process that is very much ongoing today. The debates within China based on its theological and denominational histories and traditions together with the contemporary influences, mostly from Southeast Asia and the United States, are themselves vivid example of this ongoing process. Of equal importance to these 'foreign' influences is the Chinese cultural context, which is the result of a number of traditions, of which Confucianism and socialism are the most important. Considering that much of the 'foreign' influences today are carried by individuals, who themselves grew up in both these Chinese cultural traditions, and that the Chinese mission is active on a global scale, perhaps the most pertinent question is not how Chinese culture adapts to Christianity, but how contemporary Christianity is being shaped by Chinese culture.

Note

1   The letter was signed by ten eminent Confucian scholars (including one from Taiwan) and claimed the support of ten Confucian institutions and ten Confucian web based organizations. The signatories included Kang Xiaoguang and Jiang Qing, both known for their campaigns to reinstate Confucianism as China's central ideology. Jiang Qing argued as early as 1989 that Confucianism should take the place of Marxism and become a legitimized ideology representing Chinese culture and the Chinese spirit, advocating a kingly style politics and a Confucian authoritarian regime, in which worthy men could vote for each other, which was unlike Marxism and certainly unlike liberal democracy (Ai J. 2008). Kang Xiaoguang was at the forefront of an initiative to make Confucianism China's state religion (Ownby 2009).

Bibliography

Agence France Press. (2013) Nobel Laureates Urge China to Release Liu Xiaobo. *South China Morning Post*. Available from: www.scmp.com/news/china/article/1159861/nobel-laureates-urge-china-release-liu-xiaobo (last accessed 28 February 2013).

Ai, G. (2008) Building a Harmonious Society and Achieving Individual Harmony, in *China in Search of a Harmonious Society*, Lanham, MD: Lexington Books, pp.13–34.

Ai, Jaiwen (2008) The Refunctioning of Confucianism: The Mainland Chinese Intellectual Response to Confucianism since the 1980s, *Issues and Studies* 44 (2): 29–78.

Aikman, D. (2003) *Jesus in Beijing. How Christianity Is Transforming China and Changing the Global Balance of Power*, Oxford: Monarch Books.

Amity Foundation. (2010) *Love Never Ends. On the 25th Anniversary of the Amity Foundation*, Nanjing: The Amity Foundation.

Amity Foundation. (2012) Aide Jijinhui Juban Zhuisihui Daonian Ding Guangxun Zhujiao (Amity Foundation Holds a Memorial to Commemorate Bishop Ding Guangxun). Available from: www.amityfoundation.org.cn/article/view.aspx?id=6423 (last accessed 3 December 2012).

Anagnost, A. (2004) The Corporeal Politics of Quality (suzhi). *Public Culture*, 16 (2): 189–208.

Angle, S.C. (2008) Human Rights and Harmony. *Human Rights Quarterly*, 30 (1): 76–94.

Ashiwa, Y. and Wank, D.L. (eds). (2009) *Making Religion, Making the State. The Politics of Religion in Modern China*, Stanford, CA: Stanford University Press.

Badiou, A. (2012) *In Praise of Love*, London: Serpent's Tail.

Bao, L. (2006) The Intellectual Influence of Christianity in a Modern China Society, in *Sino-Christian Studies in China*, Cambridge: Cambridge Scholars Press, pp.265–79.

Barboza, D. (2012) Billions in Hidden Riches for Family of Chinese Leader. *New York Times*. Available from: www.nytimes.com/2012/10/26/business/global/family-of-wen-jiabao-holds-a-hidden-fortune-in-china.html?pagewanted=all&_r=0 (last accessed 7 February 2013).

Bays, D. (2009) American Public Discourse on the Church in China. *The China Review*, 9 (2): 1–16.

Bays, D. (2012) *A New History of Christianity in China*, Oxford: Wiley-Blackwell.

Bergère, M.-C. (1998) *Sun Yatsen*, Stanford, CA: Stanford University Press.

Bieler, S. and Hamrin, C. (2009) *Guang Yu Yan. Tansu Jindai Zhongguo Gaige De Shiwei Lishi Mingren (Salt and Light. Lives of Faith That Shaped Modern China)*, Beijing: Zhongguo dang'an chubanshe.

Bieler, S. and Ling, S. (1999) *Chinese Intellectuals and the Gospel*, San Gabriel: China Horizon.

Birnbaum, B. (2011) Chinese Dissidents Hear Obama's Silence. *Washington Times.* Available from: www.washingtontimes.com/news/2011/feb/3/chinese-dissidents-hear-obamas-silence/print/ (last accessed 30 October 2012).

Brandner, T. (2013) Trying to Make Sense of History. Chinese Christian Traditions of Countercultural Belief and Their Theological and Political Interpretation of Past and Present History, in *Christianity in Contemporary China. Socio-cultural Perspectives*, London, New York: Routledge, pp.78–90.

Branigan, T. (2013) Chinese Intellectuals Avoid Key Issues Amid Censorship Fears, Says Author. *The Guardian.* Available from: www.guardian.co.uk/world/2013/feb/06/chinese-writers-failing-censorship-concerns (last accessed 9 February 2013).

Bruce, S. (2003) *Politics and Religion*, Cambridge: Polity Press.

Buruma, I. (2001) *Bad Elements. Chinese Rebels from Los Angeles to Beijing*, New York: Random House.

Cao, N. (2007) Christian Entrepreneurs and the Post-Mao State. *Sociology of Religion*, 68 (1): 45–66.

Cao, N. (2008) Boss Christians: The Business of Religion in the 'Wenzhou Model' of Christian Revival. *The China Journal*, 59: 63–87.

Cao, N. (2009) Raising the Quality of Belief: Suzhi and the Production of an Elite Protestantism. *China Perspectives*, 4: 54–65.

Cao, N. (2011) *Constructing China's Jerusalem. Christians, Power, and Place in Contemporary Wenzhou*, Stanford, CA: Stanford University Press.

Cao, S. (2006) The Role of Chinese Christians in the Development of China, in *Pilgrims and Citizens*, Adelaide: ATF Press, pp.147–56.

Chan, K.-K. and Hunter, A. (1993) *Protestantism in Contemporary China*, Cambridge: Cambridge University Press.

Chen, A. (2007) Xiaozu, Yizhong Kexing De Jiaohui Fazhan Moshi (Small Groups, A Plausible Model to Develop the Churches). *Wheat Seeds*, (9). Available from: www.maizhong.org/wheatseeds/2007-07.09/wz/24.html (last accessed 25 September 2012).

Chen, C. (2005) *Zhuanxing Qide Zhongguo Jidujiao. Zhejiang Jidujiao Ge'an Yanjiu*, Beijing: Dongfang Chubanshe.

Chen, Jianming. (2008) Modern Chinese Attitudes Towards the Bible, in Chloe Starr (ed.), *Reading Christian Scriptures in China,* , London: T&T Clark, pp.13–31.

Chen, Jie, Narisong, F. and Lu, C. (2010) Generalized vs. Particularized Social Capital: Social Trust and Grass-Roots Governance in Urban China, in *Toward Better Governance in China*, Lanham, MD: Lexington Books, pp.51–70.

Chen, K. (1998) Jinlai Zhongguo Wenhua Sichao Yanbian (Recent Changes in Chinese Cultural Trends). *Zhongguo Yanjiu*, 35. Available from: http://blog.boxun.com/sixiang/000408/8.htm (last accessed 21 January 2013).

Chen, K. (2004) Zhongguoren Cong Chenmin Dao Gongmin (Chinese People – from Subjects to Citizens). *Guancha.* Available from: www.epochtimes.com/gb/4/2/21/n471105.htm (last accessed 15 April 2008).

Chen, K. (2010) Zhongguo Ziyou Zhuyi Zai Wenge Zhong De Mengya (First Shoots of Chinese Liberalism During the Cultural Revolution). *Zhishi Wang.* Available from: www.21ccom.net/articles/sxwh/shsc/article_20100120203.html (last accessed 10 October 2012).

Chen, X. (2011) *Dangdai Zhongguo De Jidujiao Shenxue Fangfa (A Study of Theological Methodology in Contemporary China)*, Beijing: Zongjiao wenhua chubanshe.

Chen, Y. (2006) *Cong Zili Dao Cili. Yu Zhongguoren Tan Jidujiao (From One's Own Power to the Power of Prayer. Talking Christianity with Chinese People)*, Hong Kong: Cosmos Books.

Cheng, C. (ed.). (1989) *Sun Yatsen's Doctrine in the Modern World*, Boulder, CO: Westview Press.

Cheng, Y. (2006) 'Liangge Liu Xiaobo' He Zhongguo Zhishifenzi Zhuanxing ('The Two Liu Xiaobos' and the Transformation of Chinese Intellectuals). *Ganlanzhi*, 3: 47–8.

China Aid. (2012) China House Church Alliance's 2012 New Year's Message: Nothing Can Separate Us from the Love of God. Available from: www.chinaaid.org/2011/12/chinese-house-church-alliances-2012-new.html (last accessed 11 February 2013).

China Digital Times. (2013) One in Ten Beijingers Is a Propaganda Worker. Available from: http://chinadigitaltimes.net/2013/01/one-in-ten-beijingers-is-a-propaganda-worker/ (last accessed 7 January 2013).

Chow, A. (2013) *Theosis, Sino-Christian Theology and the Second Chinese Enlightenment. Heaven and Humanity in Unity*, New York: Palgrave Macmillan.

Christian Times. (2012) Zhuanfang Haigui Muzhe Tan Haigui Muyang (An Interview with 'Haigui' Pastors About 'Haigui' Pastoral Work) Available from: www.christiantimes.cn/special.php?sid=98 (last accessed 8 February 2013).

Chun, Y. (2009) Jianshe Hexie Shehui (Constructing a Harmonious Society). Available from: www.izuowen.com/jixuwen/xushi/21474.html (last accessed 5 February 2013).

Ci, Jiwei. (1994) *Dialectic of the Chinese Revolution. From Utopianism to Hedonism*, Stanford, CA: Stanford University Press.

Ci, Jiwei (2011) China and the Question of Freedom. *Boundary 2*, 38 (1): 53–76.

Cui, D. (2011) *Ai Yu Lun (Treatise on an Education in Love)*, Beijing: Zhongguo shehui kexue chubanshe.

Cui, Z. (2012) *Beidou You 7 Xing. Yiben Zhongguo Putong Jiating De Jingshen Chuanji (The Big Dipper Has Seven Stars. A Spiritual Biography of an Ordinary Chinese Family)*, Guangzhou: Huacheng Chubanshe.

Ding, G. (1998a) *Ding Guangxun Wenji (Collected Writings by Ding Guangxun)*, Nanjing: Yilin chubanshe.

Ding, G. (1998b) Laizi Jiefang Shenxue, De Rijin Shenxue He Guocheng Shenxue De Qifa (Inspiration from Liberation Theology, Teilhard De Chardin's Theology and Process Theology), in *Ding Guangxun wenji*, Nanjing: Yilin chubanshe, pp.188–214.

Dong, G. (2010) The First Uprising of the Cultural Revolution at Nanjing University: Dynamics, Nature and Interpretation. *Journal of Cold War Studies*, 12 (3): 30–49.

Duitournier, G. and Ji, Z. (2009) Social Experimentation and 'Popular Confucianism': The Case of the Lujiang Cultural Education Centre. *China Perspectives*, 4: 57–81.

Dunch, R. (2000) Protestant Christianity in China Today: Fragile, Fragmented, Flourishing, in *China and Christianity. Burdened Past, Hopeful Future*, Armonk, NY: M.E. Sharpe, pp.195–216.

Dunch, R. (2008) Christianity and 'Adaptation to Socialism', in *Chinese Religiosities. Afflictions of Modernity and State Formation*, Berkeley: University of California Press, pp.155–78.

Dynon, N. (2008) 'Four Civilizations' and the Evolution of post-Mao Chinese Socialist Ideology. *The China Journal*, 60: 83–109.

China Copyright and Media. (2013) 'Eight Musts' Coalesce into Consensus. Available from: http://chinacopyrightandmedia.wordpress.com/2013/01/17/eight-musts-coalesce-into-consensus/ (last accessed 5 March 2013).

Fällman, F. (2004) *Salvation and Modernity. Intellectuals and Faith in Contemporary China*, Stockholm: Stockholm University.

Fällman, F. (2008) Hermeneutical Conflict? Reading the Bible in Contemporary China, in *Reading Christian Scriptures in China*, Chloe Starr (ed.), London: T&T Clark, pp. 49–67.

Fällman, F. (2013) Calvin, Culture and Christ? Developments of Faith among Chinese Intellectuals, in *Christianity in Contemporary China. Socio-cultural Perspectives*, London, New York: Routledge, pp.153–68.

Fan, T. and Zhang, D. (2011) *Liangxin De Ziyou (Liberty of Conscience)*, Guiyang: Guizhou Daxue chubanshe.

Fan, X. (2012) *Zhe Jiu Shi Gongmin. Meiguoren De Shenghuo Yu Women You Shenme Bu Tong. (This Is the Citizens. How Our American Life Differs from Ours.)*, Beijing: Zhongguo chengshi chubanshe.

Fan, Y. (2009) The 'Mean Course' Is Gathering Momentum: The Strategic Choice. *Chinese Law and Religion Monitor*, 5.2 (July–December 2009).

Faries, N. (2010) *The 'Inscrutably Chinese' Church. How Narratives and Nationalism Continue to Divide Christianity*, Lanham, MD: Rowman and Littlefield.

Fei, X. (1992 [1947]) *From the Soil. The Foundations of Chinese Society*, Berkeley: University of California Press.

Feng, C. (2010) Charter 08 and China's Troubled Liberalism. *Asia Times Online*. Available from: www.atimes.com/atimes/China/LB26Ad01.html (last accessed 10 October 2012).

Ferguson, N. (2011) *The West and the Rest*, London: Allen Lane.

Fewsmith, J. and Zheng, Y. (eds). (2008) *China's Opening Society. The Non-state Sector and Governance*, New York: Routledge.

Fiedler, K. (2013) The Emergence of Christian Subcultures in China. Beginnings of an Inculturation from the Grassroots?, in *Christianity in Contemporary China. Sociocultural Perspectives*, London, New York: Routledge, pp.138–52.

Freud, S. (1961) *Civilization and Its Discontents*, New York: W.W.Norton.

Fu, H. and Cullen, R. (2008) Weiquan (Rights Protection) Lawyering in an Authoritarian State: Building a Culture of Public-Interest Lawyering. *The China Journal*, 59: 111–27.

Fu, H. and Cullen, R. (2011) Climbing the Weiquan Ladder: A Radicalizing Process for Rights-Protection Lawyers. *The China Quarterly*, 205: 40–59.

Gamwell, F.I. (2005) *Politics as a Christian Vocation. Faith and Democracy Today*, Cambridge: Cambridge University Press.

Gao, Shining. (2005) *Dangdai Beijing De Jidujiao Yu Jidutu. Zongjiao Shehuixue Ge'an Yanjiu (Christianity and Christians in Beijing Today. A Case Study in Sociology of Religion)*, Hong Kong: Logos and Pneuma Press.

Gao, Shining and He, G. (2011) Dangdai Zhongguo Jidujiao De Zhuyao Wenti Yu Jiejue Shexiang (The Main Problems of Christianity in China Today and Ideas for a Solution). *Zhongping Wang*. Available from: www.china-review.com/caf.asp?id=28039 (last accessed 30 October 2012).

Gao, Suijin and Guo, B. (eds). (2008) *China in Search of a Harmonious Society*, Lanham, MD: Lexington Books.

Gilley, Bruce. (2004) *China's Democratic Future. How It Will Happen and Where It Will Lead*, New York: Columbia University Press.

Goossaert, V. and Palmer, D. (2011) *The Religious Question in Modern China*, Chicago, London: University of Chicago Press.

The Guardian. (2011) China's Main Union Is Yet to Earn Its Job. Available from: www.guardian.co.uk/commentisfree/2011/jun/26/china-trade-union-global-movement (last accessed 13 September 2012).

Guo, B. and Hickey, D. (eds). (2010) *Toward Better Governance in China. An Unconventional Pathway of Political Reform*, Lanham, MD: Lexington Books.

Hao, Z. (2003) *Intellectuals at a Crossroads. The Changing Politics of China's Knowledge Workers*, New York: State University of New York Press.

Hardt, M. (2007) About Love. Available from: www.youtube.com/watch?v=ioopkoppabI (last accessed 5 February 2013).
Hardt, M. and Negri, A. (2001) *Empire*, Cambridge, MA: Harvard University Press.
Hardt, M. and Negri, A. (2004) *Multitude: War and Democracy in The Age of Empire*, New York: Penguin Books.
Havel, V. (1989) *Vaclav Havel: On Living in Truth*, London: Faber and Faber.
He, B. (1996) *The Democratization of China*, London: Routledge.
He, B. (2000) New Moral Foundations of Chinese Democratic Institutional Design, in *China and Democracy. The Prospect for a Democratic China*, London: Routledge, pp.89–110.
He, D. (2013) Trust Among Chinese 'Drops to Record Low'. *China Daily*. Available from: www.chinadaily.com.cn/china/2013-02/18/content_16230755.htm (last accessed 8 March 2013).
He, G. (n/d) 'Gongmin Shehui' Yu 'Chaoyue Jingshen' ('Civil Society' and a 'Transcendental Spirit'). Available from: http://wenku.baidu.com/view/311fc02b915f804d2b16c1e4.html?from=related (last accessed 10 April 2012).
He, G. (2011) Thirty Years of Religious Studies in China, in *Social Scientific Studies of Religion in China*, Leiden, Boston: Brill, pp.23–46.
He, G., Wang, W. *et al.* (2012) Zhongguo Shenxue Luntan Di Wujie Yantaohui Gongshi: Women Dui Jidujiao Yu Zhongguo Wenhua Guanxi De Taidu (Public Declaration by the Fifth Symposium of the Chinese Theological Forum: Our Attitude towards Relations between Christianity and Chinese Culture) *Jidu Shibao*. Available from: www.christiantimes.cn/news/201209/19/7730.html (last accessed 25 February 2013).
He, J. (2010) Rethinking a Diverse but Controversial Sector: Contradictions, Regulations and NGOs in Mainland China. LSE Seminar 18 November 2010.
Heng, S.-H. (2008) China's Cultural and Intellectual Rejuvenation. *Asia Europe Journal*, 6 (3–4): 401–12.
Holbig, H. (2009) Remaking the CCP's Ideology: Determinants, Progress, and Limits Under Hu Jintao. *Journal of Current Chinese Affairs*, 38 (3): 35–61.
Holbig, H. and Gilley, B. (2010) Reclaiming Legitimacy in China. *Politics and Policy*, 38 (3): 395–422.
Howell, J., Shang, X. and White, G. (1996) *In Search of Civil Society in Contemporary China*, Oxford: Clarendon Press.
Hsu, J.Y.J. (2012) Domestic Experiences and the Shaping of a 'China Model' of Development. Available from: www.cpsa-acsp.ca/papers-2012/Hsu1.pdf (last accessed 3 January 2013).
Hu, P. (2003) The Falungong Phenomenon. *China Rights Forum*, 4: 11–27.
Hu, Z. and Shi, W. (eds). (2008) *Hexie Wenhua Jianshelun (Theories on the Construction of a Harmonious Culture)*, Kunming: Yunnan daxue chubanshe.
Huang, J.C. (2009) *Charisma and Compassion. Cheng Yen and the Buddhist Tzu Chi Movement*, Cambridge, MA: Harvard University Press.
Huiling (2011) Beijing Huiling 11 Zhounian Jinian Kan (11th Anniversay of Beijing Huiling).
Hung, C. (2010) The Politics of China's Wei-Quan Movement in the Internet Age. *International Journal of China Studies*, 1 (2): 331–49.
Huters, T. and Wang, H. (eds). (2003) *China's New Order: Society, Politics and Economy in Transition*, Cambridge, MA: Harvard University Press.
Idao, D. (2005) The Role of Public Intellectuals. *China Rights Forum*, 1: 65–66.
Inboden, R. and Inboden, W. (2009) Faith and Law in China. *Far Eastern Economic Review*, September 2009.

Jacka, T. (2009) Cultivating Citizens: Suzhi (Quality) Discourse in the PRC. *Positions: East Asia Cultures Critique*, 17 (3): 523–35.

Ji, D. (2006) Zhongwen Wangluo Yu Jidu Fuyin Wenhua Shiming (The Chinese Internet and the Cultural Mission of the Chinese Gospel). *Wheat Seeds*, 1. Available from: www.maizhong.org/wheatseeds/2006-07.01/wz/16.html (last accessed 12 October 2012).

Ji, D. (2009) *Chuanyue Wangluo De Xinyang Sibian (Responses to Skepticism About Christian Faith on the Chinese Web)*, Houston, TX: Christian Communications Incorporated.

Jiang, D. (2009) Jiating Jiaohui De Gonggongxing Yu Zhongguo Zhengjiao Guanxi (The Public Nature of House Churches and China's Church State Relations). *Jiaohui (Church China)*, 15. Available from: https://www.churchchina.org/no090101 (last accessed 15 October 2012).

Jiang, J. (2012) Zhichi He Guli Zongjiaojie Kaizhan Gongyi Cishan Huodong (Support and Encouragement for Public Welfare and Philanthropic Activities of the Religious Sector). *Zhongguo zongjiao*. Available from: www.chinareligion.cn/zongjiaocishanzhou/cishan linian/2012-09-07/1491.html (last accessed 18 December 2012).

Jiao, G. (1998) *Xianfeng Yu Yiwu De Bianji (The Border between Sacrifice and Duty)*, Beijing: Zhongguo huaqiao chubanshe.

Jidujiao shengming zi quan (chengdu) jiaohui (Christian 'Source of Life' Church, Chengdu). (2011) *2011 Nian Zhoubao Hedingben (Collection of Weekly Reports for 2011)*, Chengdu.

Johnson, I. (2012a) Jesus vs. Mao? An Interview With Yuan Zhiming, Available from: www.nybooks.com/blogs/nyrblog/2012/sep/04/jesus-vs-mao-interview-yuan-zhiming/ (last accessed 14 December 2012).

Johnson, I. (2012b) Wary of Future Professionals Leave China in Record Numbers. *New York Times*. Available from: www.nytimes.com/2012/11/01/world/asia/wary-of-future-many-professionals-leave-china.html?pagewanted=all&_r=0 (last accessed 23 January 2013).

Kaiman, J. (2013) Going Undercover. The Evangelists Taking Jesus to Tibet. *The Guardian*. Available from: www.guardian.co.uk/world/2013/feb/21/going-undercover-christian-evangelists-tibet (last accessed 8 March 2013).

Kang, X. (2010) *NGO Yu Zhengfu Hezuo Celue (Strategic Study on NGO-Government Collaboration)*, Beijing: Shehui kexue wenxian chubanshe.

Keane, J. (2000) Secularism?, in *Religion and Democracy, The Political Quarterly*, Oxford: Blackwell, pp.5–20.

Keller, C.A. (1996) Making Model Citizens: The Chinese YMCA, Social Activism, and Internationalism in Republican China, 1919–1937, University of Kansas: Unpublished PhD Dissertation.

Kipnis, A. (2008) *China and Postsocialist Anthropology. Theorizing Power and Society After Communism*, Norwalk: Eastbridge.

Kleinman, A. (2006) *What Really Matters. Living a Moral Life Amidst Uncertainty and Danger*, Oxford: Oxford University Press.

Kleinman, A., Yan, Y. et al. (2011a) *Deep China. The Moral Life of the Person. What Anthropology and Psychiatry Tell Us About China Today*, Berkeley: University of California Press.

Kleinman, A., Yan, Y. et al. (2011b) Remaking the Moral Person in a New China, in *Deep China.*, Berkeley: University of California Press, pp.1–35.

Kwok, P.-L. (1992) *Chinese Women and Christianity 1860–1927*, Atlanta, GA: Scholars Press.

Lam, W.-H. (1983) *Chinese Theology in Construction*, Pasadena, CA: William Carey Library.

Lambert, T. (2006) *China's Christian Millions*, Oxford: Monarch Books.
Lang, G. and Lu, Yunfeng. (2011) Religion and Environmentalism in Chinese Societies, in *Social Scientific Studies of Religion in China*, Leiden, Boston: Brill.
Lee, H. (2007) *Revolution of the Heart. A Genealogy of Love in China, 1900–1950*, Stanford, CA: Stanford University Press.
Li, C. (ed.). (2010a) *China's Emerging Middle Class. Beyond Economic Transition*, Washington, DC: Brookings Institution Press.
Li, C. (2010b) Chinese Scholarship on the Middle Class: From Social Stratification to Political Potential, in *China's Emerging Middle Class. Beyond Economic Transformation*, Washington, DC: The Brookings Institution, pp.55–83.
Li, G. (2012) Jiaohui Xuyao Jingti Zui'e De Canru He Liyong (Churches Have to Be on the Guard Against Infiltration and Being Used for Criminal Activity). Available from: www.gospeltimes.cn/news/2012_11_01/23066.htm (last accessed 15 December 2012).
Li, J. (2007) Zhongguo Wenhua Jiduhua Chutan (A Preliminary Exploration of Chinese Culture's Christianization). *Wheat Seeds*, (9). Available from: www.maizhong.org/wheatseeds/2007-07.09/wz/12.html (last accessed 25 September 2012).
Li, X. and Zhang, Z. (eds). (2009) *Baling Xianzhang (Charter 08)*, Hong Kong: Open Books.
Li, Y. (2013) Debate Erupts over Official Gini Figures. Caixin Online. Available from: http://english.caixin.com/2013-01-22/100485209.html (last accessed 18 January 2013).
Lian, X. (2010) *Redeemed by Fire. The Rise of Popular Christianity in Modern China*, New Haven, CT, London: Yale University Press.
Lian, X. (2013) 'Cultural Christians' and the Search for Civil Society in Contemporary China. *Chinese Historical Review* 20 (1): 70–87.
Liang, X. (2011) *Zhongguo Shehui Ge Jieceng Fenxi (An Analysis of China's Social Classes)*, Beijing: Wenhua yishu chubanshe.
Liao, Y. (2011) *God Is Red. The Secret Story of How Christianity Survived and Flourished in Communist China*, New York: Harper Collins.
Lim, F.K.G. (2013a) *Christianity in Contemporary China. Socio-cultural Perspectives*, London, New York: Routledge.
Lim, F.K.G. (2013b) 'To the Peoples'. Christianity and Ethnicity in China's Minority Areas, in *Christianity in Contemporary China. Socio-cultural Perspectives*, London, New York: Routledge, pp.105–20.
Lin, A.H.Y. (2009) Social Welfare and Philanthropy: The Case of Guangzhou Under Chen Jitang 1929–1936. *Modern China*, 35: 495–526.
Lin, M.M. (2010) *Ethical Reorientation for Christianity in China. The Individual, Community, and Society*, Hong Kong: Christian Study Centre on Chinese Religion and Culture.
Ling, K. et al. (2005) Using Social Psychology to Motivate Contributions to Online Communities. *Journal of Computer Mediated Communication*, 10 (4). Available from: http://jcmc.indiana.edu/vol10/issue4/ling.html (last accessed 8 February 2013).
Liu, G. (2009) Zhongguo Jiaohui Muyang De Tiaozhan (Challenges for Chinese Pastoral Training). *Wheat Seeds*, 18. Available from: www.maizhong.org/wheatseeds/2009-04.18/wz/08.html (last accessed 24 September 2012).
Liu, G. (2010) Zhongguo Jiaohui Zhuanxing De Tiaozhan (Challenges for Chinese Churches in Transition). *Wheat Seeds*, 16. Available from: www.maizhong.org/wheatseeds/2008-10.16/wz/06.html (last accessed 24 September 2012).
Liu, J. (2010) Freedom of Religion: The Primary Human Right. The World Does Not Belong to Cesar. *Chinese Law and Religion Monitor*, 8 (1): 42–6.

Liu, P. (n/d) *Zongjiao Wenti Wenji (Essays on the Religious Question)*, Beijing: Pushi shehui kexue yanjiusuo.

Liu, P. (2011) On the Problem of Developing a Mechanism for the Participation of Religion in the Social Services, in *Social Scientific Studies of Religion in China*, Leiden, Boston: Brill, pp.227–44.

Liu, P. (2012) Zhongguo Xuyao Zongjiaofa – Zouchu Zhongguo Zongjiao Guanli Tizhi De Kujing (China Needs a Law on Religion – the Difficulty of Leaving Behind China's System of Managing Religion). *Lingdaozhe*, (46 and 47). Available from: www.pacilution.com/ShowArticle.asp?ArticleID=3792 (last accessed 8 November 2012).

Liu, Shigong. (2004) *Ai Yu Zhengyi. Nibuer Jidojiao Lunli Sixiang Yanjiu (Love and Justice: a Study of Reinhold Niebuhr's Christian Ethics)*, Beijing: Zhongguo shehui kexue chubanshe.

Liu, Taiheng (2005), Hexie Shehui Yu 'Ai' De Chuantong Daode Jingshen (The Harmonious-Society and The Traditional Ethical Spirit of 'Love'). Available from: http://www2.zzu.edu.cn/mzyz/showart.asp?art_id=120&cat_id=8 (last accessed 13 April 2010).

Liu, T. (2007) Zhongguo Jiaohui De Chushi Yu Rushi (The Emergence and Involvement in Society of Chinese Churches). Available from: www.liutongsu.net/test1/?page_id=41 (last accessed 26 September 2012).

Liu, T. and Wang, Y. (2012) *Guankan Zhongguo Chengshi Jiating Jiaohui (Observations on China's Urban House Churches)*, Taibei: Christian Arts Press.

Liu, Xiaobo. (2006) Bei Shangdi Xunfu De Qisa, Bei Xinyang Zhengfu De Quanli (Cesar Tamed by God, Power Subjugated by Faith). *Fangzhou*, 2: 86–96.

Liu, Xiaobo. (2010) *Zhong Guo Dangdai Zhengzhi Yu Zhongguo Zhishi Fenzi (Contemporary Chinese Politics and Chinese Intellectuals)*, Taibei: Tonsan Publications.

Liu, Xutong. (2004) Jiji Shiying Yu Fuwu Shehui: Zhongguo Jidu Jiaohui Cishan Fuwu Xianzhuang Yu Zhengce Kuangjia Yanjiu (Actively Adapting to and Serving Society: Research on the Current Status of Chinese Christian Churches' Social Service and a Policy Framework), *in Harmonious Society and Philanthropies*, Beijing: Shehui kexue wenxian chubanshe, pp.293–306.

Louie, K. (2011) Confucius the Chameleon: Dubious Envoy for 'Brand China'. *Boundary 2*, 38 (1): 77–100.

Louie, K. (1989) Love Stories: The Meaning of Love and Marriage in China, 1978–1981, *in Between Fact and Fiction*, Broadway, NSW: Wild Peony, pp.49–75.

Lu, D. (2009) Xiaoyuan Tuanqi Mianlin De Weiji Yu Kunhuo (Dangers and Difficulties for Campus Communions). *Wheat Seeds*, 18. Available from: www.maizhong.org/wheatseeds/2009-04.18/wz/10.html (last accessed 25 September 2012).

Lu, K. (2010) Zhongguo Chengshi Jiaohui Zhong Xingbie Shiheng De Wenti (The Problem of Gender Imbalance in China's Urban Churches). *Jiaohui (Church China)*, 26. Available from: https://www.churchchina.org/no101103 (last accessed 17 December 2012).

Lu, Yiyi. (2008) NGOs in China. Development Dynamics and Challenges, in *China's Opening Society*, New York: Routledge, pp.89–105.

Lu, Yiyi. (2009) *NGOs in China*, London: Routledge.

Lu, Yongjian. (2005) You Aide Dise Cai You Hexie Shehui (Only with Love as Foundation Can There Be a Harmonious Society), Available from: http://new.xinhuanet.com/comments/2005-07/11/content_3202282.htm (last accessed 9 September 2009).

Luo, B. (2011) Women Zhei Yidai (Our Generation). *Wheat Seeds*, 28. Available from: www.maizhong.org/wheatseeds/2011-10.28/wz/18.html (last accessed 25 September 2012).

Lynch, E.M. (2011) China's Rule of Law Mirage: The Regression of the Legal Profession Since the Adoption of the 2007 Lawyers Law. *George Washington International Law Review*, 42: 535–85 (last accessed 16 October 2012).

Ma, J. (2006) *Ai Shi Zhenli. Ding Guangxun Zhuan (Discerning Truth Through Love. A Biography of Ding Guangxun)*, Hong Kong: Chinese Christian Literature Council.

MacCulloch, D. (2009) *A History of Christianity. The First Three Thousand Years*, London: Allen Lane.

Madsen, R. (1998) *China's Catholics. Tragedy and Hope in an Emerging Civil Society*, Berkeley: University of California Press.

Madsen, R. (2003) Chinese Christianity. Indigenization and Conflict, in *Chinese Society. Change, Conflict and Resistance*, London: Routledge, pp. 271–88.

Madsen, R. (2007) *Democracy's Dharma: Religious Renaissance and Political Development in Taiwan*, Berkeley: University of California Press.

Madsen, R. (2011) Religious Renaissance in China Today. *Journal of Current Chinese Affairs*, 40 (2): 17–42.

Madsen, R. (2013) Signs and Wonders: Christianity and Hybrid Modernity in China, in *Christianity in Contemporary China. Socio-cultural Perspectives*, London, New York: Routledge, pp.17–30.

Madsen, R. and Strong, T.B. (eds). (2003) *The Many and the One: Religious and Secular Perspectives on Ethical Pluralism in the Modern World*, Princeton, NJ: Princeton University Press.

Mahoney, J.G. (2008) On the Way to Harmony: Marxism, Confucianism and Hu Jintao's Hexie Concept, in *China in Search of a Harmonious Society*, Lanham, MD: Lexington Books, pp.99–128.

Mai, L. (2007) Guan'ai Nide Linshe (Love Your Neighbour). *Wheat Seeds*, 8. Available from: www.maizhong.org/wheatseeds/2007-04.08/wz/17.html (last accessed 25 September 2012).

Maloney-Krichmar, D. and Preece, J. (2005) Online Communities: Design, Theory and Practice. *Journal of Computer Mediated Communication*, 10 (4). Available from: http://jcmc.indiana.edu/vol10/issue4/preece.html (last accessed 8 February 2013).

Marquand, D. and Nettler, R.L. (eds). (2000) *Religion and Democracy*, Oxford: Blackwell.

McCarthy, S.K. (2012) Serving Society, Repurposing the State: Religious Charity and Resistance in China, Oregon State University, Unpublished Conference Paper.

Mei, K. (2009) Ding Guangxun Zhujiao De Shenxue Sixiang (Bishop Ding Guangxun's Theology). *Zhongguo zongjiao*, 12. Available from: www.cssn.cn/news/153603.htm (last accessed 29 December 2012).

Mi, G. (2013) Missionary Work in Internet Ear Calls for New Management Style. *Global Times*. Available from: www.globaltimes.cn/content/757000.shtml (last accessed 6 February 2013).

Michelson, E. and Liu, Sida. (2010) What Do Chinese Lawyers Want? Political Values and Legal Practice, in *China's Emerging Middle Class. Beyond Economic Transformation*, Washington, DC: The Brookings Institution, pp.310–34.

Micklethwait, J. and Woolridge, A. (2009) *God Is Back. How the Global Revival of Faith Is Changing the World*, London: Penguin Books.

Ming Pao. (2012) Neidi 71 Xuezhe Lianshu Chang Gaige Jiao 'Lingba Xianzhang' Wenhe Ti 6 Xiang Zhuzhang (71 Scholars from Mainland China Jointly Sign a Petition Containing Six Demands, Less Controversial Than Charter 08. Available from: http://news.hk.msn.com/highlight/article.aspx?cp-documentid=251841573 (last accessed 10 January 2013).

Myers, R. (1989) The Principle of People's Welfare: A Multidimensional Concept, in *Sun Yatsen's Doctrine in the Modern World*, Boulder, CO: Westview Press.
Ng, P.T.M. (2012) *Chinese Christianity. An Interplay Between Global and Local Perspectives*, Leiden: Brill.
Nyiri, P. (2006) The Yellow Man's Burden: Chinese Migrants on a Civilizing Mission. *The China Journal*, 56: 83–106.
Olsen, M. (1965) *The Logic of Collective Action*, Cambridge, MA: Harvard University Press.
Osnos, E. (no date) Extended Interview with Zhao Xiao. Available from: www.pbs.org/frontlineworld/stories/china_705/interview/xiao.html (last accessed 17 January 2013).
Ownby, D. (2009) Kang Xiaoguang: Social Science, Civil Society, and Confucian Religion. *China Perspectives*, 4. Available from: http://chinaperspectives.revues.org/4928 (last accessed 26 February 2013).
Oxfeld, E. (2010) *Drink Water, But Remember the Source. Moral Discourse in a Chinese Village*, Berkeley: University of California Press.
Palmer, D. (2008) Labelling Heterodoxy, in *Chinese Religiosities. Afflictions of Modernity and State Formation*, Berkeley: University of California Press, pp.113–34.
Palmer, D., Shive, G. and Wickeri, P.L. (eds). (2011) *Chinese Religious Life*, Oxford: Oxford University Press.
Pan, X. (ed.). (2007) *He Zai Ai Zhong (Harmony Lies in Love)*, Beijing: Zongjiao wenhua chubanshe.
Pan, X. (2012) *Ai Zai Xingdong (Love Lies in Action)*, Beijing: Zongjiao wenhua chubanshe.
Perry, E. and Selden, M. (eds). (2003) *Chinese Society. Change, Conflict and Resistance*, 2nd Edition, London: Routledge.
Pew Research. (2012) Growing Concerns in China about Inequality, Corruption. Available from: www.pewglobal.org/2012/10/16/growing-concerns-in-china-about-inequality-corruption/ (last accessed 28 January 2013).
Pils, E. (2010) The Practice of Law as Conscientious Resistance: Chinese Weiquan Lawyers' Experience. Available from: http://papers.ssrn.com/sol3/papers.cfm?abstract_id =1564447 (last accessed 16 October 2012).
Poon, M.N.-C. (2006) *Pilgrims and Citizens: Christian Social Engagement in East Asia Today*, Adelaide: ATF Press.
Qin, Z. (2008) Cultural Construction and a Harmonious Society, in *China in Search of a Harmonious Society*, Lanham, MD: Lexington Books, pp.61–74.
Qiu, Z. (2004) Guanyu Zhongguo Fei Yingli Zuzhi Shijian Zhong De Jiben Wenti (Some Basic Issues in the Practice of Chinese Non-profit Organizations), in *Harmonious Society and Philanthropies*, Beijing: Shehui kexue wenxian chubanshe, pp.213–20.
Qiu, Z. (2010) Making Social Contributions – A 25 Year Journey, *in Love Never Ends. On the 25th Anniversary of Amity Foundation*, Nanjing: The Amity Foundation, p.5.
Radio Free Asia (2012) House Church Publications Raided. Available from: www.rfa.org/english/news/china/house-church-03282012102413.html (last accessed 11 September 2012).
Rawson, K. (1999) Come Join the Family: Helping Chinese Scholars in the West Turn to God, in *Chinese Intellectuals and the Gospel*, San Gabriel: China Horizon, pp.157–88.
Renmin Ribao (People's Daily). (2012) Xin Hui He Ai Yiqi Zou. Renmin Ribao Zhuanfang Qiu Zhonghui (Will and Love Can Go Together. Renmin Ribao Interviews Qiu Zhonghui). Available from: http://gongyi.qq.com/a/20120203/000013.htm (last accessed 3 December 2012).
Renminbao. (2005) Tiaozhan Zhonggong Zhongyang Jueding! Gao Zhisheng Panyi Jidujiao

(Challenging the Central Committee to a Decision. Gao Zhisheng Converts to Christianity). Available from: http://renminbao.com/rmb/articles/2005/11/23/38444p.html (last accessed 8 February 2013).

Rolandsen, U.M.H. (2008) A Collective of Their Own: Young Volunteers at the Fringes of the Party Realm. *European Journal of East Asian Studies*, 7 (1): 101–29.

Rujia shi xuezhe (Ten Confucian scholars). (2010) Zunzhong Zhongguo Wenhua Shengdi, Tingjian Qufu Yesu Jiaotang (Respect the Holy Land of Chinese Culture, Stop Building Qufu's Church of Jesus). Available from: www.chinarujiao.net/p_info.asp?PID=8299 (last accessed 13 February 2013).

Schak, D.C. (2011) Protestantism in China: A Dilemma for the Party-State. *Journal of Current Chinese Affairs*, 40 (2): 71–106.

Schwartz, L. (2008) A Conversation with Michael Hardt on the Politics of Love. *Interval(le)s*, II.2–III.1 (Fall 2008/Winter2009): 810–21.

Shan, M.C. (2012) *Beware of Patriotic Heresy in the Church in China: Drawing on the Historical Lessons of the Nazis' Volk Church to Analyze the Zhao Xiao Phenomenon*, Boston: Chinese Christian Theological Association.

She, H. (Ezra P.) (2011) *Zhongguo Baizihui (The Church of Tares in China)*, Washington, DC: Chinese Law and Religion Publishing House.

Shieh, S. (2012a) Can the Chinese Government Both Support and Micromanage NGOs? Available from: www.ngochina.blogspot.co.uk/ (last accessed 7 February 2013).

Shieh, S. (2012b) What Does the 18th Party Congress Augur for the Future of Civil Society. Available from: http://ngochina.blogspot.co.uk/2012/11/what-does-18th-party-congress-augur-for.html (last accessed 29 November 2012).

Shieh, S. and Deng, G. (2011) An Emerging Civil Society: The Impact of the Sichuan Earthquake on Grass-roots Association in China. *The China Journal*, 65: 181–94.

Strand, D. (1989) *Rickshaw Beijing. City People and Politics in Beijing in the 1920s*, Berkeley: University of California Press.

Tamney, J.B. and Yang, F. (eds). (2005) *State, Market and Religion Ins in Chinese Societies*, Leiden: Brill.

Tang, Y. (2007) Hexie Shehui, Aiman Tangchi (The Harmonious Society – Tangchi Is Full of Love). *Beijing Zhoubao*. Available from: www.beijingreview.com.cn/zgsy/txt/2007-07/02/content_68-57.htm (last accessed 10 April 2010).

Teng, B. (2009) Chinese Human Rights Lawyers Under Assault. *The Washington Post*. Available from: www.washingtonpost.com/wp-dyn/content/article/2009/07/24/AR2009072402940.html (last accessed 13 September 2012).

The Economist. (2012a) Working the System, 29 September 2012.

The Economist. (2012b) Defining Boundaries, 5 January 2013: 39–40.

The Economist. Middle-class Blues. Available from: www.economist.com/blogs/analects/2012/10/unrest-cities (last accessed 10 January 2013).

Thornton, P. (2003) The New Cybersects. Resistance and Repression in the Reform Era, in *Chinese Society. Change, Conflict and Resistance*, London: Routledge.

Ting, K.H. (2004) *God Is Love*, Colorado Springs: Cook Communications Ministries International.

UCA News. (2012) State Launches Religious Charity Campaign. *UCA News*. Available from: www.ucanews.com/news/state-launches-religious-charity-campaign/60618 (last accessed 7 February 2013).

Uhalley, S. and Wu, X. (eds) (2000) *China and Christianity. Burdened Past, Hopeful Future*, Armonk, NY: M.E. Sharpe.

Wang, C. (ed.). (2003) *One China Many Paths*, London, New York: Verso.

Wang, F. (2006) *Zai Aizhong Xunqiu Zhenli (Seeking Truth in Love)*, Beijing: Zongjiao wenhua chubanshe.
Wang, F. (2011) New Church to Tower over Home of Confucius. *Global Times*. Available from: www.globaltimes.cn/special/2011-01/613615.html (last accessed 14 February 2013).
Wang, J. (2010) *Jindai Beijing Cishan Shiye Yanjiu (Researching Philanthropic Activities in Modern Beijing)*, Beijing: Renmin Chubanshe.
Wang, Q. (2013) Badiu Lun Aiqing Yu Gongchan Zhuyi – Du Alan Badiu De 'Ai De Zanci' (Badiou on Love and Communism – Reading Alain Badiou's 'In Praise of Love'). *Guanchazhe*. Available from: www.guancha.cn/WangQin/2013_01_02_117850.shtml (last accessed 11 January 2013).
Wang, S. and Zhou, Y. (2009) *Da'ai Jingshen Yu Shehui Zhuyi Hexie Wenhua Jianshe (The Spirit of Love and the Construction of Socialist Harmonious Culture)*, Beijing: Renmin Chubanshe.
Wang, X. (2011) Zhongguo Shehui Renxin Shi Zenme Bian Huaide – Zhuanfang Shanghai Daxue Jiaoshou Wang Xiaoming (How Did the Heart of Chinese Society Turn Bad? A Special Interview with Professor Wang Xiaoming of Shanghai University). *Nanfeng Chuang*, 18. Available from: www.douban.com/group/topic/28443692/ (last accessed 25 January 2013).
Wang, Xiaoying. (2002) The Post-Communist Personality: The Spectre of China's Capitalist Market Reforms. *The China Journal*, 47: 1–17.
Wang, Y. (2006a) Shengyue Yu Xianzheng Zhuyi (The Covenant and Constitutionalism). *Fangzhou*, 2: 97–101.
Wang, Y. (2006b) Yu Shen Qin Zui: Jinri Zhongguo De Jiduhua He Minzhuhua (Kissing God: Democratization and Christianization in China Today). *Ganlanzhi*, 3: 32–41.
Wang, Y. (2012a) Zhe Shi Tianfu Shijie (This Is God's World), in *Chuanyue wangluo de xinyang sibian (Responses to Skepticism about the Chinese Faith on the Chinese Internet)*, Ohio: Christian Communications Incorporated. pp.12–14
Wang, Y. (2012b) The Possibility of Political Theology: Christianity and Liberalism. *Chinese Law and Religion Monitor*, 8(1): 96–118.
Wee, S.-L. (2012) Blind Dissident's Plight Revives China Rights Movement. *Reuters*. Available from: www.reuters.com/article/2012/05/16/us-china-dissident-activists-idUSBRE84F0HQ20120516 (last accessed 13 September 2012).
Wen, Y. (2012) Home Church Accused of Having US Connections to Sue Local Police. *Global Times*. Available from: www.globaltimes.cn/content/727478.shtml (last accessed 11 February 2013).
Wickeri, P.L. (2007) *Reconstructing Christianity in China. K.H.Ting and the Chinese Church*, New York: Maryknoll.
Wickeri, P.L. (2010) Seeds of Love Grow in People's Hearts, in *Love Never Ends. On the 25th Anniversary of Amity Foundation*, Nanjing: The Amity Foundation, p.113.
Wickeri, P.L. and Wickeri, J. (eds). (2002) *A Chinese Contribution to Ecumenical Theology. Selected Writings of Bishop K.H.Ting*, Geneva: World Council of Churches.
Wielander, G. (2009a) Protestant and Online: The Case of Aiyan. *The China Quarterly*, (197): 165–82.
Wielander, G. (2009b) Bridging the Gap? An Investigation of Beijing Intellectual House Church Activities and Their Implications for China's Democratization. *Journal of Contemporary China*, 18 (62): 849–64.
Wielander, G. (2011) Beyond Repression and Resistance – Christian Love and China's Harmonious Society. *The China Journal*, 65: 119–39.

Wong, E. (2011) An Online Scandal Underscores Chinese Distrust of State Charities. *New York Times*. Available from: www.nytimes.com/2011/07/04/world/asia/04china.html?pagewanted=all&_r=0 (last accessed 1 February 2013).

Wong, E. (2013) In China, Widening Discontent Among the Communist Party Faithful. *New York Times*. Available from: www.nytimes.com/2013/01/20/world/asia/in-china-discontent-among-the-normally-faithful.html?_r=0 (last accessed 22 January 2013).

World Watch Monitor. (2012) China's Christians Seize Internet Opportunities. Available from: www.worldwatchmonitor.org/english/country/china/article_1982225.html/ (last accessed 8 February 2013).

Wu, J. (2004) Zhiyu Aixin Peiyu Zhong De Cishan Wenhua (Charitable Culture Rooted in the Fostering of a Loving Heart), *in Harmonious Society and Philanthropies*, Beijing: Shehui kexue wenxian chubanshe.

Wu, Y. (2003) *Dangdai Zhongguo Daode Jianshe Yanjiun (A Study of Moral Construction in Contemporary China)*, Beijing: Zhongguo shehui kexue chubanshe.

Xiao, Y. (2007) Hao Kanwu Zai Hechu (What Makes a Successful Publication). *Maizhong*. Available from: www.maizhong.org/wheatseeds/2007-07.09/wz/06.html (last accessed 10 October 2012).

Xinhua Net. (2006) CPC Sets Moral Yardstick for Officials. *Xinhua Wang*. Available from: http://news.xinhuanet.com/english/2006-04/04/content_4384529.htm (last accessed 19 January 2013).

Xuyang, J. (2013) Without Any Care. *Global Times*. Available from: www.globaltimes.cn/content/756966.shtml (last accessed 23 January 2013).

Yan, X. (2004) Cong 'Minyun', Falungong, Dao Jiating Jiaohui (From 'Minyun' and Falungong to the House Churches). Available from: http://blog.boxun.com/hero/yanxin/46_1.shtml (last accessed 8 February 2013).

Yan, Y. (2009) The Good Samaritan's New Trouble: A Study of the Changing Moral Landscape in Contemporary China. *Social Anthropology*, 17: 9–24.

Yan, Y. (2010) The Chinese Path to Individualization. *The British Journal of Sociology*, 61 (3): 489–512. (last accessed 17 July 2012).

Yan, Y. (2011) The Changing Moral Landscape, in *Deep China.*, Berkeley: University of California Press, pp.36–77.

Yang, F. (2005) Religious Research in Communist China, in *State, Market, and Religions in Chinese Societies*, Leiden: Brill, pp.19–29.

Yang, F. (2012a) *Religion in China. Survival and Revival Under Communist Rule*, Oxford: Oxford University Press.

Yang, F. (2012b) Religious Revival and Religious Deficit in China Today. *Chinese Law and Religion Monitor*, 8 (1).

Yang, F. and Lang, G. (eds). (2011) *Social Scientific Studies of Religion in China. Methodologies, Theories and Findings*, Leiden, Boston: Brill.

Yang, G. (2009) *The Power of the Internet in China. Citizen Activism Online*, New York: Columbia University Press.

Yang, H. and Yeung, D.H.N. (eds). (2006) *Sino-Christian Studies in China*, Cambridge: Cambridge Scholars Press.

Yang, K. (2012) Basic Principles for Managing Privately Set-Up Christian Meeting Sites. *Chinese Law and Religion Monitor*, 8(1) (January–July 2012).

Yang, M.M.-H. (2004) Spatial Struggles: Post-Colonial Complex, State Disenchantment, and Popular Reappropriation of Space in Rural Southeast China. *Journal of Asian Studies*, 63: 719–55.

Yang, M.M.-H. (2008) *Chinese Religiosities. Afflictions of Modernity and State Formation*, Berkeley: University of California Press.

Yang, T. and Ge, D. (eds). (2004) *Hexie Shehui Yu Cishan Zhiye (Harmonious Society and Philanthropy)*, Beijing: Shehui kexue wenxian chubanshe.

Yang, X. (1994) *Niugui Sheshen Lu (Captive Spirits. Prisoners of the Cultural Revolution)*, Hong Kong: Oxford University Press.

Ying, F. (2009) The Regional Development of Protestant Christianity in China. *The China Review*, 9 (2): 63–97.

You, X. (2006) Christianity's Dual Meaning in Chinese Modernisation, in *Sino-Christian Studies in China*, Cambridge: Cambridge Scholars Press, pp.38–49.

Young, N. (2004) NGOs: The Diverse Origins, Changing Nature and Growing Internationalisation of the Species. *China Development Brief*. Available from: www.chinadevelopmentbrief.com/node/297 (last accessed 11 January 2012).

Yu, Jianrong. (2008) Zhongguo 'Jidujiao Jiating Jiaohui 'Xiang Hechu Qu – Yu 'Jiating Jiaohui' Renshi De Duihua (Where China's 'Christian House Church Congregations' Are Headed – a Dialogue with People from the 'House Church'). *Lingdaozhe*, 24. Available from: www.pacilution.com/ShowArticle.asp?ArticleID=3717 (last accessed 25 September 2012).

Yu, Jie. (2001) *Ai Yu Teng De Bianyuan (The Verge of Love and Pain)*, Zhengzhou: Daxiang chubanshe.

Yu, Jie. (2006) Fangzhou Jiaohui Tanfang Shangfangcun (Fangzhou Church Visits Petitioners' Village). *Ganlanzhi*, 3: 4–5.

Yu, Jie. (2010) *Shei Wei Shenzhou Li Jiu Jiang? Zhongguo De Xinyang Chongjian Yu Shehui Zhuanxing (The Reconstruction of Faith and Society in China)*, Taibei: Christian Arts Press.

Yu, Jie. (2011) *Jidutu Shequ Shi Shijie De Xiwang. Wang Yi Fantan Lu (Christian Communities Are the Hope for the World. An Interview with Wang Yi)*, Chengdu: Chengdu shengyue gongyi tushushi.

Yu, Jie and Wang, Y. (2010a) *Wo You Chibang Ru Gezi (I Had Wings Like a Dove)*, Taibei: Christian Arts Press.

Yu, Jie and Wang, Y. (2010b) *Yi Sheng Yishi De Yangwang (The Expectation for Whole Life)*, Taibei: Christian Arts Press.

Yu, R. (2012) Wenzhou Aims to Cut Red Tape for Charities Offering Free Food, Tea. *China Daily*, 16 November 2012.

Yuan, Z. (1997) God and Democracy. Reflection on the National Prayer Breakfast in Washington DC, in *Soul Searching. Chinese Intellectuals on Faith and Society*, Pasadena, CA: China Horizon, pp.56–7.

Yuan, Z. (2003) *Shizijia. Yesu Zai Zhongguo (The Cross. Jesus in China)*, China Soul for Christ Foundation.

Yuan, Z., Su B.D., Yang J., Wang C., Wu X., Huo S., Xiang R. (1997) *Soul Searching. Chinese Intellectuals on Faith and Society*, Pasadena, CA: China Horizon.

Yue, S. (2005) Dangdai Zhishi Fenzi – Jidutude Shehui Kunjing Jiexi (Contemporary Intellectuas – An Analysis of Social Difficulties for Christians). *Aiyan*, 9. Available from: www.aiyan.org/2005/05-9/13/html (last accessed 15 April 2008).

Zhang, C. (2012) *Helper*, Beijing. Available from: http://english.hdchurch.org/html/news/focus/2011/0429/196.html (last accessed 23 January 2013).

Zhang, D. (2010) Jidu Jiaohui Zai Zhongguo Gongmin Shehuizhong De Shushi Shiming (The Worldly Mission of Chinese Churches in Civil Society). Available from: www.chinesepen.org/Article/sxsy/201012/Article_20101215145914.shtml (last accessed 29 September 2012).

Zhang, E., Kleinman, A. and Tu, W. (eds). (2011) *Governance of Life in Chinese Moral Experience. The Quest for an Adequate Life*, Oxford, New York: Routledge.

Zhang, L. (2010) 'Haigui Jidutu' Yu Jinri Zhongguo Jiating Jiaohui ('Christians Returned from Overseas and Chinese House Churches Today). *Wheat Seeds*, (21). Available from: www.maizhong.org/wheatseeds/2010-01.21/wz/20.html (last accessed 25 September 2012).

Zhang, P. (2012) Yiyi Zuojiao Li Bifeng Bei Panxing 12 Nian (Dissident Writer Li Bifeng Sentenced to Twelve Years) *Neue Deutsche Welle*. Available from: www.dw.de/异议作家李必丰被判刑12年/a-16389523 (last accessed 30 November 2012).

Zhang, Q. (2006) Social Institutions, Concepts of Value and Transcendent Spirit. An Essay on the Possibility and Method of Exchange of Concents of Value, in *Sino-Christian Studies in China*, Cambridge: Cambridge Scholars Press, pp.222–9.

Zhao, J. (2010) *Jidu Xinyang Yu Zhongguo Xiandai Wenhua De Xiangyu (The Meeting of Christian Faith and Modern Chinese Culture)*, Beijing: Zongjiao wenhua chubanshe.

Zhao, S. (ed.). (2000) *China and Democracy. The Prospect for a Democratic China*, London: Routledge.

Zhao, X. (2002) Market Economy with Churches. Available from: www.danwei.org/business/churches_and_the_market_econom.php (last accessed 15 January 2012).

Zhao, X. (2010a) Wen Zongli De 'Xin, Wang, Ai' (President Wen's 'Faith, Hope, Love'). Available from: http://zhaoxiao.blog.sohu.com/146061380.html (last accessed 13 January 2013).

Zhao, X. (2010b) Dalu Gaoxiaozhong De Jidutu Zhuangkuang Baogao. Daxuesheng Xinyang Jidujiao Bili Chaoguo 10% (Report on the Situation of Christians in China's Universities. More Than 10% of Students Believe in Christianity). Available from: http://zhaoxiao.blog.sohu.com/146887940.html (last accessed 13 January 2013).

Zhao, X. (2011a) Jidu Xinyang Yu 21 Shiji De Zhongguo (Christian Faith and 21st Century China). *Conference Proceedings of the Fourth Chinese Theological Forum in Seoul*: 52–6.

Zhao, X. (2011b) Xinyang Yu Qiyejia Jingshen (Faith and Entrepreneurial Spirit). *Guanli xuejia*, (5). Available from: www.pacilution.com/ShowArticle.asp?ArticleID=2997 (last accessed 16 January 2013).

Zheng, X. (2012) Pressure Takes Its Toll on Beijingers: Survey. *China Daily*. Available from: www.chinadaily.com.cn/china/2012-10/26/content_15848105.htm (last accessed 21 January 2013).

Zhonggong zhongyang tong zhan bu er ju and Zhongguo renmin daxue fojiao yu zongjiao wenxue lilun yanjiusuo (eds). (2009) *Hexie Zhi Jing. (The Realm of Harmony)*, Beijing: Renmin Daxue Chubanshe.

Zhou, B. (2007) Chinese Liberal Culture in the Year of the Pig. *China Rights Forum*, 1: 88–92.

Zhu, Y. (n/d)Mojia De 'Jian'ai' Yu Hexie Shehui (Master Mo's 'Universal Love' and the Harmonious Society), Available from: www.rongshuxia.com/book/4417701.html (last accessed 10 August 2009).

Zhuang, Z. (2010) Yi Jiating Xiaozu Wei Danyuan Muyang Moshi (Make Small Home Groups the Only Pastoral Model). *Wheat Seeds*, 22. Available from: www.maizhong.org/wheatseeds/2010-04.22/wz/07.html (last accessed 25 September 2012).

Zhuo, X. (2000) Discussions on Cultural Christians in China, in *China and Christianity. Burdened Past, Hopeful Future*, Armonk, NY: M.E. Sharpe, pp.283–300.

Zhuo, X. (2006a) The Christian Contribution to China in History, in *Pilgrims and Citizens*, Adelaide: ATF Press, pp.157–68.

Zhuo, X. (2006b) The Significance of Christianity for the Modernization of Chinese Society, in *Sino-Christian Studies in China*, Cambridge: Cambridge Scholars Press, pp.252–64.

Zimmerman-Liu, T. and Wright, T. (2013) Making Sense of China's State-Society Relations. Unregistered Protestant Churches in the Reform Era, in *Christianity in Contemporary China. Socio-cultural Perspectives*, London, New York: Routledge, pp.220–33.

Zou, X. (2008) Hexie Shehui: Zouchu 'Ai You Dengcha' Zhi Kunjing (Harmonious Society: Escapting the 'Hierarchy of Love'). *Xuelidian*, 2: 25–8.

Zuo, F. (2005) *Shehui Fuyin, Shehui Fuwu Yu Shehui Gaizao. Beijing Jidujiao Qingnianhui Llishi Yanjiu 1906–1949 (Social Gospel, Social Service and Social Reform. A History of the Beijing YMCA 1906–1949)*, Beijing: Zongjiao wenhua chubanshe.

Glossary

ai 爱
ai de dengcha 爱的等差
Aide Jijinhui 爱德基金会
ai de jingshen 爱的精神
ai de shijian 爱的实践
aiqing 爱情
airen 爱人
aixin 爱心
Aiyan 爱延
Aiyulun 爱育论
Ai zai xingdong 爱在行动
bage bixu 八个必须
barong baru 八荣八辱
Bei Cun 北村
beipiao jiaohui 北漂教会
bo'ai 博爱
bu dui 不对
bu tan zhengzhi, bu tan shenxue 不谈政治，不谈神学
Cai Zhuohua 蔡卓华
Chai Ling 柴玲
Chen Guangcheng 陈光诚
chengxin 诚信
Chen Kuide 陈奎德
Chen Yongmiao 陈永苗
cishan 慈善
datong shjie 大同世界
danhua 淡化
danwei 单位
dao 道
datong 大同
daxue tuanqi 大学团契
Ding Guangxun 丁光训
Dongfang shandian 东方闪电

Glossary 185

Falungong 法轮功
Fang Lizhi 方励之
Fangzhou 方舟
Fan Xuede 范学德
Fan Yafeng 范亚峰
Fuyin shibao 福音时报
Ganlanzhi 橄榄枝
Gao Shining 高师宁
gao suzhi de renmin 高素质的人民
Gao Zhisheng 高智晟
Guancha 观察
guanxi 关系
Guo Feixiong 郭飞雄
Guo Yan 郭艳
haigui 海归
hai'ou 海鸥
Han Dongfang 汉东方
he er bu tong 合而不同
He Guanghu 何光沪
He Weifang 贺卫方
hexie shehui de zongjiao lun 和谐社会的宗教论
he zai ai zhong 和在爱中
Huiling 慧灵
Hu Ping 胡平
Jia Guobiao 贾国标
jiaohui 教会
jiating jiaohui 家庭教会
jian'ai 兼爱
Jiang Qing 将庆
jiaohui 教会
Jidian 基甸
jiduhua xuezhe 基督化学者
Jidu shibao 基督时报
Jiduwang 基督网
juhui 聚会
Kang Xiaoguang 康晓光
Kang Youwei 康有为
kuanguang de da'ai 宽广的大爱
Kuang Yaming 匡亚明
laogai 劳改
li 礼
liangxin 良心
liangzhi 良知
Liao Yiwu 廖亦武
Li Heping 李和平

lianghui 两会
Liang Qichao 梁启超
Li Boguang 李伯光
liumang 流氓
Liu Junning 刘军宁
Liu Peng 刘鹏
Liu Xiaobo 刘晓波
Liu Tongsu 刘同苏
Liu Xiaofeng 刘小枫
Maizhong 麦种
mingong jiaohui 民工教会
minjianxing de fei minjian zuzhi 民间性非民间组织
minkan 民刊
minsheng 民生
Mo Yan 莫言
Nanfang Renwu Zhoukan 南方人物周刊
Nanfang Zhoukan 南方周刊
Peng Qiang 鹏强
qing 情
qinggan 情感
Qiuyu zhi fu guizheng jiaohui 秋雨之福归正教会
ren 仁
renge 人格
renge jiuguo 人格救国
renmin 人民
sanmin zhuyi 三民主义
sanzi jiaohui 三自教会
Shangdi shi ai 上帝是爱
shangfang 上访
She He 舍禾
shehui fuwu 社会服务
shehui zuzhi 社会组织
Shen Helin 沈和林
Shouwang jiaohui 守望教会
suzhi 素质
Tang Chongrong 唐崇荣
Taxiang 他乡
Teng Biao 滕彪
tian 天
Tianfeng 天风
tian ren he yi 天人合一
tongqing 同情
wangluo jidu shituan 网络基督使团
Wang Mingdao 王明道
Wang Yi 王怡

weiquan 维权
Wen Jiaobao 温家宝
wenming 文明
wenming shehui 文明社会
Wu Hongda 吴弘达
Wu Yaozong 吴耀宗
xiaokang 小康
xie 邪
xiejiao 邪教
xiahai 下海
xiaozu 小组
Xin Guancha 新观察
Xinyang, xinnian, xinxin yu shigan shi women shiye chenggong de baozheng
  信仰、信念、信心与实干，是我们事业成功的保证
Xinyang zhi men 信仰之门
Xu Zhiyong 许志永
Yanhuang Chunqiu 炎黄春秋
Yan Lianke 阎连科
Yang Fenggang 杨凤岗
Yang Lili 杨莉藜
Yang Xiaokai 杨小凯
Yang Xiguang 杨曦光
Ye Jiacheng 耶家诚
yejiaotu 耶教徒
Ying Xing 殷星
you'ai 友爱
yuanze 原则
yue 约
Yue yu Fa 约与法
Yu Jianrong 余建荣
yuzhou zhi ai 宇宙之爱
Yuan Zhiming 远志明
Zha Changping 查常平
Zhang Dajun 张大军
Zhang Sizhi 张思之
Zhang Xingshui 张星水
Zhao Zichen 赵紫宸
Zhao Xiao 赵晓
zheng 正
zhengque de renshengguan 正确的人生观
Zhenjiu yu xiaoyao 真救与逍遥
zhi you ai cai you yiqie 只有爱才有一切
Zhou Enlai 周恩来
zifa jiaohui 自发教会
Zhongguo jiating jiaohui lianhe zuzhi 中国家庭教会联合组织

Zhongguo jidutu weiquan lüshi tuan 中国基督徒维权律师团
Zhongguo qingnian zhengzhi xueyuan 中国青年政治学院
Zhu Xueqin 朱学勤
Zouxiang shizijia de zhen 走向十字架的真

Index

1989 6, 25, 58, 85, 130, 133, 144, 146, 158, 162; and intellectuals 41–4, 110–12, 122, 126, 128

Africa 103, 125–7, 166
agape 36, 46, 48, 64, 106
ai see love
Aiyan 89–91, 92–103, 105, 116–17, 124, 129, 132
altruism 26, 54, 145
Amity Foundation 21, 71–8, 81–2, 84, 98, 155, 164
Association of Human Rights Attorneys for Chinese Christians 101, 139

bage bixu see Eight Musts
barong baru see Eight Honours and Eight Shames
Bible study groups 12, 17, 42–3, 60–2, 79–80, 117, 121, 161
Boss-Christians 18, 108–9

Cai Zhuohua 89, 102, 106, 124
CASS 9, 36, 52, 68, 126, 143, 147
Catholicism 23, 58, 70, 74, 145
CCIM 88, 93
CCP 18, 28, 68, 111, 123, 131–2, 146
  see also party
Chai Ling 6
Chao, Jonathan 95
charity 7, 11, 20–1, 34, 38, 55, 65–84, 115, 118, 128, 155–6
Charter 08 48, 108, 111, 122–4, 130, 132–3, 137, 142–3, 149, 157
Chen Guangcheng 118, 126, 143, 162
Chen Kuide 115, 132–3
chengxin 34, 78
China Aid Association 101, 118, 148
China Christian Council 10, 49
Chinese Christian Movement 5

Chinese House Church Alliance 19, 118
Chinese Law and Religion Monitor 102, 106, 135–6
Christian entrepreneurs 35, 96, 120, 159, 164, 167
Christian liberals 22, 35, 131–40, 143, 146, 148–9, 157
Christian Net *see* Jiduwang
Christian 'sub-cultures' 6, 18–19, 109
Christian Times *see* Jidu Shibao
Church China *see* Jiaohui magazine
church-state relations 12, 21–2, 35, 49, 83, 86, 94, 97, 100, 103, 120, 155, 163
Ci Jiwei 21, 25–6, 28–9, 34, 41, 43, 144, 153,
civil society 13, 20, 85, 97, 118, 131, 136–8, 149,
colonialism 164
communism 50–1, 54, 56–7, 59, 123, 134–5
Confucianism 28–9, 32–3, 52–3, 114, 151–4, 167
Confucius 28–9, 32, 36, 64
conscience 22, 43–4, 100, 112, 131–2, 137–8, 146–50, 157
constitution 11, 18, 85, 100–2, 107, 115–16, 124, 126, 132–6, 142–3, 147, 157
constitutional government 132, 140
constitutionalism 134–6
corruption 37, 54, 67, 70, 91, 133, 144–5, 147, 153, 157
covenant 35, 101, 134–5, 142, 147
cult 13, 18, 165
Cultural Christians 9–10, 20, 41, 111, 126, 137, 139, 156, 159
Cultural Revolution 1, 5, 10, 12, 39, 50–1, 60, 71, 116, 132

datong 28, 53
democracy activists 1, 6, 115, 131, 143, 146
democracy movement 1, 25, 85, 105, 128, 130, 144, 146
Democratic Justice Party 85, 118
democratization 108–9, 115, 131, 134, 136
Deng Xiaoping 26
denominations 3–4, 6, 8, 19, 64, 87, 128
diaspora 127, 162–3 *see also* overseas
Ding Guangxun 10, 52, 59, 63, 78, 123, 155; and theological reconstruction 7, 48–9; and Cultural Christians 9; and Amity Foundation 71–2, 74, 82, 164
Document Nineteen 10–11
Dongfang Shandian *see* Eastern Lightning

Early Rain Reformed Church 11, 17–8, 23, 81, 120–1, 134
Eastern Lightning 99, 106
education 3, 7, 14, 24, 37, 40, 42, 91, 94, 96–7, 106–7, 145, 166; moral 10, 31; in love 49, 54, 55–6; and missionaries 62, 66–7, 69; and charity 72, 77, 80, 83; rights 101–2; and intellectuals 111, 113, 116, 156
Eight Honours and Eight Shames 29–30, 157
Eight Musts 157
equality 28, 37, 45, 52 57, 68, 82, 120–1, 132–4, 137, 144, 147
English teaching 6, 117, 166
environment: protests 114, 144–5; protection 72, 97, 100
ethics 7–8, 10, 2, 24–5, 27, 29, 30, 42–3, 53–5, 58, 63, 78–9, 113, 136, 138; business 24, 33–6, 39, 44–5, 154–5, 158
evangelists 12 14, 18, 94

Falungong 13, 85, 99, 105, 116, 118, 165–6
Fangzhou church 48, 105, 118, 120, 122, 129, 130
Fangzhou magazine *see* Ganlanzhi
Fan Xuede 45, 92
Fan Yafeng 102, 111, 124, 140, 148
Fei Xiaotong 21, 25, 32, 39–40, 44, 64
folk religion 14, 166
foreign element 5–6, 9
Fuyin Shibao 89, 95–6, 98, 104–5

Ganlanzhi 118, 129, 130, 133
Gao Zhisheng 111, 122, 124, 139–40, 157
gender roles 21, 64, 104, 159–60
Gospel Times *see* Fuyin Shibao
government suppression 11–14, 126, 161–3, 165
Guancha 106, 133–4
Guo Yan 124, 140
Guo Feixiong 140, 143

Haidian Church 22, 58, 62, 87
'haigui' pastors 96–7, 119, 163
Han Dongfang 6, 116, 127
'harmonious society' 10–11, 21, 25–30, 32, 34, 36, 42, 45, 68, 153–4, 157, 166; and love 46–64
healing 13–14, 18–19, 58, 60–1, 158, 166
Healing Christians 18–9
healthcare 3, 62, 66, 80, 115, 144
hedonism 25–6, 28, 30, 40–4, 144–5, 153
He Guanghu 59, 112, 137, 151
heresy 98–9
hierarchy of love *see* love
'house churches' 2–3, 12, 48, 113, 118, 137, 163; definition of 15–20; and charity 70–1, 79; and political activism 85, 139–41; and online publications 88–91, 98–100, 103, 117; models of 97; and social make up 119–23
Huiling 21, 74–8, 82–3, 155
Hu Jintao 13, 28–9, 53
human rights lawyers *see* lawyers

immanence 49, 59
individualism 33, 113–4
intellectuals 1,4,6–8, 19–22, 50–2, 66, 71, 156–9, 166; and morality 41, 43; and love 59–60; and Christian online publications 86–9, 94, 97, 102–4; and democratization 108–29; definition of 110–13; liberal 130–3, 135–6, 140–3, 146, 151
internet 30, 38, 85–8, 91, 93, 95, 121, 133, 142, 148, 156

Jiang Zemin 26, 28–9
Jiaohui magazine 8, 89–90, 93–6, 99, 121
Jidu Shibao 96, 104, 105
Jiduwang 96, 105
justice 11, 20, 28, 33, 79, 110, 112, 115,

124, 131, 134–5, 139, 141, 146–7, 157

Kang Youwei 65, 153
Kuang Yaming 71

law 20, 90, 138; on religion 11, 80, 101, 156
lawyers 1, 79, 102, 108, 111, 124, 127, 131, 133; 142, 145–6, 157; *weiquan* 138–40, 143
lianghui 10, 96
liangxin 147–8, 150, 157
liangzhi 147–8, 150, 157
Liao Yiwu 122
Li Baiguang 111, 140
Life Quarterly 88
Ling, Samuel 95
Liu Junning 136–7
Liu Tongsu 13, 17, 62, 92, 94, 99, 119, 123, 126, 129
Liu Xiaobo 48, 102, 105, 108, 111–12, 122, 130–1, 137, 141, 146, 149, 157
Liu Xiaofeng 9, 111
love 20–1, 46–8, 60, 110, 115; and theological reconstruction 7–8, 43, 48–51; and official discourse 13, 28–9, 52–5, 58–9, 154–5; and moral reconstruction 31–3, 35–6, 44; hierarchy of 32–3, 40; and communism 56–7; and relationships 60–4, 160; and charity 65, 68, 70, 72–3, 78–9, 81; and Christian liberals 134–5; universal 32, 48, 52–3, 55;
Love Feast *see* Aiyan

Maizhong 89–90, 92–9, 121
Mao 11, 25–9, 31, 35, 54, 131, 145, 153
Mao Zedong *see* Mao
Marxism 28–9, 33, 50, 52–5, 67, 132, 167
Mayflower Compact 134, 142, 150
middle class 41, 70, 91, 97, 112, 115, 121, 142–5, 147
Middle East 103, 125, 166
migrant workers *see* migrants
migrants 15, 37, 79–80, 91–4, 97, 118–20, 165
Ministry of Civil Affairs 80, 118
minsheng 65–6, 68, 157
missionaries 2–5, 69, 78, 80, 89, 93, 117, 125, 164
modernization 3, 11, 30, 34, 47, 53, 66–7, 69, 115, 143, 163, 164
moral code 25–7, 29–30, 34, 37, 39–40, 43–4, 78, 80, 153, 158
moral constraint 114, 135–6
moral reconstruction 21, 24–7, 30–45, 145
'moral vacuum' 27
morality 10, 21, 24, 30, 43, 54, 72, 114, 140, 153–4; and Ci Jiwei 26–7; and moral reconstruction 32–4; and the individual 36–41; and political action 145–8

Nanfang Zhoukan 128, 143
National Chinese People's Political Consultative Conference 10, 49, 74, 155, 164
National Christian Council 4–5
netizens 85–6
New-Calvinists 8–9, 23, 42, 95, 113, 126, 155, 159, 162
New-Confucians 112, 136
New-Left 109, 112, 136, 139
NGOs 21, 68, 70, 73, 76–7, 81, 128, 144
nihilism 25, 43–4
NPI 76

online communities 38, 86, 88, 90, 103
online gospel 86–7, 106 *see also* online mission
online mission 21–2, 86–90, 92–5, 103, 106, 156
orthodox 4, 49, 59, 99, 166
overseas 133, 144, 159; mission on campus 6, 88; Chinese 7–8, 86, 118–19, 126, 156, 163; networks 19, 22, 72–3, 97, 109 churches 11, 16–7, 19, 45, 71–2, 81–2, 95; donors 81–2, 140; pastors 96, 104
Overseas Campus 88

Pan, Ezra 92, 99
party 2, 21, 33, 57–8, 60, 84, 149; relation with Christians/Christianity 10–12, 47, 62–4, 99, 160, 163–4; and ideology 26–31, 51, 55, 59, 152–5, 157, 166; disillusionment with 41–3, 45, 128, 145–6, 156, 158; official church and 48; liberals within 141–3, 147
pastor-intellectuals 7, 22, 126, 156–8
Pentecostal 4, 8, 14, 109, 113, 135, 160
philanthropy 68–9, 73, 83
political activism 1, 6, 115, 124, 129, 131, 143, 146
political theology 22, 35, 94, 131,

134–7, 139–40, 147
popular religion 4, 13, 52 *see also* folk religion
post-communist personality 30
Protestantism 4, 12, 70, 98, 113, 116
psychological 27, 55; health 19, 160; benefits 21, 64; dilemmas 41; needs 61–2, 79, 158, 161–2
public intellectuals 111–12

Qufu 151, 161, 167

registration: of churches 16, 18, 94, 97, 100; of social organizations 76–7
Religious Affairs Bureau 5, 12, 102
religious freedom 8, 11, 18, 100, 102, 105, 107, 120. 136–7, 139, 141, 148, 165
resistance 5, 20, 37, 49, 89, 117, 123, 145, 155; to registration 100; peaceful 131, 137; political 148–9, 162
rights defence 100, 102, 117, 124, 138–41, 149
rule of law 8, 28, 101, 124, 130, 132, 137–40, 145
rural churches 14–5, 18, 80, 90, 94, 104, 117–9, 124–5, 158–9, 166

sanmin zhuyi 65
SARA 5, 65
sects 13, 98–9, 128, 160
She He see Pan, Ezra
shehui fuwu 67
shehui zuzhi 65
Shouwang Church 17–18, 120, 148–9
Sino-foreign Protestant Establishment 4
social gospel 5, 65–7, 78–9, 83, 155
socialism 28, 51, 54–5, 59, 68, 73, 82–3
social organizations 65–6, 68–71, 75–8, 80–4, 111, 142, 148
social service 58, 65, 67, 69–70, 72, 74–6, 80, 83–4, 155
social trust 37–40, 44–5, 80, 142, 145–6, 153–4, 157, 162
social welfare 66–8, 71–2, 77, 82–4,
solidarity 56–7, 154
Sojourn 93, 97
speaking in tongues 13–4, 166
student fellowships 43, 93, 97, 119, 121
superstition 13–14, 52, 91, 166
suzhi 13–15, 54–5, 104, 117–18, 156, 158, 165

Tang Chongrong 94–5
Taxiang *see* Sojourn
T.C.Chao *see* Zhao Zichen
Teng Biao 111, 124, 139–40
The Banquet *see* Aiyan
theological reconstruction 7–8, 49
theological training 6–8, 15, 17, 41, 96–7, 117, 128, 156, 163
theology: liberal 4, 7, 50, 94, 123, 141, 149; liberation 50; modernist 4, 7, 49; conservative 104;
'three-self' churches 15–16, 83, 96, 98–100, 104, 106, 148 *see also* TSPM churches
Three Self Patriotic Movement *see* TSPM
Tianfeng 96, 98
Ting, K.H. *see* Ding Guangxun
Tong, Stephen see Tang Chongrong
transcendence 21, 36, 49, 59
transcendental values 13, 20, 22, 112, 130–1, 133, 135–7, 140, 146, 157
TSPM 2, 5, 8–10, 12–16, 19, 34, 42–3, 48, 50–1, 57, 83, 113, 123, 155
TSPM churches 7–8, 15–16, 41, 62, 82–3, 141, 159, 160–1

United States 6, 8, 45, 48, 88, 95, 101, 103, 106, 111, 113, 125–6, 128, 141, 143, 150, 162, 166–7
urban churches 2, 6–8, 14, 16, 18–9, 22, 45, 48, 62, 80, 83, 87–8, 94, 103–4, 109, 116–19, 121, 146, 158–60
utopianism 25–8, 38, 42–3, 45, 65, 144, 153

Wang Hui 52
Wang Mingdao 5, 94, 96, 100
Wang Yi 10, 13, 23, 60, 81, 94, 96, 109–11, 114, 118, 121, 124–6, 129–30; and political theology 133–6, 139–40, 142, 147
Watchman Nee 5
weiquan movement 102, 139–40,
Wenchuan 34, 69–70, 72, 94
Wen Jiabao 38, 53, 56, 122
wenming 28, 52
Wenzhou 6, 8, 18–9, 30, 35, 62, 77, 80, 89, 92–3, 97, 104, 109, 118–20, 126
Wheat Seeds *see* Maizhong
women 21–2, 95; and relationships 61–4, 155; in churches 103–4, 121, 159–60

women's liberation 62
Wu, Harry 116, 133, 149
Wu Hongda see Wu, Harry
Wu Yaozong 5, 67, 78, 123

xiaokang shehui 28–9, 53
xiaozu 161
xiejiao 99, 165

Yang Fenggang 10–11, 102
Yang Xiaokai 132, 146, 149, 187
Yang Xiguang *see* Yang Xiaokai
YMCA 3–5, 65–7, 71, 80
Yu Jie 10, 47–8, 60, 94, 102 105, 111, 118, 120, 122–3, 126, 130, 133, 143, 146, 149, 165
Yuan Zhiming 8, 88, 96, 114–16, 126, 151
YWCA 3, 5, 67

Zhao Xiao 12, 34–5, 39, 45, 53, 94, 141–3
Zhao Zichen 4, 31–2, 36, 67
Zhu Xueqin 133